Ordained Women in the Early Church

Ordained Women

IN THE EARLY CHURCH

A Documentary History

Edited and translated by

KEVIN MADIGAN *and*

CAROLYN OSIEK

The Johns Hopkins University Press   *Baltimore & London*

9 8 7 6 5 4 3 2

The Johns Hopkins University Press
2715 North Charles Street
Baltimore, Maryland 21218-4363
www.press.jhu.edu

Library of Congress Cataloging-in-Publication Data

Ordained women in the early church : a documentary history / edited and translated by
Kevin Madigan and Carolyn Osiek.
    p. cm.
Includes bibliographical references and index.
ISBN 0-8018-7932-9 (alk. paper)
1. Women in Christianity—History—Early church, ca. 30–600. 2. Women clergy—
History. I. Madigan, Kevin. II. Osiek, Carolyn.
BR195.W6W64 2005
262'.14'0820901—dc22

                                                                      2004021148

A catalog record for this book is available from the British Library.

The last printed page of this book provides the entry for Kyria of Lycaonia, which is missing
from p. 81.

Contents

Preface

In the collection that follows, we believe that we have included all known evidence for women deacons and presbyters, at least in the Greek- and Latin-speaking worlds. The existing evidence is published in many sources, some accessible to the general reader, but some published only in old and obscure reports, and a considerable amount not translated from the original languages. The sources vary widely and include church orders, conciliar decrees, funerary and dedicatory inscriptions, letters, biographies, and other literary material. Where we are aware of multiple publications of a single text, we give all the references we know of, but we have not attempted to track down every place in which a given inscription is published. What surprised us was the vast amount of information extant about women deacons, especially funerary epigraphical evidence. Much of this appears in collection here for the first time.

Kevin Madigan is primarily responsible for the Latin entries and Carolyn Osiek for the Greek entries and supporting materials, though both of us have read all entries. All translations are original. Neither of us has expertise in Christian Syriac, and while the collection contains a few Syriac inscriptions and texts, translated by others as indicated *in situ,* we do not claim to have presented an exhaustive collection in this area. If there is evidence that we have overlooked, we would be happy to receive any further examples that readers may know of.

This project began several years ago when we were both on the faculty of Catholic Theological Union in Chicago, teaching together a course called "Women in the Early Church." We became aware that, though there had been several exhaustive studies of women in church office in the early years, no one had attempted to collect all the evidence. Kevin is now at Harvard Divinity School and Carolyn at Brite Divinity School. From afar, however, we carried the common project to completion.

This has been a labor of enjoyment and even of love, as we sifted through the texts and delighted in new discoveries, especially those personal reminiscences revealed in funerary inscriptions of real women who are seldom known to a wider audience. This book is respectfully dedicated to the women deacons and presbyters who served in their church communities, and to those who attempt to do likewise today.

We are grateful to those who have helped us with the Syriac material, and who are acknowledged *in situ.* We are grateful to Giorgio Otranto of the University of Bari, who in his 1982 study of women presbyters collected the sources and did much of the groundwork in that area. He also graciously supplied the illustration of the inscription of Flavia Vitalia. Ute Eisen's recent book has also done much of the spadework for the present collection. In addition, Kevin Madigan would like to thank his research assistant, Andrew MacCarron, and his administrative assistant, Eric Unverzagt. Carolyn Osiek would like to thank Laurie Brink for both long-term and last-minute assistance at the University of Chicago library. Kim Bell, her then administrative assistant at Brite Divinity School, was of invaluable assistance in the preparation of the electronic version, as was her research assistant, Yancy Smith, on last-minute references and maps. Her biggest thanks, however, go to J. J. Leese, who some years ago offered to be a long-distance volunteer research assistant in order to learn something about women in the early church. She learned more than she bargained for, doing the first work of gathering texts and preliminary translations for this project.

A Note on Typography: In the individual entries that follow, the introductory paragraph in *italics* sets the context or summarizes the significance of the author. The text under consideration appears in **bold** type. Finally, comment on the passage is set in roman. In cases in which the selected text is very long—e.g., Theodula or the *Novellae* of Justinian—only the relevant excerpts are given, with summaries of omitted material in indented roman between them.

Source Abbreviations

AASS	*Acta Sanctorum.* Ed. J. Bollandus et al. Paris: Victorem Palme, 1863–
AC	*Apostolic Constitutions. Didascalia et Constitutiones Apostolorum* Ed. F. X. Funk. 2 vols. Paderborn: F. Schoeningh, 1905.
ACW	Ancient Christian Writers. Westminister, MD: Newman Bookshop, 1946–
AE	*L'Année Épigraphique.* Paris: Presses Universitaires de France, 1888–
AM	*Mitteilungen des deutschen archäologischen Instituts, Athenische Abteilung*
AT	Hippolytus, *Apostolic Tradition*
BCH	*Bulletin de Correspondance Hellénique*
BE	*Bulletin Épigraphique*
CCL	*Corpus Christianorum.* Series Latina. Turnhout: Brepols, 1953–
CIG	*Corpus Inscriptionum Graecarum.* Ed. August Boeckh. Hildesheim: G. Olms, 1977
CIL	*Corpus Inscriptionum Latinarum.* Ed. Deutsche Akademie der Wissenschaften zu Berlin. Berlin: G. Reinerum, 1862–
CSEL	*Corpus Scriptorum Ecclesiasticorum Latinorum*
DA	*Didascalia Apostolorum.* Ed. F. X. Funk. 2 vols. Paderborn: F. Schoeningh, 1905
DACL	*Dictionnaire d'archéologie chrétienne et de liturgie.* 15 vols. Paris, 1907–53

EG	*Epigraphica Graeca IV.* Ed. Margherita Guarducci. Rome: Istituto Poligrafico dello Stato, Libreria dello Stato, 1978
Eisen, *Women Officeholders*	Eisen, Ute. *Women Officeholders in Early Christianity: Epigraphical and Literary Studies.* Collegeville: Liturgical Press, 2000. Translation of *Amsträgerinnen im frühen Christentum. Epigraphische und literarische Studien.* Göttingen: Vandenhoeck & Ruprecht, 1996
Elm, *Virgins of God*	Elm, Susannah. *Virgins of God: The Making of Asceticism in Late Antiquity.* New York: Oxford University Press, 1994
Feissel, *Recueil*	Feissel, Denis. *Recueil des inscriptions chrétiennes de Macédoine du IIIe au Vie siècle.* BCH Supplément 8. Paris: Dépositaire, Diffusion de Boccard, 1983
Funk, *Didascalia*	Funk, Francis Xavier, ed. *Didascalia et Constitutiones Apostolorum.* 2 vols. Paderborn: F. Schoeningh, 1905
GCS	*Griechischen Christlichen Schriftsteller.* Leipzig: J. C. Hinrichs. Berlin: De Gruyter, 1879–
GRBS	*Greek, Roman, and Byzantine Studies*
Grégoire, *Recueil*	Grégoire, H., ed. *Recueil des Inscriptions Grecques-Chrétiennes d'Asie Mineure.* Amsterdam: A. M. Hakkert, 1968
Gryson, *Ministry of Women*	Gryson, Roger. *The Ministry of Women in the Early Church.* Collegeville: Liturgical Press, 1976. Translation of *Le ministère des femmes dans l'Église ancienne.* Recherches et synthèses, Section d'histoire 4. Gembloux: J. Duculot, 1972
Hermas *Vis.*	Shepherd of Hermas, *Visions*
IG	*Inscriptiones Graecae.* Berlin: De Gruyter, 1981–
ILCV	*Inscriptiones Latinae Christianae Veteres.* Ed. E. Diehl et al. Berlin: Wiedmann, 1925–85

JECS	*Journal of Early Christian Studies*
JFSR	*Journal of Feminist Studies in Religion*
JTS	*Journal of Theological Studies*
Kraemer, *Women's Religions*	Kraemer, Ross S., ed. *Women's Religions in the Greco-Roman World: A Sourcebook.* Oxford: Oxford University Press, 2004
Lampe, *Lexicon*	Lampe, G. W., ed. *A Patristic Greek Lexicon.* Oxford: Clarendon, 1961
LCL	Loeb Classical Library
LH	*The Lausiac History of Palladius.* J. Armitage Robinson, ed. Texts and Studies 6.2. Cambridge: Cambridge University Press, 1904
MAMA	*Monumenta Asiae Minoris Antiqua.* 8 vols. American Society for Archeological Research. Manchester University Press. 1928–62
Mansi, *Sacrorum conciliorum*	*Sacrorum conciliorum nova et amplissima collectio, editio novissima.* Ed. G. D. Mansi. Paris: H. Welter, 1901–27
Martimort, *Deaconesses*	Martimort, Aimé George. *Deaconesses: An Historical Study.* San Francisco: Ignatius Press, 1986. Translation of *Les Diaconesses: Essai Historique.* Rome: Edizioni Liturgiche, 1982
Mayer, *Monumenta*	*Monumenta de viduis diaconissis virginibusque tractantia.* Ed. Josephine Mayer. Florilegium Patristicum 42. Bonn: Peter Hanstein, 1938
Meimaris, *Sacred Names*	Meimaris, Yiannis E. *Sacred Names, Saints, Martyrs and Church Officials in the Greek Inscriptions and Papyri pertaining to the Christian Church of Palestine.* ΜΕΛΕΤΗΜΑΤΑ 2. Athens: National Hellenic Research Foundation, Centre for Greek and Roman Antiquity, 1986
MGH	*Monumenta Germaniae Historica.* Ed. G. H. Pertz et al. Hannover: Impensis Bibliopolii aulici Hahniani et al., 1826–

New Docs	*New Documents Illustrating Early Christianity.* Ed. G.H.R. Horsley. Macquarie University: Ancient History Documentary Research Centre, 1981
NPNF	Nicene and Postnicene Fathers
Otranto/Rossi, "Priesthood"	Rossi, Mary Ann. "Priesthood, Precedent, and Prejudice: On Recovering the Women Priests of Early Christianity." *JFSR* 7:1 (1991) 73–94. Translation with introduction of Giorgio Otranto, "Note sul sacerdozio femminile nell' antichità in margine a una testimonianza di Gelasio I." *Vetera Christianorum* 19 (1982) 341–60
PG	*Patrologia Graeca.* Ed. J.-P. Migne. Paris: Migne, 1857–66
PL	*Patrologia Latina.* Ed. J.-P. Migne et al. Paris: Garnieri Fratres, 1844–91
PO	Patrologia Orientalis
PW	*Real-Encyclopädie des klassischen Altertums-wissenchaft.* Ed. A. Pauly, G. Wissowa, W. Kroll. Stuttgart: J. B. Metzler, 1894–1972
Rahmani	*Testamentum Domini.* Ed. I. Ephraem II Rahmani. Mainz: F. Kirchheim, 1899
RB	*Revue Biblique*
RQ	*Römische Quartalschaft*
SC	*Sources chrétiennes.* Paris: Éditions du Cerf, 1941–
SEG	*Supplementum Epigraphicum Graecum.* Ed. J. J. Hondius et al. Lyon: A. W. Sijthoff, 1923–
SIG	*Sylloge Inscriptionum Graecarum,* ed. Wilhelm Dittenberger. 4 vols. Leipzig: S. Hirzel, 1915–24
Swete, *In Epistolas*	*In Epistolas Beati Pauli commentarii: The Latin Version with Greek Fragments,* ed. H. B. Swete, 2 vols. (Farnborough: Gregg, 1969)

TAM	*Tituli Asiae Minoris*
TD	*Testamentum Domini*
TS	Texts and Studies
TU	Texte und Untersuchungen
ZPE	*Zeitschrift für Papyrologie und Epigraphik*

Ordained Women in the Early Church

---------- *Chapter One* ----------

INTRODUCTION

 While there have been several studies of women in church office in recent years, none has attempted to collect all the evidence, both literary and epigraphical. That is the goal of the present volume. It builds on and supplements the collection of literary texts made by Josephine Mayer, the comprehensive studies of Gryson and Martimort, and the partial collections of inscriptions mentioned or discussed in the works of Susannah Elm, Giorgio Otranto, and Ute Eisen. Thus this volume is intended as a comprehensive resource of all textual evidence—literary, canonical, and epigraphical—in the Greek and Roman worlds, including some of the material from the Eastern churches that interfaced with those worlds. It makes available under one cover to an interested audience not versed in the original languages all the evidence for women in the recognizable titles and functions of church office.

The majority of this evidence comes from texts and epigraphical collections that are accessible in a theological and classical research library. The reader who wishes to consult the original texts can easily find them there. Some, however, come from very obscure and old publications, difficult for any but the dedicated scholar to access. In these cases, we have given the original text in a note. This is also the case with the key Latin inscriptions of presbyters, even though they are published in *CIL*.

Since it is clear from texts and contexts that the role of prophet and the order of virgins were not considered church offices, and were not commissioned by ordination, they are not included here. In most cases, the same is true of widows. But there are some exceptions: a few texts about widows suggest that they are ordained and/or are members of the clergy in specific churches. In a few other cases, they are confused with deaconesses. Only such texts about widows are included. Our general cutoff date is 600 CE, though we have included some key documents from after 600 that bear on the interpretation of earlier texts. For example, later commentators are included such as Atto of Vercelli, who takes for granted that women deacons or presbyters did exist at an earlier date, even if he knows of none in the Western church of his day. The earlier diachronic studies of Gryson and Martimort show that the institution of the female diaconate continued to exist and develop for many centuries after 600, most extensively in the East but also to some extent in the West.

One of the most delicious and tantalizing of the Western diaconal inscriptions is unfortunately known to be a forgery. First published in 1749, it was still thought to be genuine by Henri Leclercq in 1920.[1]

PREVIOUS STUDIES

The study of women's ministry in the early church is not new. There have been several major and thorough studies published in the twentieth century and earlier, even specifically on female deacons.[2] The earliest collection of texts, Mayer's *Monumenta* from 1938, begins with the New Testament and continues into the Middle Ages, bringing together literary, historical, canonical, and legal texts in Greek, Latin, and Latin translations of some Syriac texts. It includes no inscriptions. It is fairly comprehensive for legal texts, less so for the rest, but offers no definition of office or analysis of the material, and it does not attempt to distinguish office from recognizable organization, so that consecrated virgins and widows are included along with female deacons. In this regard, it is useful for its inclusiveness, though perhaps it would be more so if Mayer had included titles like prophet and teacher, as Eisen did.

Roger Gryson, *Ministry of Women,* offers a comprehensive interpretive study of literary and canonical texts, using some epigraphical evidence as support. He began, with the help of a student seminar, to compile a complete collection of inscriptions but abandoned the effort before its completion.[3] Georges Martimort, in his *Deaconesses,* went on to do the most comprehensive study exclusively of female deacons, but neither does he attempt a full collection of sources. Susannah Elm's *Virgins of God* is really about the development of female asceticism in the context of the wider ascetic movement, but it contains good discussion and some helpful epigraphical references to female deacons.[4] Giorgio Otranto's groundbreaking article on female presbyters in the West (Otranto/Rossi, "Priesthood"), collects and discusses all known inscriptions of female presbyters that can be interpreted as referring to officeholders. Finally, the recent fine book by Ute Eisen, *Women Officeholders,* has the most comprehensive, though not complete, collection to date of inscriptional evidence, though some of it is only summarized because of the wide scope of her study. Her collection is much less thorough with literary sources. In order to go more thoroughly into the specific offices of deacon and presbyter, we have not tried to cover the more difficult topics of apostles, prophets, teachers, and bishops, as Eisen does.

CORRECTING ASSUMPTIONS

In sifting through the evidence, we have found several frequent assumptions proven false. The first is that there were never women officeholders in the West. While the preponderance of evidence for female deacons is clearly in the East, the West is not without its references, often conciliar prohibitions, which must be presumed to have been enacted to control or suppress actual practice. There is inscriptional evidence for the West too, though it is far less than in the East. Much of this is often overlooked and needs to be taken seriously. Otranto and Eisen especially have brought some of this material to the fore. One of the intriguing factors is that the evidence for women presbyters is greater in the West than in the East.

A second false assumption is that the title of deaconess displaced that of female deacon by the late third century. While evidence for exactly what such women did is vague, the title *diakonos* for women continues through the sixth century. This is a subject that will receive further comment below.

A third assumption is that all women officeholders were celibate, either virgin or widowed. Again, the majority of the canonical, literary, and epigraphical evidence does suggest this, and many of these women were buried in solitary graves (Athanasia at Delphi and Tetradia in Thessaly were determined to keep the graves solitary by threatening eschatological punishment to anyone else!), or some with other ascetics (Posidonia, Theodosia). Many others were buried in family groupings that say nothing about the marital status of the female officeholder. But there are exceptions and ambiguities. It seems that in some times and places, this was not such a hard and fast rule. Many had surviving children, but may have been ordained as widows. A few buried husbands, Basilissa, Domna, or Eistrategis for example, and one wonders if they could have been ordained so quickly after their husbands' deaths; of course, the monument could also have been set up at a later time. Agathē at Philippi may have been married at the time of her death. The presbyter Leta in Calabria definitely was; it was her husband who commemorated her. Given the general pattern of older men marrying younger women, more widows than widowers are to be expected in such a burial population. Although in many instances virginity or widowhood was required for diaconal ordination of women, it cannot be assumed that one of these states was required everywhere and at all times.

A fourth assumption is that by the fifth and sixth century the title deaconess was simply being given to female monastic superiors. Again, while certainly many superiors of convents by this time carried the title of deaconess, not all did. Sometimes there seem to be deaconesses in the communities who are not superiors (e.g., Lampadion in Macrina's monastery; Elisanthia, Martyria, and Palladia in Olympias's monastery), and many deaconesses in these centuries were not monastics, for example, those who ministered in the great church of Hagia Sophia under Justinian and those commemorated by their children and siblings. Indeed, many female deacons were deeply embedded in family systems, as is evident from their burials in family tombs (see Appendix F on deacons' relationships). Eisen noticed that none of the commemorations from Palestine indicated any family relationship.[5] The sample from Palestine is perhaps too small, but the reason for this absence may also have been because of the ascetic character of the church there, which was by the end of the fourth century a major monastic center. By far the largest number of family relationships attested of women deacons is in the group from central Asia Minor, but that is also the area from which the largest number of inscriptions comes. It was also not known as a major center of monastic life, as were Palestine and Egypt, for example.

Henri Leclercq in his 1920 *DACL* article suggested that the female diaconate evolved from the order of widows.[6] After placing deaconesses among those with ordination (*cheirotonia*) and a privileged place among the clergy, he equates their ordination with a blessing because they did not share the deacons' sacramental role. While the nature of their ordination is contested, it is also clear that widows continued to exist in the church as a distinct group at the same time that the order of female deacons was flourishing. Likewise, Elm assumes that by the fifth century the role of deaconess had subsumed those of widow and virgin and was synonymous with abbess of a monastery.[7] Both assumptions prove incorrect in the face of the complete evidence.

METHODOLOGICAL PROBLEMS

There are several methodological problems to be considered. The first is that the reference to Phoebe the *diakonos* at Rom 16:1 cautions us that whatever the function of a *diakonos* in a first-century Pauline church, in the early years any reference to *diakonoi* as a group must not be understood necessarily to refer only to men. We have not collected every early mention of deacons where this could be true, such as in Phil 1:1 or the Letters of Ignatius, but this ambiguity must be kept in mind. It is only in the third century, with the rise of the specifically female diaconate, that the term *diakonos* is more likely to be understood as referring exclusively to men, and even after that the title is still in use for women.

A second problem is the tendency on the part of some modern writers to assume that every major female figure in the early church was a deacon, in spite of an absence of specific mention of their ordination. This is especially true of significant ascetic figures like Paula, the two Melanias, or Macrina.[8] None of their biographers makes reference to such an ordination. In the absence of sound evidence that is not based on later assumptions, we have omitted these references.

A third and most important methodological problem is the possible discrepancy between ancient and modern concepts of ordained ministry and clergy, as well as chronological and geographical variations. Some distinctions must be made that are often ignored by historians and modern commentators. It is necessary to keep in mind the differences between three aspects of church leadership that affected women: ordination, membership in the clergy, and special group status. Sometimes all three designations overlap, but often they do not. For example, the widows of Tertullian's Carthage were apparently not ordained, but they do seem to have been considered members of the clergy, seated with the presbyters in formal assembly and present with them for disciplinary hearings. The widows and female presbyters of the *Testamentum Domini* were probably not ordained either, yet they had a privileged role to play in liturgical assemblies. In some cases, deaconesses clearly were ordained (*DA, AC*) yet did not have a sacramental role at the altar. But commentators too easily dismiss their absence at the altar as an absence from liturgical roles, failing to distinguish between liturgical and sacramental. Except in monastic traditions, those in today's liturgically impoverished West, with its fixation on sacrament and preaching, can too easily forget that recitation of the Divine Office is an essential component of the liturgy. There is ample evidence that female deacons exercised leadership in this role. Then there are the intriguing pieces of evidence of female presbyters who do indeed seem to have exercised a ministry at the altar, even in the West, as documented by Otranto.

SACRAMENTAL ORDINATION?

The question whether the ordination of female deacons was considered "sacramental" is fraught with problems of anachronistic interpretation. Martimort doubts the sacramental nature of their ordination even in the *Apostolic Constitutions*. Gryson accepts it on the basis of the sequence of ordination rites there: that of the deaconess comes between that of the deacon and those of subdeacon and lector, both of the latter being seen as true ordinations. Martimort tries too hard to fit the ancient evidence into "the concepts of our modern theology," whereas Gryson is willing to see the ancient evidence on its own terms.[9] One author tried to make a case that *cheirotonia* was a general term for appointment, while *cheirothesia* had a more specific meaning of sacramental ordination.[10] But another scholar argued just the opposite: that *cheirotonia* meant ordination by laying on of hands, reserved only to bishop, presbyter, deacon, and deaconess, while lesser orders received a simple blessing or establishment.[11] Gary Macy has shown that well into the twelfth century, the terminology of ordination in the Latin Church was not precise, and deaconesses and abbesses even in the West were considered as fully ordained as male clergy. Abbesses were expected to perform certain sacramental roles, such as preaching and hearing the confessions of their nuns.[12]

There is no doubt that in some times and places the ordination of female deacons was seen as sacramental, even if not for exactly the same purposes as that of male deacons. In 1995, the (Roman Catholic) Canon Law Society of America reached that conclusion and offered suggestions for contemporary reintroduction of the order.[13] By contrast, the 2002 document of the Vatican's International Theological Commission on the diaconate acknowledges that at one time deaconesses were members of the clergy, but it stresses the differences between their order and that of deacons, and it refrains from judgment on the sacramentality of their ordination.[14]

So what did deaconesses do?

Once a sense of clerical status had developed, that is, by the early third century, it is fairly clear that ordained or clergy women ordinarily did not perform the same role as their male counterparts. The role of the female deacon as a special ministry to women is briefly described in the *Didascalia* and in more detail in the *Apostolic Constitutions* dependent on it: assistance at the baptism of women, including anointing of the body of the female baptizand, pastoral visits and religious instruction with women, welcoming and maintaining order among women at the assembly, and travel and authorized representation of the church. They were the liaison between women and the bishop and accompanied women who visited him.[15]

But these canonical descriptions do not explain all the textual references, for example, the activity of the deaconess Lampadion in Gregory of Nyssa's *Life of Macrina,* who evidently was some kind of leader but not the monastic community superior (a title reserved to Macrina), or the reference in Justinian's *Novellae* 6.6 to both men and women's apparent participation in sacred rites (*aporrētoi, sebasmiōtata mystēria*) and administration of (not assistance at) baptism. A close study of some of the literary sources fleshes out that description better. Female deacons prepared women for baptism and offered them hospitality during the transitional time before and after (Manaris, Romana). They provided hospitality and protection to socially vulnerable women (unnamed deacon of Caesarea). They were advocates and agents for laywomen in the church (Susanna). They traveled with women pilgrims (Theophila). They embarked on pilgrimages themselves (Severa of Jerusalem). Some were monastic superiors (Eugenia, Jannia, Olympias, Theodula, Valeriana). Some were trusted teachers (unnamed deacon of Theodoret). Others were members of monastic communities but not superiors (Lampadion, Elisanthia, Martyria, and Palladia). Some supervised important centers of pilgrimage (Marthana, Matrona of Cosila). Others lived in their own house (Eusebia). They supervised liturgical roles of women and led them in liturgical prayer (Elisanthia, Martyria, and Palladia). In fifth and sixth-century Edessa, some canonical texts grant that religious superiors of women who were deaconesses performed a variety of liturgical roles, even to the point of pouring the wine and water in the chalice at the Eucharist and doing other actions in the sanctuary in the absence of a priest or deacon. They also read the Gospel and other Scriptures in assemblies of women.[16] At least one raised a foster child (Athanasia of Korykos). They sometimes owned slaves (Eirene of Thebes). Like others in the church, they dedicated mosaic pavements (Agrippianē, Andromacha, Matrona of Stobi, Zoe), columns (Aretē, Celerina), and altar screens (Zaortha). They are sometimes buried in ecclesiastical contexts, sometimes in familial contexts. They sometimes came from families with many members of the clergy, sometimes not. Female monastic leaders were sometimes deacons, and in other cases, one or more female deacons resided in a monastery but did not hold the place of superior.

Oddly, two texts that do not identify their women characters as deacons may in fact give us a clue to some of the liturgical activities of female deacons. In Cyril of Scythopolis's *Life of Theodosius* (236.19–237.1; the narrative time is about 450 CE) Cyril relates that Theodosius, an aspiring Palestinian monk, being new to the ascetic life, was sent by his superior to a holy woman named Hikelia (who is given no title) who was building the church of the Kathisma of the Mother of God between Jerusalem and Bethlehem, so that he could be useful to her in the office and ministries of the church. Surely some of Hikelia's work refers to charitable activities. But Cyril also relates that Hikelia introduced there the celebration of the feast of the Presentation of Jesus in the Temple with the use of candles. She received Theodosius and made him a cantor in the church and member of the ascetic group under her authority there. When she died, he was appointed steward of the church, which, it is clear in the narrative, was not the same office as superior of the ascetic community.

Cyril's *Life of Cyriacus* (233.27–28) also mentions a woman cantor at the Church of the Anastasis in Jerusalem. While neither text says that the woman in question was a deacon or held any other official ecclesiastical position, both women clearly exercised liturgical leadership. Hikelia was a liturgical innovator as well as coordinator. These are the kinds of functions that female deacons, whether they were ordained or not, may have been exercising widely in the East at the time.

Women who were wives of deacons usually did not hold the title of deaconess, as often became true in the case of wives of presbyters. This is clear, for instance, from two inscriptions from Hadrianopolis in Phrygia, in which wives commemorate their deceased deacon husbands, with no mention of a title for the wives.[17]

DEACONS OR DEACONESSES?

The earlier title is *diakonos* with feminine article, already used in Rom 16:1–2 of Phoebe. Most assume that Pliny's *ministrae* are the equivalent, but we do not know that for sure. The later term *diakonissa* appears in a datable Greek text for the first time in Canon nineteen of Nicaea. It is used in the Latin translation of the *Didascalia,* but neither the date of the translation nor the term used in the original Greek is known.[18] It also appears in the *Apostolic Constitutions,* usually thought to date to the late fourth century (*AC* 3.11.3, a passage independent of the *Didascalia*). Book Eight, after one alternative form, *diakonē* (8.13.14), uses *diakonissa* throughout. But this must mean that the title was already in general use. From then on, both terms are used in both literature and inscriptions, with no perceivable difference of time or place, and in Latin another version, *diacona,* comes into use. Eisen, *Women Officeholders,* tries to form conclusions about regional usage, but the samples are so small that nothing can be stated for sure. Apart from the small samples from any particular region there is also the difficulty that a number of inscriptions abbreviate the title of office to *di, diak,* or something similar, which could be either *diakonos* or *diakonissa.*

In the literature, the same person can be called by different titles by different persons. John Chrysostom calls his aunt Sabiniana a *diakonos,* while Palladius calls her a *diakonissa.* John's friend Olympias is consistently a *diakonos.* Even in some of the latest canonical texts, both terms are in use in both the West and East (e.g., the Councils of Orange, 441 CE, and of Epaon, 517 CE and the *Life of Saint Radegunda,* ca. 600 CE: *diacona;* epitaph of Theodora of Ticini, 539 CE: *diaconissa;* Justinian's regulations use both terms, once switching between them in the same article, *Novellae* 6.6). We can only conclude on the basis of present evidence that the terms were interchangeable. English translations tend to be inexact about this, assuming that "deaconess" is the appropriate term for a woman (even sometimes for Phoebe in Rom 16:1!). In the translations in this book, we have tried to keep the difference straight by rendering "deacon" for *diakonos* or *diacona,* "deaconess" for *diakonissa*—and noting the uncertainty for the abbreviation *diak.*

PRESBYTERS

There is of course much less evidence for women presbyters than for women deacons, yet it is clear that something along these lines was happening in certain times and places, perhaps under the influence of Montanism in the East beginning in the early third century, and the Prisicillianist movement in the West. Heresiologists like Tertullian, Epiphanius, and Augustine want to give the impression that only in these "deviant" groups are such practices done. Yet the existing evidence cannot be confined to members of these movements. Documents like the Synod of Nimes and the Letter of Gelasius are addressed to their own people and bishops. What exactly the practices were is unclear. What can be said with certainty is that the claim that women have never functioned as presbyters in the "orthodox" church is simply untrue.

CONCLUSION

Most previous studies of female deacons have focused on the nature of their ordination and sacramental role, or lack thereof. We have given some consideration to this question, but we hope that by expanding the presentation of evidence, we can move beyond these juridical questions to a greater appreciation of these women for who they were and what they actually did.

Certainly the evidence for women presbyters is far less, but it cannot be confined to fringe or "heretical" groups. The intriguing profile that emerges is the larger number of references in the West than in the East, in spite of the determined efforts of various councils to eliminate them.

Notes

1. See Martimort, *Deaconesses,* 202. This is *CIL* 5.180: DACIANA DIACONISSA QUE V AN XXXXV M III ET FUIT F PALMATI COS ET SOROR VICTORINI PRESBRI ET MULTA PROPHETAVIT CUM FLACCA ALUMNA V A XV DEP IN PACE III ID AUG (Daciana deaconess, who lived 45 years 3 months, and was daughter of Palmatius, consul, and sister of Victorinus, presbyter, and prophesied extensively, with Flacca, foster child who lived 15 years. Buried in peace, August 13). First published by Francesco Scipione Maffei, *Museum Veronense hoc est Antiquarum Inscriptionum atque Anaglyphorum Collectio cui Taurinensis adjungitur et Vindobonensis* (Verona: Seminary Press, 1749), 179; included as genuine by Henri Leclerq, "Diaconesses," *DACL* 4 (1920): 733. Palmatius is unknown on the consular lists but appears in the late *Acts of Callistus* (*AASS* 54, pp. 439–41, October 14).

2. See, for example, Henri Leclercq, "Diaconesses," *DACL* 4 (1920): 725–33, and Adolf Kalsbach, *Die altkirchliche Einrichtung der Diakonissen bis zu ihrem Erlöschen* (Freiburg: Herder, 1926). A bibliography of major studies can be found in Gryson, *Ministry of Women,* 121–23. Eisen's extensive bibliographies do not include a collection specifically on this topic.

3. See his note 158, pp. 153–54.

4. See her discussion, *Virgins of God,* 170–83.

5. *Women Officeholders,* 162.

6. See note 1.

7. *Virgins of God,* 180–82.

8. For example, Kyriaki Karidoyanes Fitzgerald, "The Characteristic and Nature of the Order of the Deaconess," *Women and the Priesthood,* ed. Thomas Hopko (Crestwood, NY: St. Vladimir's Seminary Press, 1983) 75–95.

9. The discussion is laid out in an appendix of Gryson, *Ministry of Women,* 115–20 and 156, n.1–2, in response to Martimort's rejoinder to the original French edition of Gryson's book.

10. C. H. Turner, "*Cheirotonia, cheirothesia, eipthesis cheirōn* (and the Accompanying Verbs)," *JTS* 24 (1922/23): 496–504.

11. Cipriano Vagaggini, "L'ordinazione delle diaconesse nella tradizione greca e bizantina," *Orientalia christiana periodica* 40 (1974): 146–89.

12. Gary Macy, "The Ordination of Women in the Early Middle Ages," *Theological Studies* 61 (2000): 481–507.

13. *The Canonical Implications of Ordaining Women to the Permanent Diaconate,* Report of an Ad Hoc Committee of the Canon Law Society of America, presented to the 57th Annual Meeting (Washington, DC: Canon Law Society of America, 1995).

14. *Quaestiones de Diaconatu,* International Theology Commission, July 2002.

15. The *Apostolic Constitutions* greatly expand on the duties of deaconesses but at the same time seek in some ways to lessen their authority. See discussion in Gryson, *Ministry of Women,* 54–63.

16. Summarized with partial quotations in Martimort, *Deaconesses,* 139–43. The texts are of Rabbula (412–35), John bar Qursos (538), and James of Edessa (683–708).

17. *MAMA* 7.175: "Aurelia Domna Papados to her own dear husband Klaporinios (Calpurnius) deacon, erected to his memory while she was still living" (p. 35); *MAMA* 7.176: [A presumably different, or twice-married] "Aurelia Domna erected this memorial to her own husband Gaius deacon, in loving memory" (p. 35). But see, for instance, Brian Brennan, "'Episcopae': Bishops' Wives Viewed in Sixth-Century Gaul," *Church History* 54.3 (1985): 311–23, about the wives of presbyters (*prebyterae*) and of bishops (*episcopae*) who with their newly ordained husbands embraced celibacy, but continued to live with them and sometimes exercise a great deal of influence in the Merovingian church.

18. Martimort speculates that the original Greek term in the *Didascalia* was *hē diakonos* (*Deaconesses,* 41).

Chapter Two

NEW TESTAMENT TEXTS AND THEIR
PATRISTIC COMMENTATORS

 The New Testament texts most frequently understood to refer to women in church office and that have been commented upon favorably with respect to women deacons are Rom 16:1–2 and 1 Tim 3:11. While today scholars are divided on whether the women of 1 Tim 3:11 are deacons or wives of deacons, the ancient consensus, in a world in which women deacons were known, was the former. It is clear that each of the authors below understood the text from his own context. Pelagius and Ambrosiaster did not know the office of deaconess in the West, but Pelagius acknowledged its existence in the East. John Chrysostom was very familiar with women in the diaconate. The discussion of enrollment of widows in 1 Timothy 5 also muddied the waters for some, like Pelagius, who conflated the two offices or functions of widow and deacon.

Of course, 1 Tim 2:11–15, a passage that rejects the authority of women to teach, was also quoted ubiquitously against the leadership of women, especially against "heretical" groups that practiced it in more expanded ways. Gnostics and Marcionites came in for special criticism here.[1]

Phil 1:1 also needs brief mention. Here, contrary to his usual custom of addressing "the church" or "the saints" in a specific place, he addresses at Philippi "all the saints in Christ Jesus" in Philippi with the *episkopoi* and *diakonoi*. The translation of these terms used in a predominantly Gentile Christian gathering in the middle of the first century is problematic. Sometimes they are translated "bishops and deacons," but certainly the term *episkopos* carried none of the connotations that the word "bishop" does today, or even after Ignatius of Antioch. It is a term borrowed from management functions, meaning a supervisor or overseer.[2] Neither does the other term, *diakonoi*, carry the connotations that it would acquire in the next century. What is clear, however, is that these terms in Phil 1:1 need not be understood as referring to an all-male group, in light of Rom 16:1–2, where Phoebe has the same title. Moreover, the importance of Evodia and Syntyche in Phil 4:2 in the context of the whole appeal for unity in the letter may suggest that these two women are among the *episkopoi*, probably leaders of local house churches.[3] It is interesting to note that Theodore of Mopsuestia read Phil 4:2 as a struggle of the two women for leadership.[4] But there is no direct reference to women in Phil 1:1, and we do not know what duties *diakonoi,* including Phoebe, had at the time. Most probably the office included representation of the community as its agent, perhaps in business or in relationships with other churches.[5]

The use of the term *diakonia* in other New Testament writings also needs to be figured into the attempt to grasp the evolving contextual understanding of the semantic field in the first century. Particularly Luke 10:40 and Acts 6:1–6 must be considered. In the first, the famous Mary and Martha incident, Martha has much *diakonia* and complains that her sister has left her alone to *diakonein.* Given the use of the same vocabulary in Acts 6, Martha's service may be more than just table service. In the passage in Acts, the Twelve find that they can no longer leave the daily *diakonia* to the widows (Acts 6:1), so they delegate the table service (*diakonein trapedzais*) to seven other males (*andres*). That way, the Twelve can then devote themselves to the *diakonia* of the word and prayer (Acts 6:4). Thus, *diakonia* in Christian context is not limited to table service but involves preaching as well. It gets more confusing in the next passage when Stephen, one of the seven chosen for table service, preaches. Contrary to impressions, no one is ever called a *diakonos* in this passage. The exact meaning remains unclear.

ROMANS 16:1–2

Phoebe, Romans 16:1–2

Paul concludes his letter to the Romans by mentioning all those to whom he sends greetings. But first he writes his note of commendation of the probable bearer of the letter, Phoebe. There has been some question whether chapter sixteen of the letter was not originally part of a letter of Paul to Ephesus, now lost, since some of the names (e.g., Prisca and Aquila) are at this later date in Paul's life associated with that city, and because of the argued implausibility of Paul knowing so many people in a city he had never visited.[6] However, the intended audience does not affect the impact of the data: whether to Rome or Ephesus does not matter for our purposes.

> Now I commend to you our sister, Phoebe, being a deacon (*diakonos*) of the church at Cenchreae, in order that you may receive her in the Lord in a manner worthy of the saints and come to her aid in whatever she may need from you, for she has been a benefactor (*prostatis*) of many and of me also!

The language of the passage is typical of a letter of commendation. Phoebe is first called a *diakonos* of the church of Cenchreae, the eastern seaport of Corinth. Figuratively, Paul will refer to himself and other missionaries by this title (e.g., 1 Cor 3:5; 2 Cor 3:6, 6:4), but Phil 1:1 shows us that it was also a title of some kind of function or office in local churches (see also 1 Tim 3:8–13). What exactly a deacon did at this point is not clear, but it may have involved not only local ministerial service but also some kind of official representation of the community, which seems to be the case here, for Phoebe is about to travel and her travel is the occasion for Paul's writing the letter. She may have been traveling on her own business or that of the churches of Cenchreae and Corinth.

Certainly there is no suggestion that her ministry was a ministry especially to women, the kind of female ministry that will later develop in the Syrian churches. The male title is used here, not to be confused with the third-century institution of deaconess. Though incorrect, "deaconess" is often the translation given to *diakonos* in this passage, on the assumption that the proper title for a female deacon is always deaconess. As we shall see below, that is not always the case, even to the sixth century. Phoebe is the only deacon of a first-century church whose name we know. (The seven men appointed by the Twelve in Acts 6:1–6 are called to *diakonia* of the table but are never called deacons.)

Phoebe is also called *prostatis,* benefactor or patron, of Paul and many others. This places her in the social system of patronage as a relatively high-status person to whom Paul is indebted as client for financial support. That is, she is relatively wealthy and probably higher in social ranking than Paul. A plausible comparison is Junia Theodora of first-century Corinth, originally from Lycia, who provided a center of hospitality and advancement for Lycians passing through this commercially strategic city. Her patronage consisted of providing hospitality for traveling Lycians in her own house and cultivating the Roman authorities in their favor; so her favors were not only directed to the Lycians but also performed on their behalf with the political powers. The decree of the Lycian city of Telmessos speaks of her *prostasia* in the context of hospitality and mediation.[7]

Origen, *Commentary on Romans* 10.17 on Romans 16:1–2[8]

Origen (185–253), the preeminent biblical exegete and theologian of his day, was head of the famous catechetical school in Alexandria from early in the third century until 231. At that point, he was ordained in Palestine. His local bishop, Demetrius of Alexandria, deprived him of his priesthood for the irregularity of his ordination (and perhaps out of envy), at which time Origen left for Caesarea, where he founded another great theological school. For some two decades, he continued his writing, teaching, and preaching there. During the Decian persecution (249–51), he was tortured and, perhaps as a consequence, died in 253. He was among the most prolific, profound, and influential authors in the history of Christianity. Many of his voluminous writings were lost because they contained views later thought to be erroneous. Others, including the text here, survive in the Latin translation of the monk Rufinus (345–410).

"I commend to you Phoebe . . ." This passage teaches by apostolic authority that women also are appointed (*constitui*) in the ministry of the church (*in ministerio ecclesiae*), in which office Phoebe was placed at the church that is in Cenchreae. Paul with great praise and commendation even enumerates her splendid deeds . . . And therefore this passage teaches two things equally and is to be interpreted, as we have said, to mean that women are to be considered ministers (*haberi . . . feminas ministras*) in the church, and that such ought to be received into the ministry (*tales debere assumi in ministerium*) who have assisted many; they have earned the right through their good deeds to receive apostolic praise.

Martimort argues that Origen meant to suggest here that women were called to serve the church in the same role as Phoebe—in acts of charity and hospitality, essentially—and that such acts should be honored.[9] The "ministry" treated here "is thus the consecration by the church of charitable activities performed for the sake of one's Christian brethren." He goes on to argue that when Origen declared "'there are women deacons in the Church,' it is inadmissible to infer from this statement that he was talking about an institution that existed in the church of Alexandria of his day or, indeed, in any other particular church of that time." Martimort concludes "Neither widows nor deaconesses were in [Origen's] mind included in the sacred hierarchy."[10] Gryson, with whom Martimort explicitly agrees, had already argued that Origen "never mentioned deaconesses among the ministers of the church" and that "wherever the Alexandrians mentioned deacons or widows, they referred to the past, not to the present."[11]

It is regrettable that the text survives only in Latin translation, which makes it more difficult to arrive at any definitive interpretation. It may well be true that the exact juridical status of the female ministers, their relationship to male hierarchy, ritual induction, and qualifications (other than a record of charity and assistance) are left unclear here. It is even unclear whether *ministra* should be here translated "minister" or "deaconess." Likewise *ministerium* could signify "diaconate" rather than "ministry." The most literal translation is presented here simply on the principle of caution. But it is not impossible, *pace* Martimort, that Origen had the institution of deaconesses and the ministry of the female diaconate in mind.

John Chrysostom, *Homily* 30 on Rom 16:1–2[12]

John Chrysostom (c. 347–407) was a well-educated citizen of Antioch, ordained deacon and presbyter of that city in 381 and 386. He became so well known as a preacher that he received his nickname Chrysostom ("golden-mouth"). His fame became so great that he was appointed bishop of the capital, Constantinople, in 398, where his downfall began. Strong in eloquence, he had no sense of "political correctness" and soon found himself on the wrong side of certain powerful persons in the imperial court, especially the empress Eudoxia. At the same time, he was staunchly defended by other friends, among them the deaconesses Olympias, Pentadia, and Procla. He was finally tried, deposed, and sent into exile, where he died four years later. He is considered the greatest preacher of the patristic church and is one of the four doctors of the Eastern Church.

"I commend to you our sister Phoebe, a deacon of the church of Cenchrae." See how much he distinguishes her, for he mentions her before all the others and calls her "sister." It is not a small thing to be called Paul's sister, and he adds her status by calling her "deacon." "That you receive her worthily of the saints." That is, for the sake of the Lord, that she be honored through you. The one who is received for the sake of the Lord, even if not very important, is received with great care. Since she is holy, think of what great care she is worthy. This is why he adds "worthily of the saints," as they should be received. There is double occasion for her to be cared for by you, for she is to be received for the sake of the Lord, and because she is holy" . . . How can she not be blessed, who enjoys such a witness from Paul, who is able to help him who set the whole world straight? This is the finishing touch on her good deeds, since he goes so far as to say "and of me as well" (e.g., that she is patron, *prostatis*). What is this "and of me as well"? Of the herald of the world, of the one who suffered so much, of the one who satisfied countless numbers of people. Both men and women, let us imitate this holy one!

In these quick remarks on the text of Romans, Chrysostom acknowledges Phoebe's rank of deacon, probably equating it with the office of deaconess that existed in his day, and with which he was quite familiar (see his relationship, for instance, with Olympias). He waxes eloquent about Phoebe's holiness in a rather unusual but pleasing way, designed to attract his listeners, both male and female. Unfortunately, in the passage between the quotes given here, he does not comment on the term *prostatis* applied to Phoebe by Paul.

Theodoret of Cyrrhus, *Commentary on Romans* 16:1–3[13]

Theodoret (c. 393–460) was raised in Antioch and educated in monastic schools, then entered a monastery. He was pulled from it in 423 to become bishop of Cyrrhus in Syria. He became involved in the christological controversy between Nestorius and Cyril of Alexandria, with greater sympathy for the Nestorian arguments. This put him in conflict with Cyril and his successor Dioscurus, and he was one of those deposed at the "Robber Council" of Ephesus in 449; he was restored by the new rulers Pulcheria and Marcian in 450 and was active at the Council of Chalcedon in 451. A century later, his writings against Cyril were condemned at the Council of Constantinople of 553. Many of his writings have survived, especially biblical commentaries.

"Now I commend to you our sister, Phoebe, a deacon of the church at Cenchreae, in order that you may receive her in the Lord in a manner worthy of the saints and come to her aid in whatever she may need from you, for she has been a patron of many and of me also! Greet Priscilla and Aquila, my co-workers in Christ Jesus." Cenchreae is a large village of Corinth. It is worth admiring the strength of the preaching. In a short time not only the cities, but also the villages were filled with piety. Such was the significance of the church at Cenchreae that it had a female deacon, honorable and well known. Such was the wealth of her accomplishments that she was praised by the apostolic tongue.

"For she has been a patron of many and of me also." I think what he calls patronage (*prostasia*) is hospitality (*philoxenia*) and protection (*kēdemonia*). Praise is heaped upon her. It seems she received him in a house for a little time, for it is clear that he stayed in Corinth. He opened the world to her and in every land and sea she is celebrated. For not only do the Romans and Greeks know her, but even all the barbarians.

Cenchreae is actually one of the two seaports of Corinth, on the eastern or Aegean side. Theodoret suggests that the size or importance of Cenchreae is related to the community having a female deacon. This probably says more about the church as Theodoret knows it than about the church in first-century Corinth. But he certainly has some inspiring things to say about Phoebe. He also understands the function of patronage as care exercised from a more powerful social position than the recipient's.

Ambrosiaster, *Commentary on Romans* 16:1[14]

Ambrosiaster ("Pseudo-Ambrose") is the name given to the author of the oldest Latin commentary on the Pauline letters. Based on internal evidence (such as a reference to Damasus [366–84] presiding as pope hodie *["today"]), the commentary has been dated to the late fourth century. Throughout the Middle Ages, it was mistakenly attributed to Ambrose, Archbishop of Milan (340–97), a "doctor of the church," and so it enjoyed considerable authority. In the sixteenth century, Erasmus proved the ascription spurious; since then, the author has been known as Ambrosiaster. In much of his commentary on Paul, Ambrosiaster is, as Gryson has observed, "extremely harsh toward women."[15]*

"I commend to you our sister Phoebe, a deaconess of the church at Cenchreae that you may receive her in the Lord as befits the saints, and help her in whatever she may require from you, for she has been a helper of many and of myself as well." He says she is a minister (*ministram*) of the Church at Cenchreae. And because she was a help to many, he says she too ought to be helped on account of her journey.

For Ambrosiaster, *ministra* does not signify a distinct, well-recognized category of ecclesiastical office, nor is Phoebe to be enumerated among the "deacons" of the churches. As Gryson has correctly observed, Ambrosiaster understood the term *ministra* "in a non-technical sense."[16] As far as he was concerned, this simply meant that she was a "helper" of many and had ministered to them in this nonjuridical, general capacity. That Latin commentators like Ambrosiaster confronted the Bible only in its Latin version helped to prevent some from recognizing a *ministra* as the equivalent of "female deacon" or "deaconess."

Pelagius, *Commentary on Romans* 16:1[17]

Pelagius's is one of the most famous names in ecclesiastical history. He is often associated with the view, eventually condemned as heretical, that humanity could take the initial step toward salvation apart from the operation of divine grace. (This is a somewhat crude expression of his fundamental views.) Less controversially, this British ascetic, born sometime in the mid-fourth century, certainly became leader of an austere, lay, aristocratic movement in Rome. From Rome, he moved on to North Africa. After his departure for the East, Pelagius and his views were condemned by two North African councils in 416, a condemnation recapitulated the following year by Pope Innocent. He is probably most famous for having occasioned (as did his followers and defenders, most notably Bishop Julian of Eclanum) many of Augustine's writings on the interconnected ideas of original sin, free will, grace, and anthropology. Pelagius wrote voluminously. However, much that he wrote has been lost. Some has been transmitted under other names. For example, his commentary on the Pauline corpus, completed early in the fifth century, often traveled under the name of Jerome. The following is an extract from his Commentary on Romans *(ca. 405–9), probably completed when Pelagius was active among the aristocracy in Rome at the end of the fourth century and before he became involved in the controversy that now bears his name.*

> "I commend to you our sister Phoebe, a servant of the church in Cenchreae" (Rom 16:1) Just as even now in the East, deaconesses (*diaconissae*) are seen to minister in baptism to those of their own sex, or in the ministry of the word, so we have found women who have taught in private (*privatim docuisse feminas invenimus*), as did Priscilla, whose husband was named Aquila.

This text can be interpreted in two ways. First, one might suppose that Pelagius presumes that the female diaconate in the West, once extant, no longer exists. This may well be an indication that it no longer existed in Rome. (However, other evidence, inscriptional and literary, suggests that it would exist in other parts of the West long after Pelagius was active in Rome.) Alternatively, Pelagius might presume that the office had never existed in the West.[18] If this is true, the text could be interpreted to mean that Pelagius was not yet aware of the existence of the office in the West. Following Eisen, this could be because the "explicit attestation of women deacons begins [only] in the fourth century" or "only became a problem in the fourth century" and Pelagius was thus ignorant of the office and of evidence pointing to its existence. In either case, Pelagius interestingly observes that he has known women who taught privately. This would reflect, as de Bruyn has suggested, "the custom of his day, when aristocratic women both sought and gave instruction in the privacy of their homes."[19]

1 TIMOTHY 3:8–11

A scholarly consensus dates 1 Timothy to the late first century, written by a follower of the Pauline tradition who also probably wrote the Letter to Titus and perhaps 2 Timothy a generation or two after Paul's death. The Letter to Titus reinforces the need for fidelity to the tradition received and the surrogate family structure of the community (see 5:1–19).

> **In the same way, deacons are to be serious, not given to double-talk, not with a tendency to much wine, not eager for dishonest profit, holding to the mystery of faith with a clear conscience. And let them first be approved, then let them perform their diaconal ministry blamelessly. In the same way, women are to be serious, not irresponsible talkers, sober, faithful in all things.**

It is not clear whether the women of verse 11 are female deacons or wives of the male deacons of the previous verses, since Greek does not have different words for "woman" and "wife" nor for "man" and "husband." Two factors suggest that female deacons are referred to here. First is the mention of the female deacon Phoebe at an earlier stage of the development of ministerial structures in the Pauline churches (Rom 16:1–2). Second, the structures of verse 8 about men and verse 11 about women are parallel: the first three words of the Greek text are exactly the same except for gender changes. If female deacons were still referred to by the masculine designation as in Rom 16:1, there would be no other way to make a gender distinction in verse 11, the generic term *diakonoi* already having been used in verse 8. Some modern commentators opt for wives of male deacons here, but as we see below, quite a few early commentators understood the text as referring to female deacons.

John Chrysostom Homily 11 on 1 Timothy 3:11[20]

"Likewise women must be modest, not slanderers, sober, faithful in everything." Some say that he is talking about women in general. But that cannot be. Why would he want to insert in the middle of what he is saying something about women? But rather, he is speaking of those women who hold the rank of deacon. "Deacons should be husbands of one wife." This is also appropriate for women deacons (*diakonoi*), for it is necessary, good, and right, most especially in the church.

The point that John makes is still disputed in the interpretation of the text from Timothy (see discussion on the text itself above). Here the commentator is clear which option he favors. In John's churches in Antioch and Constantinople, female deacons or deaconesses were well known. His application of the one-marriage rule to women deacons seems to suggest that in late-fourth-century Antioch, they were allowed to marry and so need not have been celibate.

Theodoret of Cyrrhus, *Commentary on 1 Timothy* 3:11[21]

"In the same way, women" that is, the deacons (*diakonous*), "are to be serious, not irresponsible talkers, sober, faithful in everything." What he directed for the men, he did similarly for the women. Just as he told the male deacons to be serious, he said the same for the women. As he commanded the men not to be two-faced, so he commanded the women not to talk irresponsibly. And as he commanded the men not to drink much wine, so he ordered that the women should be temperate.

Theodoret is another commentator on 1 Timothy who interprets the women as deacons. He understands that the author has the same expectations about the virtuous conduct of both male and female deacons.

Theodore of Mopsuestia, *Commentary on 1 Timothy* 3:11[22]

Theodore of Mopsuestia (350–428) was one of the most prolific and influential Greek commentators on the Bible of his era. After studying rhetoric in Antioch, he entered the school and monastery of Antioch for ten years. In 392, he was made bishop of Mopsuestia. He was twice condemned, at the Councils of Ephesus (431) and Constantinople (553) for christological dualism, though modern scholars have given good reasons for believing such condemnations to have been ill founded. His commentaries on the minor epistles of Paul survive only fragmentarily in Greek, more fully in Latin translation.

"The women likewise must be serious, no slanderers, but temperate, faithful in all things." Paul does not wish to say this in this passage because it is right for such [deacons] to have wives; but since it is fitting for women to be established to perform duties similar to those of deacons.

For Theodore, as for his Greek contemporaries, there is an order of deaconesses that is parallel in status and function to the male diaconate. Accordingly, he goes on to comment that such women must be discreet (*non accusatrices*), capable of keeping confidences so as to prevent arguments and divisions (*divortia*) in the community.[23] When he comments on 1 Tim 5:9, we learn more about how he views their status and place in the hierarchy.

Ambrosiaster, *Commentary on 1 Timothy* 3:11[24]

"The women likewise must be chaste, not slanderers but sober, faithful in all things" ... But the Cataphyrgians seize an occasion for error. Because women are spoken of after deacons, they argue with a vain presumption that female deaconesses (*diaconissas*)[25] ought to be ordained (*debere ordinari*), although they know that the apostles chose seven male deacons. Was it that no woman was found to be suitable (*idonea*), when we read that, among the eleven apostles, there were holy women? But—as is the wont of heretics, who build their thought on the words of the law rather than its sense—they oppose the Apostle by using his own words. Thus, when he orders women to be silent in the church, they on the contrary attempt to vindicate for her the authority of her ministry.

Ambrosiaster assigns the origins of the office of deaconess to "the Cataphrygians"—the name that he and (as we shall see) Augustine and John of Damascus give to the Montanists. Here he uses the holiness of the women among the apostles to underline their unsuitability for diaconal ministry. *Despite* their holiness, their gender excluded them from such ministry. Oddly, he uses the apostolic injunction against speaking in church to suggest that women were excluded from a form of ministry that did not require, or even allow, female speech there. In his *Commentary on Romans,* he resorts to philological grounds to deny the institution of the female diaconate.

Pelagius, *Commentary on 1 Timothy* 3:11[26]

The women likewise must be chaste [*pudicas*] (1 Tim 3:11). He orders that they be selected similarly to the way in which deacons are chosen. Apparently, he is speaking of those who still today (*adhuc hodie*) in the East are called deaconesses (*diaconissas*).

Pelagius, writing around 410, sees here apostolic foundation for the female diaconate. Again, his comment suggests that he believes the Western diaconate no longer exists at the same time that it suggests its Eastern counterpart does. In his eyes, then, there is a vestigial practice in the East for which the church of Rome had no parallel. There is allusion here to qualifications for induction to the diaconate—*pudica* means "chaste" or "pure"—but no reference to liturgical or pedagogical function, or to ecclesiastical status.

1 TIMOTHY 5:3–13

For an introduction to 1 Timothy, see the previous section.

> Honor widows who are really widows. If any widow has children or grandchildren let them first learn to honor those of their own house and to repay the services of their parents, for this is pleasing before God. But the true widow who has been left alone has hoped in God and remains in prayer and supplication night and day. But the one who continues in self-indulgence, has died while still alive. Commend these things so that they might turn out to be above reproach. But if anyone does not provide for one's own and especially a member of one's household, that one has denied the faith and is worse than an unbeliever.
>
> Let a widow be enrolled if she is not less than sixty years old, has been married only once, is seen to have done good works, has raised children, provided hospitality, washed the feet of the saints, helped those in distress, and pursued every good work. But refuse younger widows, for whenever they may feel the impulse that alienates them from Christ, they want to marry. They incur judgment because they set aside their first faith. But at the same time, they also learn to be idle, running around to houses, not only idle but even gossips and busybodies, saying what they should not say.

It seems that two different practices about widows are spoken of here. First, widows who truly have no means of family support should be maintained by the Church. Second, there are qualifications for being accepted into this group that imply further services: a successful career as wife and mother and proven ability to provide hospitality. Probably this is an early reference to what later develops in many places as an "order of widows," which served as the service organization of the early church, especially for works of charity to needy women and hospitality to visitors. Given average life expectancy in antiquity, sixty was an advanced age. The sharp words about widows as wandering gossips reflect the informal female communication network that functions in most traditional cultures, which men typically disdain because they are excluded from it. It will be a repeated stereotype in later literature.

Theodore of Mopsuestia, *Commentary on 1 Timothy* 5:9 [27]

"No widow may be put on the list of widows unless she is over sixty, has been faithful to her husband, and is well known for her good deeds, such as bringing up children, showing hospitality, washing the feet of the saints, helping those in trouble and devoting herself to all kinds of good deeds."

Above all, the Apostle believed he had designated the age which those to be received into the order of widows (*in ordinem viduarum*) ought to have attained. Some people, however, not considering his reasons for wanting to indicate this age, have wondered whether it was fitting that deaconesses (*diaconissas*) be ordained (*ordinari*) before this age.

One is frustrated by this being translation from the Greek. Nonetheless, from what we know about widows and deaconesses from other texts, we can draw certain conclusions. First of all, for Theodore (unlike for Epiphanius of Salamis), widows seem to be part of an "order" and thus part of the clergy. The same might be said of deaconesses. Indeed, they are ordained so far as Theodore sees it; this in fact corresponds to what was happening in the Eastern church from the fourth century on.

Pelagius, *Commentary on 1 Timothy* 5:9 [28]

"Let a widow not less than sixty years of age be chosen . . ." (1 Tim 5:9) He wanted such deaconesses to be chosen so that they might be examples of living for all.

Here Pelagius identifies widows and deaconesses and sees their role as an exemplary one in the community.

CONCLUSION

Generally, wherever female deacons are already known and accepted, the biblical texts are read to support the practice that is already done. John Chrysostom,

Theodoret, and Theodore know and accept women deacons. The possible exception here is Origen, for it has been argued that, other than this passage, there is a total lack of evidence for women deacons in Egypt, and so he could not have been writing about the church of Alexandria. There is much more possibility that he knew the rise of the female diaconate in Caesarea, however, or other places in his extensive travels. Be that as it may, he is the strongest to claim "apostolic authority" for the institution. Pelagius knows of it, but only in the East, and seems neutral to it. But he conflates widows with deacons in 1 Timothy. Ambrosiaster, never known as someone favorable to women, prefers to put Romans 16 in a general framework of ministry, and resists the reading of women deacons in 1 Tim 3:11. But the biblical texts are only the first step.

Notes

1. E.g., Epiphanius, *Panarion* 49.3, where against Montanist use of Gal 3:28, he quotes Gen 3:16b; 1 Tim 2:12; 1 Cor 11:9 (out of context); and 1 Tim 2:14.

2. See, e.g., Frederick W. Danker, *A Greek-English Lexicon of the New Testament and other Early Christian Literature*, 3rd ed. (Chicago: University of Chicago Press, 2000) 379–80.

3. For more, see Carolyn Osiek, *Philippians Philemon* Abingdon New Testament Commentaries (Nashville: Abingdon, 2000) 110–13.

4. *Peri prōteiōn* 4.3. Swete, *In Epistolas,* 1.245. Thanks to Yancy Smith for this reference.

5. See John N. Collins, *Diakonia: Re-interpreting the Ancient Sources* (New York: Oxford University Press, 1990).

6. Karl P. Donfried, "A Short Note on Romans 16," in *The Romans Debate,* ed. Karl P. Donfried, revised and expanded edition. (Peabody, MA: Hendrickson, 1991), 44–52.

7. Roz Kearsley, "Women in Public Life in the Roman East: Junia Theodora, Claudia Metrodora, and Phoebe, Benefactress of Paul," *Ancient Society: Resources for Teachers* 15 (1985): 124–37; *New Docs* 6.3, pp. 24–25.

8. *Der Römerbriefkommentar des Origenes,* ed. Caroline P. Hammond Bammel (Freiburg: Herder, 1990–98), 3.832–33; Mayer, *Monumenta,* 8–9.

9. *Deaconnesses,* 82–83.

10. Ibid., 83. See also Anonymous, "On the Early History and Modern Revival of Deaconesses," in *Church Quarterly Review* 47 (1898–99): 302–41, which makes the same point emphatically on pp. 308–9.

11. *Ministry of Women,* 32.

12. *PG* 60.663–64.

13. *PG* 82.217; Martimort, *Deaconesses,* 117.

14. *CSEL* 83 (1966): 476–77.

15. *Ministry of Women,* 92.

16. Ibid., 97.

17. *PL* 30.714.

18. See Eisen, *Women Officeholders,* 185. Eisen also observes that "in previous centuries they bore the title *diacona* and were thus terminologically invisible within the group of *diaconi*"

(ibid.)—a term which could have embraced both male and female deacons. This, too, could explain why Pelagius is unaware of female deacons in the West.

19. Theodore de Bruyn, *Pelagius's Commentary on St. Paul's Epistle to the Romans* (Oxford: Oxford University Press, 1993) 151 n.2.

20. *PG* 62.553; Mayer, *Monumenta,* 18; reference in Martimort, *Deaconesses,* 118.

21. *PG* 82.809; Martimort, *Deaconesses,* 118.

22. Swete, *In Epistolas,* 2.128.

23. Ibid.

24. Ambrosiaster, *Commentarius in Epistulas Paulinas, CSEL* 81 (1969): 267–68.

25. The editor Vogels puts *diaconas* in parentheses after *diaconissas* without explanation.

26. *PL* 30.880.

27. Swete, *In Epistolas,* 2.128.

28. *PL* 30.883.

WOMEN DEACONS IN THE EAST

Literary Texts, Literary Allusions, Inscriptions

 It is clear that the office of female deacon or deaconess was much more present in the East than in the West. We can probably assume that Phoebe and other unnamed women deacons like her in the first and perhaps second century belonged to an office or function that was not distinguished by sex (see discussion in chapter 2). Phoebe's first-century office, whatever it was, was nothing like that of later deaconesses. In the East, the new office only for women first appears with the *Didascalia* in the early third century. However, none of the literary or epigraphical evidence of actual women deacons surely belonging to this office can be dated before the fourth century, with the obvious exceptions of Phoebe and 1 Timothy 3:11, as discussed in chapter 2, and the two references in the *Shepherd of Hermas* and Pliny's letter to Trajan.

Graptē (*Hermas Vis.* 2.4.3) is included here because of her role that corresponds to later deaconesses' tasks, though she is not given the title. Pliny's slave *ministrae* are also uncertain as to their role, and there is question whether the name, perhaps translated by Pliny himself, is really equivalent to *diakonoi*. However, these two second-century texts may describe women doing what in the next century evolved into the office of deaconess.

When we look at the references to real historical female deacons, whether in literary allusions or inscriptions, a picture emerges that can then be supplemented by prescriptive texts and comments. But it is wise to look first to the reality before examining legislation and official clerical views. The evidence ranges from the third to at least the seventh century, from Armenia to Gaul.

LITERARY TEXTS

The texts on Graptē and the *ministrae* of Pliny are discussed first, since they are clearly earlier than the rest. Graptē, the woman to whom Hermas in Rome entrusts his revelation for communication to the widows and orphans (*Hermas Vis.* 2.4.3) should technically be considered Western, not Eastern. But since both clearly Western deacon references are so much later (sixth century), because Graptē does not actually carry a title, because the underclass Greek-speaking community of Rome can be assumed to have Eastern origins, and because she seems to have a ministry to women and children that foreshadows that of later deaconesses, she is included here. The allusion to *ancillae ministrae* in Pliny's Latin letter is commonly assumed to refer to female deacons who were also slaves. As we shall see, that identification is quite possible but not certain.

After that, the texts are given in alphabetical order, since some are more difficult to date than others. A few are the stuff of legend (e.g., Eusebia [Xenē] and Justina), but most are stories about historical deacons. These references and the legal texts given in chapters 4 and 5 are keys to what female deacons did and how they functioned.

Graptē

Hermas Vis. 2.4.3[1]

The Shepherd of Hermas *is a long apocalyptic and paraenetic document probably written in or near Rome in several editions during the first half of the second century CE. This passage comes from the beginning of the first of three sections and refers to the first piece of revelatory teaching dictated to the recipient Hermas by an elderly woman later identified as the church.*

> Therefore, you will write two small scrolls, and you will send one to Clement and one to Graptē. Clement will send [it] to the cities abroad, since that has been entrusted to him. But Graptē will admonish the widows and orphans.

Hermas is instructed to make two written copies of the revelation he has received and meanwhile to deliver the message orally to the church with its presbyters. One copy goes to Clement, probably to be identified, whether historically or as a literary allusion, with the author of the First Letter of Clement, a prominent leader in the Roman church of the late first century. The other copy goes to an otherwise unknown female teacher who is responsible for the instruction and spiritual development of an identifiable group of widows and their children. Though Graptē receives no title in the text, she exercises an important function as pastoral leader and teacher of a group of women and their children, the role that deaconesses will later play.

Pliny the Younger, *Epistle to Trajan* 10.96[2]

Around 110 CE a number of Christians in Bithynia and Pontus (imperial provinces south of the Black Sea) were executed simply as Christians by the imperial legate, Plin-

*ius Secundus. After the execution, Pliny proceeded to outlaw by edict all sodalities (*hetaeriae*). Although the publication of the edict apparently curtailed some Christian activity (the common meal especially), "the crime," as Pliny put it, "kept spreading." Soon he received an anonymous accusation containing the names of many Christians. In response, Pliny required the new defendants to pray to the gods and to make an offering of incense and wine to the image of the Emperor Trajan (98–117). He also required them to anathematize Christ. However, Pliny wished to find out more about the cult practices of the forbidden sodality. In his celebrated* Letter to Trajan, *Pliny provides the following account of how he did so.*

> I believed it was necessary to find out from two female slaves (*ex duabus ancillis*) who were called deacons (*ministrae*),[3] what was true—and to find out by torture (*per tormenta*).

This is the earliest Latin text that appears to refer to female deacons as a distinct category of Christian minister. For that reason alone it is of great interest. Note, however, that the text says nothing about the status and function of these women in the Christian community. Accordingly, it would be hazardous to link these *ministrae* with allusions to "deaconesses" or "deacons" or "women" elsewhere in early Christian literature. It is possible that these female deacons were, in function and status, not unlike the women referred to in 1 Tim 3:11. But it is not at all certain. It is probably best to conclude that *ministra* signifies a reasonably well-defined and acknowledged role in the community and to recognize that we can say nothing very exact about it. That the two deacons are designated "slaves" (*ancillae*) is of some interest, though any significance attached to this must be in the context of Pliny's statement, later in the letter, that Christians were drawn in these provinces from all classes and he adds, all ages, both sexes, and from city and countryside. In any case, the text does suggest the origin *in nuce* of women deacons in Asia Minor.

Amproukla

John Chrysostom, *Letters* 96, 103, 101[4]

John Chrysostom (347–407) was one of the most eloquent preachers and classically educated scholars of the early Church, but not one of the most politically savvy. He was born in Syria about 347, and baptized in 368 after a time of study in Antioch with Libanius, the most famous rhetorician of the day. After Christian study, he spent some years in the eremetical life and cultivated an appreciation of solitude. By 386, he was a presbyter of the church of Antioch, making a mark with his learned and inspiring sermons. Because of these strengths, he became bishop of Constantinople in 398 (against his will), and thereafter was in a situation where he was over his head. His straight-

forward character could not cope with the intricacies of imperial politics, and soon opposition to him was mounting, not only from clerics and other bishops but from the empress Eudoxia. By 404, he was in his second and permanent exile somewhere east of Antioch, where he died three years later. His correspondence from exile is plentiful, and many of his letters are addressed to women. His most loyal supporter was Olympias. For more on John Chrysostom, see Pentadia, below.

> Letter 191: "To Amproukla deacon"
> Letters 96 and 103: "To Amproukla deacon and those [fem.] with her"
> Letter 103 calls her "my most honored and revered lady"
> Letter 191 calls her "my most honored and adorned lady"

We know nothing more of this *diakonos* beyond her apparent location in Constantinople and her loyal support of John. His letters to her are familiar and warm, thanking her for her correspondence and support, asking her to write soon about her health and general situation, and theologizing on his situation. The addresses in *Letters* 96 and 103 that include "those [fem.] with her" are taken to mean that she is head, or at least member, of a monastery. Yet elsewhere in the letters he refers to desiring news about her whole household (*oikos*), which could mean relatives and slaves. This reference does not sound as if she is in a monastery, unless it is in her own house. Then again, it is said of Olympias that she gathered in her monastery many of her relatives and fifty of her chambermaids (*Life of Olympias* 6). Amproukla could be the same as the deacon Procla in Palladius' *Dialogue* 10.50 (see sources from Pentadia and Olympias below).

Anastasia

Severus of Antioch, *Letters* 69, 70, 71, 72[5]

Severus (c. 465–538) was educated in Alexandria and Beirut, baptized in 488, and then became a monk. By 508, he was active in Constantinople on behalf of persecuted Monophysite monks. He became bishop of Antioch in 512 after the deposition of Flavian II from that office, but was deposed by emperor Justin in 518 because of his Monophysite beliefs. He went into exile in Egypt and was formally excommunicated by a synod of Constantinople in 528. He was an important theologian of the moderate Monophysite position. His many writings are still being edited. At least 125 homilies and 400 letters survive, mostly in Syriac translation from the original Greek.

*   The four letters to Anastasia were probably written after his exile from Antioch. There is no accurate knowledge of where Anastasia lived, but she had embraced*

monastic life.[6] Letter *69 is quite long. It begins by acknowledging her request for an explanation of the parable of the nocturnal request for hospitality (Luke 11:5–13). A long allegorical exegesis ensues and leads into discussion of the rewards of asceticism, all enriched with many quotations and allusions from biblical sources, Gregory of Nyssa, Basil, and Sozomen. It also contains an allusion, drawn from an apocryphal gospel, to the virgin Mary being kept in the Temple. Toward the end, Severus comments on her previous statement that she felt in order to be perfect that she must feel detached from her brother Innocent and her "sisters in the faith," perhaps her monastic community. He encourages her, on the contrary, not to think in this way but to continue her affection for them as well as for himself. The other letters are briefer comments on various passages of Scripture and the ascetic life and contain no contextual information, perhaps because this material has been removed in the editing.*

All four letters are addressed: "To Anastasia the deaconess"

The Syriac word for deaconess is *mshamshānîtâ,* the usual term. Only the allusion to concern for her "sisters in the faith" in *Letter* 69 might suggest that she is a superior. Nothing else indicates this. As we also see in the case of Lampadion in Asia Minor two centuries earlier and the deaconesses in the monastery of Olympias contemporary with this text, a deaconess in a monastery is not necessarily the superior. This becomes even clearer when one considers Severus' letter to Eugenia (see below), which specifies that she is both deaconess and superior. There, Severus finds it necessary to address her by both titles, which would seem to indicate that they are not co-terminus.[7]

Axia

Theodoret of Cyrrhus, *Letter* Patmos 48 (44)[8]

Theodoret (c. 393–460) was born in Antioch and became bishop of nearby Cyrrhus in 423. In the controversies surrounding the Council of Ephesus, his christology made significant contributions to the Antiochene position. Because of it, he was deposed from his episcopate at the "Robber Council" of Ephesus in 449, where Alexandrian interests prevailed, but restored at the Council of Chalcedon in 451.

To Axia, deacon

The brief letter is a message of condolence to a *diakonos* on the death of a woman named Susanna, whom Theodoret said was renowned for her wisdom, goodness, and care. Nothing more is known either of Susanna or of Axia. The date of the letter is unknown. For other letters of Theodoret, see Casiana and Celerina.

Basilina

Cyril of Scythopolis, *Life of John the Hesychast* 218.21–219.7; 219.19–220.4[9]

Cyril was born about 525 in Scythopolis, the Hellenistic-Byzantine name for the ancient city of Bet Shean at the south end of Galilee in the Jordan Valley. He first encountered Saint Sabas in his home city in 531, and left home to embrace the eremitical life in 543. After his conversion to the eremitical life, he traveled to Jerusalem, then lived for a while as a hermit beside the Jordan River. By 544 he was in the monastery of St. Euthymius in the Judean desert. That community dissolved over theological disputes stemming from the Origenist controversy, but he was part of its refounding by Orthodox monks in 555. Two years later, he transferred to the nearby monastery of St. Sabas, which still exists. At some point before the writing of the Lives, he was ordained presbyter. The lives of seven famous Palestinian monastic leaders that he wrote are important sources for the history of Palestinian monasticism from 405 to 558.

John the Hesychast, or the Silent One, was born about 454 in Nicopolis, Armenia. He embraced the ascetic life at eighteen after his parents died. By 481 he was bishop of Colonia in Armenia, against his will. He traveled to Constantinople, then to Jerusalem, where he took up residence in a hospice as a lay monk and met St. Sabas, who convinced him to come to his new monastery. There he labored at menial tasks for many years. When Sabas, convinced that John should become a presbyter, brought him to Bishop Elias of Jerusalem for ordination, John confessed that he was already a bishop and asked that his secret be respected. From there he lived in the desert for seven years until Sabas persuaded him to return to his monastery, where he died about 558. Both he and Sabas were personally known to Cyril and exercised considerable influence on him.

A certain woman from Cappadocia named Basilina, a deacon of the great church of Constantinople, came to Jerusalem with a high-ranking nephew who was otherwise devout but not in communion with the Catholic Church, since he belonged to the Severan sect. The deacon was trying hard to change his mind and bring him into union with the Catholic Church. With that end in view, she asked every righteous man to pray for him. Having heard of the grace surrounding the holy John, she wanted badly to put herself at his feet. But when she heard that it was not permitted for a woman to enter the laura, she sent for his disciple Theodore and pestered him to take her nephew to the holy old man, convinced that through his prayer God would remove his hardness of heart and find him worthy to be in union with the Catholic Church.

So the disciple took him to the old man and knocked on his door in the usual way. When the elder was about to open the door, both prostrated. The disciple said, "Bless us, Father." The old man opened the door and said, "You

I bless, but this one is without blessing." The disciple said, "Let it not be so, father." But the old man answered, "Surely, I will not bless him until he separates himself from the thinking of the Aposchists and confesses communion with the Catholic Church." When the young man heard this, he was astounded at the old man's gift of insight and, changed by the wondrous event, agreed to be in full communion with the Catholic Church. Then the old man blessed him, raised him up, and shared with him the holy mysteries, since he had eliminated all doublemindedness from his heart.

When Basilina learned about this, she wanted all the more to go see the holy man with her own eyes and plotted to put on masculine dress so as to visit him in the laura and thus set out her own soul before him. But this was revealed to him by an angelic vision, so he sent a message to her, saying "Know that if you come, you will not see me. Don't try, but remain where you are staying. I will come to you in a dream, hear what you want to say, and tell you whatever God inspires me to say." Hearing this and trusting in it, she received the vision clearly. He appeared to her in her sleep and said: "Behold, God has sent me to you. Tell me whatever you want." She gave an account of her soul and received a fitting answer. She arose giving thanks to God and told the disciple, when he came, about the form and appearance of the old man.

I heard this from the deacon Basilina herself, and so put it here in the text.

This charming story illustrates the compassionate attitude of the holy monks, even while they kept to the rules about the company of women. Basilina is far from home, perhaps in Jerusalem for church business. Her strong convictions with regard to orthodoxy as well as her firm faith complete the story that Cyril received directly from the one who experienced it.

The Severus to whose party the nephew belonged is understood to be Severus of Antioch (see Anastasia).

Casiana

Theodoret of Cyrrhus, *Sirm. Letter* 17[10]

Theodoret was bishop and Antiochene theologian in the early fifth century. For more on him, see Axia and Publia.

To Casiana, deacon

This second condolence letter to a *diakonos* (see Axia) reminds Casiana that she is one already accustomed to live according to the Scriptures. She should give to both women and men an example of "philosophy," that is, of virtuous outlook and conduct. We have, he says, a living image in our memory of the child who used to be among us. Though the time and place of the letter and Casiana's location are unknown, this suggests that the occasion for the writing of the letter was the death of a child.

Celerina of Constantinople

Theodoret of Cyrrhus, *Sirm. Letter* 101[11]

This letter can be dated to or near 448. Unlike Theodoret's other two letters to female diakonoi, *this is not a letter of condolence. It is part of a group of letters written by the bishop to influential people in Constantinople on the occasion of a representative delegation of Syrian bishops who risked the dangers and inconveniences of travel in winter to go to the capital to argue the case of the Antiochene bishop-theologians against their politically powerful opponents from the Alexandrian party. Theodoret does not yet seem to know that on November 22, 448, his position had been vindicated in the condemnation of Eutyches. In the following year, Theodoret would be deposed from his bishopric in the triumph of the Alexandrians at the "Robber Council" of 449 in Ephesus, only to be reinstated at the Council of Chalcedon in 451.*

To Celerina deacon

This letter is to a politically and theologically influential woman deacon in Constantinople. Theodoret refers to the urgency that has prompted some bishops to leave their churches and travel in winter. He very briefly explains his Antiochene christology, then cuts the topic short, reminding himself that he does not need to say these things to her. He urges Celerina to do everything she can to further the true faith and the peace of the church. This suggests that she was in a position to receive and influence bishops who were wavering in their theological positions and to win them over.

Dionysia, mother of Saint Euthymius

Cyril of Scythopolis, *Life of Saint Euthymius* 8.20–9.9; 10.5–14; 10.22–11.2[12]

Euthymius (377–473) was born at Melitene in Armenia, where he was ordained a presbyter. By 405 he was in Palestine, where he lived as a hermit in several places in the vicinity of Jerusalem, and then in the community he founded in the Judean desert between Jerusalem and Jericho. This laura, or grouping of solitaries with some aspects of community life, grew to be very famous after his death, so much so that it became heavily embroiled in the Origenist controversy of the sixth century.

Otreius was bishop of Melitene in Armenia 374–384, one of the champions of

Nicene orthodoxy. He was a correspondent of Basil the Great (Letter 181) and was present at the Council of Constantinople (381), where Nicene christology and trinitarian theology were further clarified.
For more on Cyril, see Basilina.

The heavenly citizen Euthymius had as parents Paul and Dionysia, who were not of undistinguished lineage, but the most noble, and they were adorned with every divine virtue. Their fatherland and home was Melitene, the greatest metropolis of Armenia. The blessed Dionysia after having lived with her husband many years had not borne a child, but was sterile. They were both very discouraged about this and for a long time begged God to give them a child. Going to the holy shrine of the glorious and victorious martyr Polyeuctos in the same neighborhood, they endured many days there in prayer, as the word has come down to us from those of old. On one of those nights, while they were praying alone, a divine vision appeared to them and said: "Take courage. Take courage. Behold, God has bestowed on you a child who will bear the name 'encouragement' (*euthymia*), for with his birth, the one who gives him to you will encourage his churches." (8.20–9.9)

When the child is born, his parents offer him to God.

After three years, his father Paul ended his life. The blessed Dionysia had a well-educated brother named Eudoxios, who held a position of authority as councilor to the bishop. Making him her adviser and intermediary, she brought the child to the great Otreius, at that time ruler of the holy church of Melitene, who had been a leading figure at the holy Council of Constantinople. Thus she fulfilled what she had promised, offering him as an acceptable sacrifice to God as the well-known Anna did with Samuel. (10.5–14)

Bishop Otreius hears the story of the boy's conception and birth, and accepts him into his church and household, baptizing him and making him a lector (at the age of two!). Euthymius from then on lives in the bishop's house.

But blessed Dionysia, since she was so devoted to God and the things of God, he ordained deacon of the holy church. (10.22–11.2)

The widow Dionysia, who no longer has familial duties since her son's care is provided, is ordained deacon (*echeirotonēsen diakonon*). We hear no more of her in the life of her son. The same information is repeated in a later text:[13]

Otreius, who presided over (*praeerat*) the church of Melitina [in Armenia] . . . ordained (*ordinat*) his (Euthymius') mother Dionysia deaconess (*diaconissam*) of his church, in order that she might assiduously serve the divine.

Essentially the same information is repeated in the considerably later *Life of Euthymius,* except that the reason for her ordination is added. It seems to imply some kind of liturgical function. The motif of the prodigious child born to parents of advanced age and dedicated to God from childhood is, of course, modeled on 1 Samuel 1.

Elisanthia, Martyria, and Palladia

Life of Olympias 7[14]

For background on the Life of Olympias, *see under Olympias. The context of this passage is that Olympias has made over to the church, in the person of its bishop, John Chrysostom, all her remaining property. John then acts to ordain more women deacons for Olympias' monastery. Elisanthia later was the second successor to Olympias as superior of the monastery, after Olympias' goddaughter, Marina.*

> **He also ordained (***cheirotonei***) deacons (***diakonous***) of the holy Church her three relatives, Elisanthia, Martyria, and Palladia for the monastery, so that by the four diaconal services (***diakonia***), the established procedure might be carried on by them unbroken and without interruption.**

John ordains three more deacons for the monastery alongside Olympias, who had been ordained by his predecessor. The previous paragraph (6) describes their entry into the monastery, all three sisters in the same family. With them came Olympias' niece of the same name, but she is not mentioned in the ordination passage. The number of four deacons seems to have been thought appropriate for the monastery. The language of the second part of the text is very obscure. We do not know what is the "established procedure" that went on in the monastery, but it is called *diakonia* and must have had something to do with liturgy. It has been suggested that since there were four of them, each would have taken a turn of six hours at some activity that went on continuously. Since some women deacons seem to have been leaders of the monastic choir (see Lampadion), perhaps it was the Divine Office or some form of liturgical singing. It must be remembered that in both Eastern and Western monastic traditions, the Divine Office is every bit as much liturgy as is celebration of Eucharist.

Eugenia

Severus of Antioch, *Letter* 110[15]

For background on Severus of Antioch, see Anastasia. The letter is a very brief allegorical development of Prov 23:1–2 for ascetics. It contains no contextual information, which has probably been edited out.

To Eugenia, deaconess and monastic superior

Eugenia is called in the Syriac translation *mshamshānîtâ* and *rîshat dayrâ,* the usual Syriac equivalents of *diakonissa* and *archimandritē,* or monastic superior. Here the two offices are combined in the same person, yet Severus thinks it necessary to use both titles in addressing her, an indication that the two positions did not automatically go together. Similarly, Anastasia, a deaconess to whom Severus addresses four letters, is not called a monastic superior and therefore probably is not. Nothing further is known about Eugenia. For two other deaconesses who are superiors of monasteries, to whom Severus writes, see Jannia and Valeriana.[16]

Eusebia of Constantinople

Sozomen, *Ecclesiastical History* 9.2[17]

For background on Sozomen, see Olympias.

A certain woman by the name of Eusebia, a deacon of the Macedonian sect, had a house and garden in front of the walls of Constantinople.

As with his references to Olympias, here too Sozomen keeps the original term *diakonos* in its masculine form. The "Macedonian sect" began with a rival claimant to the episcopacy of Constantinople about 340 and was later associated with denial of the divinity of the Holy Spirit. The rest of the story concerns Eusebia's concealment of the relics of the forty holy martyrs in her own tomb on her property in the early fifth century. She therefore owned and determined the disposition of her own burial property.

Eusebia, or Xenē, of Mylasa

Caria, *Vita Sanctae Eusebiae*[18]

This legendary life of Eusebia is located in the first century but was probably written in the fifth, with many anachronisms, by an unknown author. Another major character is a bishop St. Ephrem, who is distinguished from "the Syrian." The account twice refers to the story of Paul and Thecla, but as the editor points out, the two stories bear little similarity.

According to the story, Eusebia was a Roman virgin who fled to Cos to avoid marriage. There she lives with a group of virgins, meets Paul, and begs him to teach them the way of salvation. Paul is leader of a group of brothers in a monastery of the holy apostle Andrew in Mylasa. He brings her and her companions there, where she refounds her monastery and a shrine of St. Stephen protomartyr. No one knows where she is from, and when asked, she says that her name is Xenē, "traveler" or "pilgrim."

> After a long time when bishop Cyril died in the Lord, the city elected in his place the lord Paul, and he was ordained bishop of that city. So going into the women's monastery, the lord Paul persuaded lady Xenē and ordained her deacon (*diakonon*).

The story continues with a description of her great virtue and heroic asceticism.

Jannia

Severus of Antioch, *Letter* 7.2[19]

For background on Severus of Antioch, see Anastasia.

This letter is dated by the editor before the episcopate of Severus, which began in 512. It could therefore have been written in Egypt, where he had previously lived.

To Jannia, deaconess and monastic superior

Jannia is called in the Syriac a *mshamshānîtâ* and *rishat dayrâ*, the usual words for deaconess and monastic superior, or in Greek, *archimandritē*. The fact that both titles are used indicates that they are not co-terminus. See the background on Anastasia, Eugenia, and Valeriana. The letter exhorts Jannia to continue to be merciful to a sister in her monastery who has committed some kind of unspecified lapse—unless the fault corrupts the others, in which case she should be expelled. It ends with the reminder that she must above all give good example of the way of life that she teaches.[20]

Justina

Fourth-century legend; *Lives of Saints Cyprian and Justina* [21]

The Lives of Saints Cyprian and Justina *is a compilation of stories that may or may not be about historical people. According to some versions, Cyprian is a magician of Antioch hired to cast a spell on a virgin named Justa. Instead, she converts him to Christianity, and he changes her name to Justina. He becomes a bishop, and they are tried and executed together, either under Decius at Damascus (249–251) or under Diocletian at Nicomedia (early fourth century). In some versions, Cyprian is confused with St. Cyprian of Carthage: the converted magician of Antioch survives persecution and moves to Carthage, where he becomes bishop. Gregory Nazianzen (Oration 18 [24]) makes this confusion and waxes eloquent on the occasion of his feast day, without mentioning Justina.*

The truly distinguished virgin Justa, whom he renamed Justina, having added her to the deacons, he entrusted with the leadership of those in the monastery and appointed her as a mother to them.

Justina is a *diakonos*. Though this account has no historical value, it is an early legend that again witnesses to the prevalence of women deacons, and to the frequency with which the superior of a women's monastery held the title. Though all versions of the legend say that she converted him, in this case he assumes the role of ecclesiastical superior who ordains and appoints her. At the moment of their martyrdom by the sword, he asks that she be killed first, since he is "mistrusting of feminine weakness" (*PG* 115.880), that is, he fears she might relent if he is not there to strengthen her. After she is killed, he too receives the sword.

Lampadion of Annesi

Gregory of Nyssa, *Life of Macrina* 29 [22]

Gregory of Nyssa (c. 330–c. 395), younger brother of Basil the Great and Macrina, is, with Basil and his friend Gregory Nazianzen, one of the "Cappadocian theologians" who were influential in the development of fourth-century Trinitarian theology. Unlike the other two, he was married and did not study at a major intellectual center. He was ordained bishop by Basil in 372 to a small country bishopric, where he spent little time and was never successful as administrator and pastoral leader. His gifts lay rather in scholarship and theological and mystical writing, and he was a major figure at the council of Constantinople in 381, after which he traveled and wrote extensively until his death sometime after 394. On his way home from a synod in Antioch, shortly after the untimely death of his older brother Basil in 379, he visited his eldest sister Macrina, superior of a monastery at Annesi in Pontus, northern Asia Minor. He was present at her death shortly after.

Macrina, eldest sister of Saints Basil and Gregory of Nyssa, with her mother and others began a double monastery at the family estate at Annesi in Pontus sometime in the second half of the fourth century. Macrina was the superior and revered figure. Her brother Gregory recounts the events surrounding her death. Here, he and another important figure in the monastery named Vetiana are debating whether to clothe Macrina in better clothing for her burial than the very poor garments she had worn during life.

There was one in the diaconal rank who was a leader of the choir of virgins, Lampadion by name, who said she knew exactly what Macrina wanted for her burial. When I asked her about these things, she was very helpful to our deliberations.

Lampadion is a member of the diaconal status or rank (*en tō tēs diakonias bathmō*), so it is not possible to know exactly what her title was. That one of her duties is leadership of the choir of virgins (she is *protetagmenē*, placed first) may suggest some kind of liturgical role, though Gregory uses the same expression elsewhere simply to refer to the group of ascetic women with no liturgical connotations. So she exercised some kind of leadership, but just what kind is not clear. She is not "abbess," for Gregory calls his sister *hēgoumenē*. See Justinian, *Novellae* 59.4 for the existence of a musical group of virgins with accompanying role at the liturgy two centuries later.

As the narrative continues, Lampadion emerges as a close confidante of Macrina who knew her burial wishes. Lampadion's role as deacon may have been one of instruction and liturgical supervision, as in *AC* 3.15.1–4. Perhaps she had already been ordained deacon before she entered the monastic community. The story reveals that the role of deacon in a female monastic community was distinct from that of superior.

Magna of Ancyra

Nilus of Ancyra, *Letter* [23]

Nilus of Ancrya, (sometimes called of Sinai) studied at Constantinople as a disciple of John Chrysostom and later founded a monastery near Ancyra, from which he had wide influence on the ascetic movement through his writings. He died about 430. Later legends had him with his father as ascetics at Mt. Sinai and eventually ordained presbyters, hence the connection of his name with Sinai.

On Voluntary Poverty, to the most distinguished deacon Magna

A long treatise on religious poverty (*aktēmosynē*) is addressed to a *diakonos* named Magna, about whom we know nothing else from this reference except her presumed level of literary culture. However, she is probably the same person as in the following source.

Palladius, *Lausiac History* 67 [24]

For background on Palladius, see Olympias.

In that city of Ancyra many other virgins lived, perhaps two thousand or more, who practiced self-control and were outstanding. Among them, one stands out for praise, a most distinguished woman named Magna. I do not know by which name to call her, virgin or widow. She was forcefully married to a man by her own mother, but many say that by deceiving him and putting him off, she remained untouched. When he died after a little while, she gave herself over entirely to God and gave the utmost care to her own household, living an ascetic and sober life, conducting herself in such a way that even bishops respected her for her abundant virtue. She supported the needs of hospices, the poor, and traveling bishops without cease, doing it in a hidden way by herself and through trustworthy house slaves, and she never left the church at night.

This is probably the same Magna to whom Nilus dedicated his letter, but we cannot be sure. Here she does not have a clerical title, but we do get a little more information about her life, though it is cast in stereotyped language. The rumor that despite being married she retained her virginity is also found in Palladius' brief description of Olympias.

Manaris of Gaza

Mark the Deacon, *Life of Porphyry, Bishop of Gaza* 102[25]

Porphyry was born in Thessalonica about 347, ordained presbyter in Jerusalem in 392, and bishop in 395. As bishop of Gaza, he struggled as representative of a Christian minority against a still-pagan majority. One of his triumphs was succeeding in the imperial condemnation and destruction of the Temple of Marnas in Gaza. He died in 420.

Mark the Deacon came from Asia to Palestine, where he was ordained about 397. The next year he was sent by Porphyry to Constantinople with the mission of getting the decree of condemnation against the Temple of Marnas. His biography is virtually the only source of information on his bishop, Porphyry. The manuscript was discovered in 1556.

Toward the end of the narrative, Porphyry encounters an orphaned girl of fourteen who, with her aged grandmother, desires baptism. The grandmother is baptized immediately because of her ill health, and the girl, Salaphtha, soon after.

Then it happened in those days that the old lady came to her rest and went to the Lord. Then calling the girl, he sent for the deacon Manaris, whose name means in Greek Photeinē [light]. He gave Salaphtha over to her, giving her the dress of a *kanonikē*, and commending them to God, dismissed them in peace.

Manaris is a *diakonos* who is entrusted with the care of the girl. The name Manaris perhaps derives from a Syriac root meaning "brilliant" or "bright."[26] The text goes on to describe the ascetic lifestyle that is then adopted by Salaphtha, suggesting a connection between the status of *kanonikē* and asceticism.[27] The role of the deacon Manaris is not asceticism, however, but church responsibility. There are

other contexts in which it is suggested that one of the chief roles of the female deacon is the instruction of women for baptism (see Romana). But in this case it is
protection and patronage of a young girl without family.

Marthana

Egeria, *Pilgrimage to the Holy Places* 23.3 [28]

*There is much about this fascinating travelogue to the Holy Places, discovered late in
the nineteenth century, which is not absolutely clear, beginning with the date of its
composition, intended audience, and author. Scholars are generally agreed, however,
that the text was written in the early fifth century, certainly no later than 417 CE. (The
date of the actual pilgrimage, however, is unclear.) The author was very possibly a nun,
abbess, or consecrated virgin writing to other women religious. There is some evidence
to suggest that she was the daughter of a Spanish-born official of the imperial court,
perhaps that of Theodosius (379–95), through whom she may have arranged to have
escort to the Holy Land. In any case, the pilgrimage was undertaken by a devout
woman who visited Jerusalem, as well as holy places in Egypt, Palestine, Syria, and
elsewhere. On her pilgrimage she makes a special trip to Seleucia in Isauria (modern
Silifke on the Turkish coast), about sixty miles southwest of Tarsus. Seleucia was the site
of the shrine of St. Thecla, a legendary disciple of Paul, who was immortalized in the
second-century* Acts of Paul and Thecla *(see Tertullian,* On Baptism *17.4) and
the* Life of St. Thecla, *traditionally attributed to Basil of Seleucia.*[29] *At the shrine of
Thecla, she finds a community of monastic cells for men and women and an old friend.*

> I found there a very dear friend of mine named Marthana, a holy deaconess
> (*diaconissa*) whom I had met in Jerusalem, where she had come to pray, to
> whose way of life all in the East bore testimony. She was governing (*regebat*)
> these monastic cells of apotactites or virgins (*aputactitae vel virginum*).

Marthana is the only contemporary mentioned in the entire travelogue. The term
aputactitae is perhaps a Latin transliteration of the Greek *apotaktitai*. A remark
later in the same chapter, and one in chapter 28 of the diary, indicates clearly that
she was presiding over (*regebat*) both men and women. Thus the term *apotaktitai*,
transliterated as *aputactitae*, was likely the native term for a particular kind of
monk and nun. It has been argued, in fact, that the term refers to male and female
monks who observe a particularly strict regimen of fasting and self-discipline.[30] In
late-antique Latin, *vel* does not inevitably distinguish two classes of things; thus it
is difficult to say for sure whether *aputactitae* represents a separate category from
virgins. In any case, it is clear that the deaconess Marthana was something like an
abbess presiding over what we might call a "double monastery" of men and women.

Matrona of Cosila, near Chalcedon

Sozomen, *Ecclesiastical History* 7.21[31]

This chapter in Sozomen's Ecclesiastical History *relates the finding of the head of John the Baptist and its translation to Constantinople in two stages. As the story goes, the head was miraculously discovered by some monks of the Macedonian sect in Cilicia, in southeast Asia Minor (for the Macedonians, see Eusebeia). The emperor Valens (328–78) gave orders that the relic should be brought to the capital, but when the cart was in the district of Pantichium in the area of Chalcedon, the mules pulling it refused to move any further. This was taken as a divine sign, and the head was left in the village of Cosila. Later, the emperor Theodosius I (379–95) wanted it brought to Constantinople. For more on Sozomen, see Olympias.*

> The only one who opposed the move was Matrona, a holy virgin, who was its deacon and guardian. Putting aside the use of force, he tried mightily, and finally by entreaty gained from her a reluctant consent, because she remembered what had happened when Valens tried it. He clothed the box encasing it royally and took it to the place called Hebdoma in the suburbs of Constantinople, where he raised a large and beautiful church for it. Though the emperor tried with many pleas, he could not persuade Matrona to change her allegiance, for she was of the Macedonian sect.

The narrative continues with the contrasting story of a Macedonian presbyter by the name of Vincent, who was the chaplain of the relic. He, like other Macedonians, had taken an oath never to change his beliefs, but he said that if John the Baptist could follow the emperor this time, so could he. The story concludes with the following:

> But Matrona remained in the village of Cosila to the end, living with great holiness and wisdom as leader of a group of virgins. Even now it is said that their virtuous lives are worthy of their teacher.

Matrona's title is *autē* (dative singular) *diakonos*, that is, its (the relic's) deacon. It is therefore possible that the term *diakonos* is used in a more general sense of minister or caretaker of a relic. But given that the most common term for deacon is used, a term that had a definite ecclesiastical meaning at the time, it is more likely that she was a female deacon with a special responsibility. She is also superior of a group of virgins, which she probably was before the head arrived. It was therefore in her and their monastery that the relic resided. That she belonged to the Macedonians, as probably did her whole monastery, and that John the Baptist's head was thus entrusted to them, does not seem to have bothered the emperors.

Nektaria

Sozomen, *Ecclesiastical History* 4.24 [32]

Nektaria and those associated with her had shady reputations. Elpidius, bishop of Satala in Armenia, was associated with malpractice and causing uproar. One of the factors that contributed to his deposition was that he had reinstated a presbyter named Eusebius. For more on Sozomen, see Olympias.

Eusebius had been deposed because he considered Nektaria worthy of the diaconate, despite the fact that she had been excommunicated for violating agreements and perjury. This was clearly against the laws of the church.

It is never said who ordained Nektaria, and her title is not given; it is clear only that after excommunication, Eusebius tried to reinstate her as a member of the diaconate. If her supporters were deposed, we can be sure that she was, too, and that she was of sufficient social status to be heavily embroiled in ecclesiastical politics.

Nicarete

Sozomen, *Ecclesiastical History* 8.23 [33]

[Nicarete, a noble lady from Bithynia residing in Constantinople] made a point of concealing her virtuous ways by her humility. Thus she considered herself unworthy both of the honor of the diaconate and appointment as leader of the "ecclesiastical virgins," even though John had often urged her to accept.

The context of the passage is a series of stories about persecution of the followers of John Chrysostom after he had been deposed from his position as bishop and expelled from Constantinople. Even though she was of advanced age, Nicarete was one of those who fled the city voluntarily because they did not feel safe in the midst of military attacks and looting. She had vowed perpetual virginity and was renowned for her virtue and generosity to the poor. Yet she declined ordination to the diaconate (*axiôma diakonou*, the dignity of being *diakonos*) or another ecclesiastical role with the group of consecrated virgins. This last group is well attested in other sources as a community of women who at first lived privately in their family homes, but by this time many lived together in community in urban settings as an alternative to desert monastic life. Olympias presided over one such community in the city monastery she founded. This passage among others shows that the office of deaconess was not simply one who presided over such a community.

Olympias

Born about 365 of a noble family, Olympias was one of the wealthiest, most powerful, and best-known women of her time. Her grandfather was Ablabius, pretorian prefect and consul in 331, one of the new Christian nobility created by Constantine. As a young girl, Olympias knew Gregory Nazianzen during his brief occupation of the episcopate of the capital in 381. He was later invited to her wedding; he did not attend but sent a poem as a gift. In about 385 she was married to Nebridius, a second marriage for him, who was likely much older than she. He became prefect of Constantinople in 386 but soon died. At about the age of twenty, Olympias was already a widow. From then on, she refused to remarry, in spite of pressure from even the emperor Theodosius I, who for a time deprived her of the right to administer her vast properties until she should reach the age of thirty, thinking this would dissuade her. Instead, she adopted the ascetic life and founded a women's monastery in Constantinople next to the cathedral, which became a center of spiritual life, works of charity, and, because of her high position and connections, embroilment in politics.

She was ordained deaconess by Bishop Nectarius while still in her thirties, though canon law specified a minimum age of sixty. (About fifty years later, the Council of Chalcedon would reduce the minimum age to forty.) The exception made here might have been because of her extraordinary patronage of the bishop and close position as his personal and political adviser. She was also very generous to other bishops, priests, and ascetics of both sexes, so that she was widely known. Gregory of Nyssa dedicated his commentary on the Song of Songs to her. Her most famous friend was John Chrysostom, Nectarius' successor, and she was John's most loyal supporter. She was thus involved in the conflict that led to his exile in 404. Between then and his death in 407, he wrote to her seventeen surviving letters. After his exile, she was also put on trial and exiled because of her support of him. She died in exile, probably in either Cyzicus or Nicomedia, sometime between 407 and 419. She is a saint of the Eastern Church but also is mentioned in the Roman martyrology.

The anonymous fifth-century author of the Life of Olympias *may have been a contemporary and eyewitness to the events of her life. There is another text about her, the* Narration Concerning St. Olympias *by Sergia, a successor of Olympias as superior of the monastery, probably about 630. Her document recounts the miraculous events surrounding the transfer of the bones of Olympias from her original burial place outside the city to their final resting place in the monastery. It does not allude to her office as deacon.*[34]

Life of Olympias 6[35]

Then by the divine will she was ordained deacon (*diakonos*) of the holy and great church of God and built a monastery at the south corner of it. All the houses situated near the holy church and all the workshops at that corner were torn down for it. She made a passageway from the monastery to the narthex of the holy church. In the first section, she enclosed her chambermaids, fifty of them, all living in purity and virginity. Then Elisanthia her relative, seeing the good work pleasing to God that divine grace had led her to accomplish, she also being a virgin, wished to imitate her holy zeal and renounced all the ephemeral and vain things of this life, with her two virgin sisters Martyria and Palladia. The three entered with all the others, after having made over to the monastery all their possessions. Likewise Olympia, niece of Olympias, with many other women of noble families, according to the grace and good pleasure of God who desires the salvation of all, being inspired by divine love, chose the kingdom of heaven, despising all earthly things that drag us down, so that the number of women gathered by the grace of God into the holy sheepfold of Christ were two hundred fifty, all adorned with the crown of virginity and living the sublime life that is fitting for the saints.

Olympias' ordination as deacon while she was superior of her monastery might lead to the conclusion, sometimes made, that in later centuries deacon or deaconess was simply another title for monastic superior. However, at a later date, her three sibling relatives were also ordained by the successor to Bishop Nectarius, John Chrysostom (see Elisanthia, above), and at the time of John's exile, there were two other deacons in the monastery, Pentadia and Procla (see below).

Palladius, *Dialogue on the Life of John Chrysostom* 10.50–67 [36]

Palladius (c. 365–425) was born in Galatia and studied and lived monasticism in Palestine and Egypt, especially with Evagrius of Pontus, one of the great monastic writers. Palladius eventually became bishop of Heliopolis in Bithynia, then of Aspuna in Galatia. He wrote the Dialogue *about 410 to defend the memory of John Chrysostom, and his more famous* Lausiac History *(about 419), an important collection of stories about the history of monasticism and monastic personalities.*

In the narrative, cast as a conversation between Palladius and a Roman deacon, John Chrysostom has just been told that the sentence of condemnation has been pronounced, and he has received the order from the emperor to leave Constantinople. He leaves the episcopal palace, amid much lamentation of his supporters. It is important to remember that this is not a report of events, but Palladius' reconstruction.

Going into the baptistery, he [John Chrysostom] called Olympias, who was constantly in the church, with Pentadia and Procla, that is, the three deacons (*diakonoi*), and also Silvina, wife of the blessed Nebridius, who was adorned with distinction in her widowhood, and said to them: "Come here, daughters, and listen to me. 'I see that the end of my affairs is in sight. I have run my course, and likewise, you will no longer see my face.'[37] But this is how I exhort you: let none of you cut short your customary devotion to the church. But whoever is led, not by his own will, to ordination (*cheirotonia*), with the agreement of all and without having schemed for it, to him bow your heads as you would to John, for the church cannot be without a bishop. May you thus receive mercy. Remember me in your prayers." Overcome by tears, they prostrated at his feet. Then catching the attention of one of the distinguished presbyters, he said: "Take them away from here, lest the crowds revolt." Thus after they had clung to his feet for a little while, they gave way.

Olympias, Pentadia, and Procla, the three *diakonoi* of the monastery, seem to be recognized as the leaders and spokespersons for the monastery. Of Olympias alone, this would be perfectly understandable because of her social position and special relationship to John, but that he calls the three together indicates some kind of shared leadership.

Palladius, *Dialogue on the Life of John Chrysostom* 16.179–90 [38]

> The deacon speaks: Now, if it's not too much trouble, tell us about Olympias, if you have some knowledge of her.
> The bishop: Which one? There are several.
> The deacon: The deacon of Constantinople, who was the bride of Nebridius, the former prefect.
> The bishop: I know her well.
> The deacon: What kind of woman is she?
> The bishop: Do not say "woman," but "such a person" (*anthrōpos*), for she was a man (*anēr*) despite her bodily appearance.
> The deacon: How is that?
> The bishop: By her life, her asceticism and knowledge, and her patient endurance in trials.

This constructed Socratic dialogue praises Olympias for her courage and virtue. It is typical of the gender rhetoric of the time that the highest praise a woman could be given was to call her a man. "Woman" symbolized weakness of the flesh; "man" symbolized courage and strength. Grammatically the Greek word *anthrōpos* means a human person of either sex, while *anēr* is a male, but there was much slippage between the two terms owing to the predominance of thinking from a male perspective. Compare 1 Cor 7:1, where "it is good for an *anthrōpos* not to touch a woman."[39] The passage goes on to narrate an incident in her life in which Theophilus, bishop of Alexandria, spoke of her insultingly because he accused her of harboring some monks whom he had dismissed from his church.

Palladius, *Dialogue on the Life of John Chrysostom* 17.122–30 [40]

The theme of Olympias' role in sheltering the monks mistreated by Theophilus is resumed in chapter 17.

> These are those whom priests and levites passed by, and to the shame of men, a manly (*andreia*) woman took them in, and to the shame of bishops, a female deacon (*diakonos*) gave them hospitality, she whose praise resounds in the churches for many other reasons, in imitation of that Samaritan, whoever he was. Going down from Jericho and finding a man beaten by thieves and half-dead, he put him on his own mount as far as the inn, mixing the oil of compassion with the wine that heals, and treated his wounds.

This comparison of Olympias to the Good Samaritan also appears in chapter 5 of the *Life of Olympias*. Here the text goes on to recount her early widowhood, the proposed remarriage to Elpidius, and her refusal in favor of a life of asceticism, details also recounted in the *Life*. Palladius says that her marriage to Nebridius lasted twenty months but that the public belief was that she remained a virgin (17.137). This idealization of virginity was typical of the era. It is said in several places that her patronage included the total maintenance of the bishop of Constantinople, both Nectarius and John, and that she was also a generous benefactor of many other bishops, among them Basil and the two Gregories. In the *Lausiac History* 56, written about 419, Palladius speaks of her as an illustrious figure of the past, and borrows for her from the age of martyrdom the term "confessor," previously reserved to those who had suffered for the faith; Olympias certainly suffered for her loyalty to John. Here the time of her marriage is shortened to several days, probably better to correlate with the belief in her continued virginity. In this short passage, her generosity to the needy and support of bishops are praised, and we are told that she is venerated as a confessor at Constantinople. This text does not mention her office as deacon, nor does another passing reference to Olympias in *Lausiac History* 61.3, where she is praised as one who had disposed of her luxurious garments in gifts to the church, as had Melania the Younger.

Sozomen, *Ecclesiastical History* 8.9 [41]

Sozomen was a lay historian born near Gaza in Palestine. He arrived at the royal court in Constantinople after 425 and wrote a history of the church of the previous century, heavily dependent on previous sources for the earlier years.

> For this woman [Olympias] was from a prominent family and although she was a young widow living a virtuous life according to the law of the church, Nectarius ordained [her] deacon.

Nectarius, John's predecessor who died in 397, ordained her (*cheirotonein*) as a female deacon (*diakonos*) in disregard of the canonical age limit, which was probably sixty. It is unclear what would be the role of a monastic female deacon at the cathedral of the imperial capital. She and her monastery were known for their charity to the poor, and this may have been part of her role as deacon. Sozomen gives us the information about her ordination at a later time in his narrative, when opposition to John Chrysostom, Nectarius' successor, was building in Constantinople. One of the factors in this opposition was the resentment of an archdeacon from Egypt named Serapion, because of John's advice to Olympias. She had, in John's estimation, been disposing of her property unwisely by giving some of it to those not in need. He advised her to put it at his disposal, and he would see that it went to those who really needed it. According to the *Life*, this she readily did. Understandably, this concentration of immense power and wealth in the hands of John would cause a great deal of resentment from those who had previously benefited from it.

Sozomen, *Ecclesiastical History* 8.24[42]

In this difficult situation Olympias the deacon (*diakonos*) showed herself to have manly courage (*andreia*).

For the ascription of manly courage to a woman as a compliment, see comment on Palladius, *Dialogue on the Life of John Chrysostom* 179–90, above. The situation alluded to is the aftermath of the exile of John Chrysostom from Constantinople. His supporters and detractors came to blows at the cathedral, and in the confusion, the church caught fire and burned. Each side accused the other of setting the fire. Many of John's supporters were exiled, or their property confiscated, or they were otherwise punished. Many, like Nicarete, fled. One of the cathedral lectors was tortured to death. Olympias was roughly treated under interrogation and accused of setting the fire. She disdained the tribunal and would not defend herself, refusing also to have anything to do with John's successor, Arsacius—quite to the contrary of the advice John supposedly had given her, at least as composed by Palladius in *Dialogue* 10, quoted above. Most of her property was confiscated, and she left the city, whether of her own volition or in exile, to Cyzicus, not far from Constantinople, where she died in the next few years.

Pentadia

John Chrysostom *Letters* 94, 104, 185[43] ❧

For background on John Chrysostom, see Amproukla.

To Pentadia, deaconess

Before the accession of John to the episcopate in Constantinople, Pentadia was known as the wife of an exiled consul, Timasius. Sozomen relates that when Timasius was banished to Egypt, where he subsequently died, Pentadia tried to take refuge in a church of the capital, but Eutropius, the imperial eunuch responsible for the trouble, refused it to her and dragged her out of the church as part of his continuing policy not to honor church asylum (Sozomen, *Ecclesiastical History* 8.7). During his exile (404–7), John Chrysostom wrote three extant letters to this woman, who was by then a *diakonissa*. In them, he is warmly supportive of her efforts to keep him updated on news, and he notes that he has heard of her good health and prosperity, and that of all her household (*oikos*) and those who are with her (gender unspecified; see discussion under Amproukla). It does not necessarily sound as if she is in a monastery. The brief letter 185 includes a plaintive "Why haven't I heard from you lately, how you are?"

In Palladius' *Dialogue on the Life of John Chrysostom,* the two deacons, Pentadia and Procla are summoned with Olympias in the church before the forced departure of John into exile (*Dialogue* 10.50). This is probably the same Pentadia. Her companion Procla may be the same as Amproukla, Palladius having confused the name, or she may be a different person.

Publia

Theodoret of Cyrrhus, *Ecclesiastical History* 3.14[44]

Theodoret (c. 393–c. 466), a native of Antioch, was consecrated bishop of Cyrrhus in 423. As bishop, he became drawn into the christological controversies then dividing the Eastern churches. He probably held heretical Nestorian views until at least 435, for which he was deposed at the Second Council of Ephesus (449), but seems to have abandoned them sometime after the Council of Chalcedon anathematized Nestorius in 451. Some of his works were condemned by the Second Council of Constantinople (553). Among the few works of his that have survived is his Ecclesiastical History, *which, in five books, continues Eusebius' famous history down to the year 428. In the third book of his history, Theodoret tells of Publia (or Poplia), a high-born deacon in Antioch, who ruled over a monastery in her house during the reign of Julian the Apostate (361– 63). Once he became emperor, Julian attempted to weaken the church by reinvigorating worship of the old gods, secularizing education, withdrawing many of the privileges Constantine and his successors had showered on the church, and even incarcerating Christians merely for practicing their religion.*

Theodoret's Ecclesiastical History *identifies Publia as a deacon (*diakonos*) only in the title at the beginning of the chapter. Theodoret may well have inferred Publia's* *diaconal status from her having been the choir mistress* (didaskalos; *Latin,* magistra*)* *of her community. It is also possible that Theodoret, writing some half-century after* *Publia's death, is reflecting a local tradition (very possibly based on fact), that Publia* *was a deacon. As other texts in this collection indicate, it was not uncommon for lead-* *ers of communities of virgins in Syria and elsewhere in the East to have been conse-* *crated as deacons.*

Title of the chapter: "About Artemios the official, and Publia the deacon, and her godly boldness (*parrēsia*)"

After a brief statement about Artemios' opposition to idolatry:

Here I will add to the narrative a story about a distinguished and praiseworthy woman, for women, armed with divine zeal, treated his [Julian's] rage with contempt.

At that time, there was a certain Publia, well known and celebrated because of her exceptionally virtuous person and deeds. Having borne the yoke of marriage for a short time, she offered its best fruit to God, for from it sprang John, to whom she gave birth, who was for a long time the leader of the presbyters at Antioch. He was often elected by common vote to the Apostolic See,[45] but he always fled from the honor.

This woman had with her a group of virgins, who were professed to perpetual virginity. They used to praise the Creator and Savior God assiduously. Once when the Emperor was passing by, they all sang together more loudly, regarding the persecutor as contemptuous and laughable. They sang especially the Psalms in which the weakness of false gods is derided, and said with David, "The idols of the nations are silver and gold, made by human hands."[46] They then added, having expounded on the stupidity of idols, "those who make them will be like them and so will all who trust in them."[47]

When Julian heard them, he grew incensed and demanded that they keep silence while he was passing by. But she, with little consideration for his laws, encouraged the chorus of virgins to greater zeal. With the Emperor passing by, she ordered them to sing a second time, "Let God and all his enemies be scattered."[48]

When this occurred, Julian grew bitter with rage and commanded that the teacher (*didaskalos*) of the choir be brought to him. Although he saw her venerable age, he neither respected her bodily gray hairs nor her high character of soul. Instead, he commanded one of his bodyguards to strike her on either side of the face, and to bloody her cheek with his hands. She, however, took this insult as the highest honor and returned to her house. She cast him out with spiritual music, just as the author and teacher of that music quieted the evil spirit that was troubling Saul.[49]

Publia seems to have been a high-born woman and a deaconess who presided over a monastic community in her home. Swan argues that, in addition, "there were several deaconesses in the community."[50] She is sometimes said to be a martyr, perhaps because she died in 362–63, during Julian's reign and after the punishment she received from one of his men. Her feast day is October 9, and all who write about her celebrate her as a courageous opponent of the wicked, apostate emperor. Even today, organizations of widows regard her with special affection.

Romana

The Life of St. Pelagia, the Harlot [51]

This Life, *a delightful and deeply moving piece of ancient Christian literature, was very likely written by a deacon named James in the fifth century. About James, we know nothing except that he served the bishop Nonnus (diocese unknown), who is one of the main characters in the story. James wrote the original in Greek, but the story survives only in Syriac[52] and Latin. The narrative has to do with the conversion of a notorious prostitute in Antioch who lived in the late fourth century, possibly the unnamed woman to whom John Chrysostom refers in a homily on Matthew. Her* Life *was very popular in the medieval Latin West and was influential as a literary model in hagiographical texts of the period.*

*As the story begins, the beautiful (and half-clad) Pelagia rides by an assembly of bishops on a donkey. According to the Syriac version of the text, her appearance was such as to cause all, including the Bishop Nonnus, to fall in love with her. Nonnus also denounces her as a cause of lust and a stumbling block to many. Through an act of "merciful providence," Pelagia appears in church on a day Nonnus is preaching on the eschatological judgment of sinners. She is moved to tears. She soon writes Nonnus for an audience with a group of bishops, which she is granted. Arriving in their presence, she immediately throws herself on the ground in obviously sincere agonies of guilt and penitence, then begs the bishops (themselves now in tears) to be baptized. After some hesitation, Nonnus agrees, but not before sending his deacon James (i.e., the author) to locate a deaconess. With the help of a local bishop, James returns with "the lady Romana, the first of the deaconesses" (*dominam Romanam primam diaconissarum*). The bishop then exorcises and baptizes Pelagia.*

And her sponsor (*pater spiritalis*) was the holy lady Romana, first of the deaconesses, who took her and went up to the place for catechumens.

Romana is present for the sake of propriety. Thus, when the text says she "took" Pelagia, we are meant to understand she received her from the baptismal waters. Note that the sponsor here, though the equivalent of "godmother," is in the masculine: Romana is said, literally, to be Pelagia's "spiritual father." Her being designated a *domina* suggests high social standing. After the baptism, Satan cries out for the loss of Pelagia, who signs herself with the cross and routs the demon by breathing upon him.

After two days, sleeping with her spiritual mother, the holy Romana (*sancta Romana commatre sua*) in her chamber, the devil appeared by night and awoke the handmaiden of God, Pelagia.

Again, Pelagia rebukes the devil, and he vanishes. Note that the deaconess is now the constant companion of the newly baptized Pelagia. The next day, Pelagia has a list made of all her worldly goods to give to the church.

She immediately called for Nonnus the holy bishop through her spiritual mother, the holy Romana.

Romana brings the message to the bishop both for the sake of propriety and because a catechumen like Pelagia would have been confined to her cubicle until the eighth day after her baptism. On the eighth day, she rises in the middle of the night and, unknown to anyone, including Romana, she puts on the tunic of Nonnus; she is never again seen in Antioch.

The holy Romana wept most bitter tears, but holy Nonnus used to console her by saying: "Do not cry, daughter, but rejoice with great joy. Pelagia has chosen the better part, as did Mary, whom the Lord preferred to Martha in the Gospel." She, however, went to Jerusalem and constructed for herself a cell on the Mount of Olives, where the Lord prayed.

The Syriac version of the story tells us that Romana had provided food and all of Pelagia's requirements from her own pocket. She quickly became like a fond mother and considered Pelagia her own "beloved daughter." Thus she is stricken with grief and, according to the Syriac version, despondently but incessantly inquires as to Pelagia's whereabouts.

At the end of the text, James goes to Jerusalem with Nonnus' blessing in order to inquire for a certain brother Pelagius, "a monk and eunuch." James unwittingly encounters Pelagia in Jerusalem before discovering "Pelagius" had died. When "Pelagius" is carried out of his cell for the body to be anointed, it is discovered that "Pelagius" is in fact a woman—the erstwhile harlot Pelagia. She is buried with great ceremony, with scores of virgins from Jericho and the Jordan present.

We hear nothing more of Romana in the Latin version once Bishop Nonnus attempts to console her. Her story is an interesting depiction of religious patronage from the high-born that develops into an intense, maternal fondness for a young daughter in faith, and also of the ongoing role of the deaconess in the spiritual development of the women she has assisted in baptism.

Sabiniana

John Chrysostom, *Letter* 13 [6 to Olympias][53]

John, in exile in Armenia, writes to Olympias, in exile in Cyzicus:

> My lady Sabiniana the deacon (*diakonos*) arrived the same day that we did, worn out and overwhelmed with fatigue, for she is of an age when it is difficult even to move. But she is young in her willingness and insensitive to her sufferings. She declared herself ready to go to Scythia, since the rumor is that that is where we will be taken. She says she is ready never to turn back, but to live wherever we are. The church people welcomed her warmly with much solicitude and care.

This is probably the same Sabiniana, John's aunt, of whom Palladius also spoke.

Palladius, *Lausiac History* 41[54]

Palladius is listing a number of virtuous women he has known. For background on Palladius himself, see Olympias.

> I encountered at Antioch a distinguished woman who conversed with God, the deaconess Sabiniana, aunt of John bishop of Constantinople.

John in his mention of Sabiniana in his letter above does not call her his aunt, nor does he give her the same title as here, *diakonissa*. It is sometimes doubted, therefore, that these two women are the same: "It is hardly likely that Chrysostom would have spoken of her to Olympias simply as 'my lady Sabiniana, the deaconess.'"[55] On the contrary, that is exactly how he would have spoken of her, with formal respect, to one who already knew their family relationship. Palladius situated her in Antioch, from whence John came, and was keenly interested in John, having composed his *Dialogue on the Life of John Chrysostom* (see Olympias). These two references taken together may show that the titles *diakonos* and *diakonissa* were interchangeable for women.

Severa of Jerusalem

Evagrius Ponticus, *Letters* 7.2, 8.2, 19.2, 20[56]

Evagrius of Pontus (346–99) was ordained deacon at Constantinople by Gregory Nazianzus in 379. A few years later, he sought out the monastic settlements of Judea and Egypt, spending a short time with Melania and Rufinus in their monastery on the Mount of Olives in Jerusalem. But by 383 he was in the desert of Nitria in

Egypt, where he lived the rest of his life developing an ascetic spirituality based on the theology of Origen. These letters must therefore date to sometime after his stay in Jerusalem.

Melania the Elder (c. 342–c. 410) was a wealthy Roman aristocrat who, on the death of her husband about 365, adopted the ascetic life. She left Rome about 372 to visit the monasteries of Egypt; she then settled in Jerusalem where she built a double monastery in 381 on the Mount of Olives with Rufinus. About 400, she returned to Italy for a few years but went back to Jerusalem before the Gothic invasion of Italy, and died there. She was revered in early Christian monastic circles for her asceticism and piety, though she became involved in the political intrigues between Jerome and her monastic companion, Rufinus.

Rufinus of Aquileia (c. 345–c. 410) was a friend and student companion of Jerome in Rome. About 373–80, he lived in the monasteries of Egypt, where he met Melania and was a student of Didymus the Blind, who put him in contact with the teachings of Origen. In 381 he joined Melania in their double monastery on the Mount of Olives in Jerusalem. When his old friend Jerome arrived and set up another double monastery with Paula in Bethlehem, Rufinus and Jerome became embroiled in a bitter and long feud over the orthodoxy and correct interpretation of Origen's writings. Rufinus returned to Italy in 397 and died in Sicily during the Gothic invasion of Italy.

These letters therefore can be dated between 383 and 397, and presumably were composed all at the same time.

The situation that seems to be behind the four letters is that a female deacon named Severa in Melania's community in Jerusalem wanted to undertake a rigorous pilgrimage to some of the more remote holy places, as did Egeria around the same time. Evagrius writes to convince those who could dissuade her to do so, fearing for her safety and that of those who would accompany her. Letter 7 addressed to Rufinus has the following to say about the situation.

> With regard to the chaste deacon Severa, I praise her intent but cannot accept the deed. I don't know what she can gain from this long journey on a laborious itinerary. But by the Lord, I can show her and those with her how much damage they can suffer. So I entreat your holiness to stop those who have left the world from proceeding on such a difficult way, for I marvel how in all this distance they will not drink the water of Gihon[57] either in their minds or in their actions. These things are foreign to those living in chastity.

Letter 8 addressed to Melania says the following, which though indirect, seems to be about the same situation.

> Teach your sisters and daughters[58] not to go on long journeys in deserted places and to take in doubtful locations. All of this is foreign behavior to every soul that has renounced the world.

Letter *19 is again addressed to Rufinus.*

> I wanted very much to give the chaste virgin something useful toward her salvation but time would not allow. So what we already said to her we pass on, that she should pray in her mind unceasingly about this desire, by necessary moderation to curb desire through restraint, and anger through meekness. By such ideas [as hers] the word of God is choked, but by the power in us it is fulfilled, and wants to be seen in us through the virtue of our hidden works and to show forth our secret Father and Creator.

Finally, Letter *20 is addressed to Severa herself. It speaks of the situation only in general terms, and spends more time on praise of the hidden monastic life. Perhaps by the time Evagrius composed it, she had relinquished her plans. The document to which Evagrius refers is presumed to be his* Treatise to a Virgin, *which may therefore have been composed expressly for her as consolation for the canceling of her pilgrimage.*

> Your spiritual intention has reached me, and I marvel at your love of learning and I rejoice at your progress, because having put your hand to the plow and not looking back to the mortal world and transitory things, you fight the good fight so as to be crowned with the crown of justice[59] and seek your chosen spouse through good works. This is the true search, to seek the Lord through good deeds. No one who does evil seeks justice, nor does one who hates one's neighbor do good, nor does a liar seek truth. This is seeking the Lord: keeping the commandments with unmitigated faith and recognition of the truth. The model for this you will learn from the document I sent you, which teaches you the narrow and difficult path[60] that leads to the knowledge of heaven through good works.

If the four letters are related, as we think they are, a number of points emerge. Severa is a members of Melania's community and a *diakonos*. It is never said that Melania is ordained; therefore, as in Macrina's community, the superior did not need to be ordained but other members could be. It is interesting that the idea of actually forbidding her to set out on her pilgrimage is mentioned only in *Letter* 7 to Rufinus. One would think that Melania would be the likely candidate to do this, but as extensive as female leadership was in women's monasteries, the closest male leadership seems to have dominated the authority structure; or perhaps Melania took the easy out by deferring to Rufinus or Evagrius. Nevertheless, even when Evagrius uses the language of forbidding (*kōluein*), and that only once, still the principal approach is that of dissuasion.

We do not know if Severa was dissuaded. If she did go anyway, she would not have been alone in her travels. Other women, such as Egeria, made extensive pilgrimages to the holy places at this time.

Susanna

Acta Sanctorum [61]

Susanna, according to tradition, was born in the late third century in Palestine. Her father Artemios was a pagan, and her mother Martha, Jewish. Susanna became Christian, gave away her wealth, freed her slaves, disguised herself as a man, and lived as a monk in a Jerusalem monastery. When a nun fell in love with her, she asked the bishop Kleopas of Eleutheropolis[62] to summon two deaconesses and two consecrated virgins, to whom she revealed her sex. She was acclaimed for virtue, ordained a deaconess, and put in charge of a monastery. She died in prison as a confessor in the brief persecution of Christians under the emperor Julian (361–63).

The text takes up at the point at which she is accused of seducing the nun. She has prostrated herself before the bishop.

Rising from the ground, she said to the bishop: "I beg you in the Lord, sir, call quickly for two deaconesses and two virgins. I have something to show them which will deal with your concern." The bishop sent immediately to Eleutheropolis, to send quickly two deaconesses and two virgins. When they arrived, the holy Susanna took them and went into the diakonikon of the monastery, and disrobing before them, she showed them that she was female by nature and a virgin like them from birth. In order to save her soul, she had put on the angelic habit and changed her name to John, though her real name was Susanna. Those honorable women, seeing and hearing these things, cried out in astonishment with a loud voice, saying: "Great is God who gave you this gift and perseverance!" When the bishop, monks, and laity with them heard the cry, they were disturbed and ran to know why the cry had arisen, for they thought that something shameful had happened to them. Then the deaconesses and the virgins went to the bishop and said: "Truly we have seen a new Susanna!"

The four women then repeat to the bishop the story of what they have learned.

When they had heard all these things from the revered deaconesses and virgins, they marveled at the great faith, modesty, and purity of holy Susanna, and they praised the holy God in victory songs because no contentious evil was found in her.

But her fellow monks are not pleased and prepare to stone the false ascetic. Susanna, however, falling to the ground, dissuades them. Bishop Kleopas then takes her under his care.

After all this, the thrice-holy bishop took holy Susanna and brought her to Eleutheropolis and put her at the head of the monastery of virgins, also making her a deacon of the holy church, since she was revered, pious, and a virgin. This became known in that whole region, and she was honored and revered by all. The Lord healed many who had various illnesses and diseases through her holy prayers, and he also cleansed many from unclean spirits and evil possession through her prayer. She had special concern for the poor, and she shone brightly as a shining star sent by God to this land.

Elements of the story are certainly legendary. The theme of a holy ascetic woman who disguises herself as a man is common in early monastic stories; usually her sex is only discovered after her death. While the two ordained witnesses are *diakonissai,* Susanna is ordained *diakonos.* Probably here, as elsewhere, the two terms were interchangeable. It is not clear why Susanna asks for four witnesses, two deaconesses and two consecrated virgins who were not ordained, when traditionally two witnesses sufficed. Perhaps the witness of the ordained carried special authority, while the two virgins held the same status as Susanna, unordained ascetics. There is no indication that the two deaconesses held any position in a monastery. More likely, they served in the bishop's church in Eleutheropolis, while the virgins lived in a monastery. By this time, however, the head of a women's monastery was frequently—though not always—ordained, as Susanna later was. The sequence of monastic headship and ordination in this text, however, shows along with other texts that the superior of a monastery did not have to be a deacon; the two positions were not the same.

Theodula

Life of St. Euphrasia or Eupraxia [63]

Eupraxia (also called Euphrasia) was a relative of Thedosius the Great. She lived approximately 380–410. Her mother of the same name, on the death of her husband Antigonos, left Constantinople with her seven-year-old daughter and retired to her estate in the Thebaid of Egypt, near a women's monastery, which she frequently visited and where she offered money in exchange for the prayers of the nuns for her deceased husband and her orphaned daughter.

*Theodula the deacon, spokesperson and superior of the monastery, first appears at 2.7 to tell the mother that she need not give offerings to get their prayers. She then continues to appear and to speak throughout the narrative. She is called alternately deacon, deaconess, the great one (*hē megalē*), abbatissa, archimandritēs and hēgoumenē (religious superior), and despoina (lady). While this charming legendary story is named after Eupraxia, it is really about the growing relationship between Eupraxia and her deacon superior, Theodula.*

One day the deacon Theodula said to the girl kindly: "Lady Eupraxia, do you love this monastery and the sisters?" She answered, "Yes, my lady, I love you in every way." So the deacon said to her kindly: "If you love us, stay with us in the monastic habit." The girl said to her: "Truly, if it would not grieve my lady mother, I would never leave this place." (2.7)

The mother, learning of this, objects that she is too young, since she is only seven years old. She tries to get the daughter to leave.

The girl said to her: "I am staying here with the lady deacon." The deacon said to the girl: "Go, lady, you cannot remain, for no one can stay here unless you are joined to Christ." The girl said to her: "And where is Christ?" The deacon kindly showed her the image of Christ. The child went up to it and kissed it, and turning, said to the deacon: "Truly I will join myself to Christ and will go away no more from my lady." The deacon said to her: "You have no place to sleep, child, and you cannot remain here." The girl said to her: "Wherever you sleep, my lady, so will I." (2.8)

Since it was evening, her mother and the deacon tried hard [to get her to leave], but they were not able to put her out of the monastery. For many days, her mother and the deacon tried to soften her resolve but could not persuade her to leave. The deacon said to the girl: "If you want to remain here, you have to learn to read and to pray the Psalter and to fast like all the sisters." The girl said: "I will fast, and I will learn everything. Only let me stay here." The deacon said to the girl's mother: "My lady, leave the girl here. I see that the grace of God has enlightened her, and the just deeds of her father and your holy life and the prayers of both of you have procured for her eternal life." So Eupraxia the mother rose, took her daughter, and brought her to the image of the Lord, and extending her hands to heaven, cried out with tears: "Lord Jesus Christ, you will take care of this child because she desires you and she has given herself to you." Turning to the child, she said: "May the God who set the foundations of the immovable mountains strengthen you in fear of him, child." And having said this, she gave her over into the hands of the deacon, and went out of the monastery weeping and beating her breast so that the whole group gathered wept with her. (2.9)

The next morning, the deacon took Eupraxia into the chapel and after prayer clothed her in the monastic habit. (2.10)

The mother then sees her in the monastic habit and praises God, accepting her daughter's call to monastic life.

Twelve years passed, when she strengthened herself for the contest. At first, she ate only once a day, in the evening, then every two days, then every three . . .

If any of the sisters suffered testing by the devil in dreams, they would immediately inform the deaconess. She would then with tears beseech God to keep the devil from her. She ordered stones to be prepared and placed under the bed of the sister, under the mat, and ashes to be scattered on the skin on top, and the sister to sleep upon it for ten days.

Eupraxia is tested at night and puts the rocks and ashes on her bed without telling Theodula.

The deacon, seeing the ashes on Eupraxia's bed, smiled and said to one of the older sisters, "Truly the girl has had testing by the devil." And the deacon prayed, saying: "O God, who created her and commanded her to take this monastic habit, do you yourself strengthen her in reverence for you." Calling Eupraxia, she said to her: "Why did you not tell me, child, about the testing of the devil, but hid it from me?" She fell at the feet of the deacon and said to her: "Forgive me, my lady, because I was ashamed to tell you." The deacon said to her: "My child, be strengthened [*andrizou,* literally, act like a man], so that you may conquer and be crowned." (3.14)

Various other stories follow about Eupraxia's temptations, and the help and intercession of other sisters in the monastery, all of whom defer to the strength and wisdom of Theodula. All temptations are to be reported to her, and each time, she provides the appropriate prayer and guidance. One sister, Julia, tells Eupraxia that Theodula has such wisdom about temptations because when she was young, she endured so many of them. By this time, Eupraxia is twenty-five years old.

Only Theodula can fast all week, but Eupraxia asks permission and then does it, to the amazement of all (3.19). Once, the devil afflicts Eupraxia so severely by attacking her with an axe that she is thought to be dead.

But the superior brought water to her face, and anointing and embracing her, said to her: "My child Eupraxia, why do you not respond? Get up and speak to the sisters." She, looking up, said to the superior: "Do not weep, my mother, my soul is still in me." The superior gave her the saving seal on her forehead and prayed thus: "Lord Jesus Christ, heal your servant, who suffers for you." And seizing her rough foot, raised her up, and giving her a hand, led her into the monastery. (4.23)

Everyone in the city and surrounding region brought their sick children to this monastery to the distinguished women there, and the Great One [Theodula] would take them into the chapel and pray to God on their behalf, and the children would be immediately healed of all illness, and their mothers would receive them back healthy, so that they would go around rejoicing and praising God. There was in that monastery a woman who suffered from her youth, brought to the monastery in hope of healing. She had a controlling spirit, so that bound hands and feet, she behaved madly, grinding her teeth, crying out so loudly that everyone who heard her cowered with fear. Many times, the Great One along with the elder sisters prayed for her healing, but they were not able to do it. (5.26)

Later (5.31), Eupraxia is able to exorcise the possessed woman as an act of obedience to the command of the superior, after having also healed a sick child. One day, Theodula is greatly disturbed and does not want to tell the sisters why, but she finally does: she has had a dream of the death of Eupraxia (6.32).

The deacon came and stood outside the doors [of the chapel] and recounted the dream to the elder sisters, thus. "I saw two distinguished men who arrived, looking for Eupraxia, to take her. They said to me: 'Send her off, because the king is looking for her.' Again, others came and said to me: 'Take Eupraxia and bring her to the Master.' Taking her immediately, we went with them. When we arrived at some doors that were more glorious than I can tell, they opened by themselves and we went in and saw there incomparable glory, a heavenly palace, an everlasting bridegroom, a bridal chamber not made by hands. I was not able to go any further inside, but the holy ones took Eupraxia to the Master and she kissed his undefiled feet. I saw there myriads of angels and an uncountable number of saints, and they all stood beholding the scene. And the mother of the Lord took Eupraxia and showed her the palace, the bridegroom, the bridal chamber, and the crown prepared for her. A voice spoke to Eupraxia thus: 'Behold your reward and your rest. Go now, and after ten days you will come and enjoy all of this for eternity.' Today is the ninth day since I saw the vision, which means that Eupraxia will die tomorrow." (6.33)

The next day, Eupraxia develops a fever and dies, at the age of thirty. She is buried in the tomb with her mother (6.36). Three days later, her friend Julia, who had taught her to read and to pray the psalter, announces that she too will die—she had previously asked Eupraxia while still alive, to take her along. Five days later, Julia dies and is buried in the same tomb.

Thirty days later, the deacon called together the leading sisters of the monastery and said to them: "Choose for yourselves a mother and put her in my place to be able to guide you." They said to her, "Why, mistress? You have never said this to your servants." She said, "The Lord has called me. The lady Eupraxia has prayed for me and has showed me many trials in prayer, so that I might be worthy of the heavenly bridegroom. Julia has received her portion because of Eupraxia and has entered into that palace not made with hands and now has joined the unconquered choir. Now I hastened to be found worthy to be with them." When the sisters heard about the glory in which Eupraxia and Julia were, they rejoiced and prayed that they too might be worthy of that bridegroom. They chose one of the sisters, Theogneia, to govern them. Then the Great One [Theodula] called her and said to her: "They all witnessed to you and made you guide and leader to be entrusted with the traditions and the succession of leadership of the monastery. I adjure you by the undefiled and homoousian Trinity, that you not acquire to this monastery money or property. Do not turn the mind of the sisters to earthly things and futile worries, so that by despising temporal things, they might set their sights on the heavenly." And again to the sisters, she said: "Since you know well the life and manner of the lady Eupraxia, let us make haste to imitate her and strive in the same way, so as to be worthy to share her portion." When they had all said "Amen" she gathered them, went into the chapel, and closed the doors, announcing that no one should enter until sunup. Early the next morning, when they went in, they found her asleep in the Lord. Singing to God, they placed her in the tomb of Eupraxia. From that day, no other body was buried in that tomb. (6.37)

Then many signs and healings happened at that tomb, and demons were expelled, crying: "After death, Eupraxia has overpowered us and pursues us!" Such was the life of the noble Eupraxia, who was worthy of the noble assembly of heaven. Let us too hasten to the same discipline, humility, submission, labor, meekness, long suffering, so that we might enjoy the same passing and joy, with our great king and savior Jesus Christ, to whom is the glory and the power now and forever and for the ages to come. Amen.

Because the story does not center on Theodula, her role in the narrative is all the more interesting. Many monastic superiors of women at this time were ordained; some commentators have even thought, without adequate examination of the evidence, that by this period, ordination as a female deacon was synonymous with governing a monastery. Through this hagiographical account, we may see some of the roles of a monastic superior of women, who was often a deacon: discernment and admission of new members, spiritual guidance, discipline, intercession, model asceticism, and animation of community consensus. All in the monastery owe absolute obedience to her, and she sometimes provides special tests of obedience by commanding difficult tasks. When before her death the community chooses another superior to replace her, nothing is said about diaconal ordination for the successor. Nor is it clear what aspects of the superior's role, if any, arose from her ordination. We are thus left with the impression that ordination was not required for a superior. The same is true in the *Life of Macrina*, where not she the superior but another member of the community, Lampadion, is a deacon.

Theophila of Chersonesus

Life of St. Parthenius [64]

St. Parthenius was bishop of Lampsacus in the Crimea, on the Asian side of the Hellespont, during the reign of Constantine. The brief Life *by his disciple Chrysippus recounts his virtues and miraculous powers. This account was probably amplified by Simeon Logothetēs, (a.k.a. Metaphrastēs), a ninth- or tenth-century Byzantine author of a number of saints' lives. Parthenius is commemorated on February 7. In the midst of recounting his miracles performed while he was bishop:*

> A certain woman deacon (*diakonos*) named Theophila from Asērmos, a village of Chersonesus, and with her Rufina, a lifelong child (*aeipais*) from the same village who was paralyzed by an unclean spirit, were brought to the holy man. For a few days, he sprinkled water on them and prayed, and by the power of the Lord they were sent away healed.

The account of the healing is in the plural, but there is no mention of an illness on the part of Theophila. She more likely accompanied the possessed woman on the pilgrimage. We may have here another role of the female deacon: to accompany the sick on pilgrimage to places or persons of healing.

Her sick companion is an *aeipais,* literally a "perpetual child." This was another way of speaking of an *aeiparthenos,* a person consecrated to perpetual virginity.

Valeriana

Severus of Antioch, *Letter* 7.1 [65]

For background on Severus of Antioch, see Anastasia.

The addressee's name is probably Valeriana, which would be rather common, or Valeriana, a more unusual form. Severus exhorts her to supervise her sisters in the practice of asceticism and the sharing of goods in common. Female slaves of women who have joined the monastery, if they show sincere interest, may be admitted, but without any contact with their former mistresses, who may not keep attendants for their personal use. The editor dates the letter to the period of Severus' episcopacy, so perhaps the intended monastery was in or near Antioch.

To Valeriana, deaconess and monastic superior

The titles are the usual terms in Syriac (see Anastasia, Eugenia, and Jannia). Valeriana is both *diakonissa* and *archimandritē,* two distinct roles in the monastery.

Unnamed daughters of Count Terentius

Basil of Caesarea, *Letter* 105 [66]

Basil the Great (330–379), brother of Gregory of Nyssa and Macrina, belonged to an illustrious Christian family of Pontus. Two more of his brothers became bishops and his eldest sister superior of a monastery. As presbyter and then bishop of Caesarea in 370, he was an effective administrator, pastor, and theologian. With the other two "Cappadocian theologians," his brother Gregory and his friend Gregory Nazianzen, Basil was responsible for important advances in trinitarian theology. To him is attributed the monastic rule that is still paramount in the Eastern Church. This letter is from 372.

To the deacons, daughters of Count Terentius

Terentius was governor of Cappadocia, removed from office the next year for embezzlement, at which time Basil performed the role of patron by writing three letters to influential men on his behalf. The daughters are *diakonoi*; we do not know the number of them in the family. Basil writes to them a brief letter to encourage them to keep his trinitarian theology in the midst of questioning and uncertainty about the divinity of Son and Spirit.

Unnamed deaconess

Callinicos, *Life of Hypatius* 8.13–17 [67]

Hypatius was probably born in Phrygia about 366 CE. According to this account, he left home at the age of eighteen to pursue the ascetical life. After living in several other monastic foundations, he was ordained presbyter in 406 and the same year refounded with some companions the monastery of Rouphinianes near Chalcedon on the Bosphorus. (The early foundation by Flavius Rufinus, consul and praetorian prefect in 392, was abandoned soon after the patron's death. The Council of the Oaks that decided the exile of John Chrysostom in 403 had been held there.) Disagreements over leadership led to his going voluntarily to another place for some time, but at the time of his death in 446, Hypatius was superior of the monastery. Alongside it, a church dedicated to Saints Peter and Paul was consecrated in 395, with relics of the saints brought from Rome.

Callinicos, probably originally from Syria, and was a monk of the same monastery by 426. He may have been the second superior after Hypatius, but this is not clear. He bequeathed his work, written 447–50, to the third superior.[68]

[The monastery chapel] was large and in poor repair, so that in winter it was filled with snow. One day when they did not have enough to eat, two [of the three there] went to the city to buy what they needed by the labor of their hands. A certain woman who was rich and very Christian was praying in [the church of] the Apostles. Passing from there, she heard that there was a monk in the monastery. Leaving her slaves outside, she entered alone, to test the ascetic—for she herself was a very ascetic deaconess—and throwing herself at his feet, said: "O Christian man, bless me and receive me to stay with you." But in anger he cried out: "Get behind me, Satan! Have you come here to drive us out? We won't be here many days yet. Take what is here and stay as long as you wish." And he left in a hurry. Then she signaled to her slaves to stop him, saying: "I tested you to see if you are a true monk." Knowing that they were three, she immediately sent for provisions that would take care of their needs.

The story is told to show how they were miraculously given food when they needed it. The *diakonissa* is, besides being wealthy, *panu christianē* and *askētikōtatē,* not an unusual combination in the fourth and fifth centuries when wealthy women like the Melanias and Olympias were embracing the ascetic life and using their wealth to support monasteries and the poor.

Unnamed female deacon

Theodoret of Cyhrrus, *Ecclesiastical History* 3.14 [69]

For background on Theodoret, see Publia.

    This story is one of several related by Theodoret about Christian resistance to the emperor Julian (361–63), who tried to restore Greco-Roman religion and stamp out Christianity. It was too little too late. His death in battle after only two years on the throne was taken by the Christians as divine vindication.

    A certain young man, son of a [pagan] priest, brought up in impiety, at that time wanted to turn to piety [i.e., become a Christian]. A woman who was distinguished in piety and who had been worthy of the charism (*charisma*) of the diaconate (*diakonia*) was very close to his mother. She often visited her when he was a child, gave him attention, and encouraged him to the faith. When the mother died, the young man used to go to her to profit from her teaching (*didaskalia*). When he had firmly accepted the counsel given, he asked his teacher (*tēn didaskalon*) what to do, and how he could flee from his father's superstition and participate in the truth preached (*kēruttomenē*) by her.[70]

As the story continues, she replies that he should leave his father and go to another city to avoid the emperor, while she takes care of the situation. (The location of the story is Antioch. Daphne, mentioned below, was a suburb of that city.) The young man replies:

"I will come, and I hand over my life to you."

Soon there is a religious festival in Daphne that lasts seven days, at which the father, the young man, and his brother appear to perform a cultic function. After the first day, the young man leaves and returns to the deacon, asking her to keep her promise by protecting him. She brings him to a holy man named Meletius who hides him in his house. The father searches all of Daphne, then Antioch. When he is in the neighborhood of Meletius, he looks up and sees his son watching him from the railing of an upper balcony. He runs into the house, seizes him, takes him home, beats him severely, tortures him with a red-hot instrument, locks him up in the house, and returns to Daphne. The young man tears up all the pagan images in the house, then, fearing his father's return, asks Christ— for whom he had suffered—to help him, whereupon the bolts on the door fall off and the door opens. (Theodoret adds here that he heard the story from the young man himself, in his old age.) The story continues in the first person.

I ran to my teacher (*tēn didaskalon*), who dressed me in women's dress and went with me in a covered carriage back to the holy Meletius. He took me to the bishop of Jerusalem [Cyril, who was in Antioch at the time] and thence by night we made off to Palestine.

After the death of Julian, the young man returns to his father and converts him to the true faith.

This story is remarkable not only for its content but for some of its language. The general thinking about the role of female deacons is influenced by the descriptions given in the *Didaskalia* and *Apostolic Constitutions*, which restrict their work to ministry with women. But here is a story of a female deacon instructing a young man privately, with no apparent disapproval from anyone. Theodoret, not known to be any more pro-women than any of his contemporaries, calls her twice by the official (masculine) title of teacher, *didaskalos* and refers to what she does as "teaching" (*didaskalia*).[71] This is the terminology used when prohibiting women from teaching, from 1 Tim 2:12 on[72]—though the prohibition is usually understood to mean public teaching, and here it is done in private. Moreover, the instruction she has given is also called truth that is "preached" (*kēruttomenē*, using the Attic stem in the past participle). This story gives indirect evidence that perhaps the activity of female deacons as given in the church orders is more prescriptive than descriptive.

Unnamed female deacon of Caesarea

Palladius, *Lausiac History* 70.3[73]

Palladius (see Olympias) tells a story in which an innocent lector, falsely accused, is miraculously vindicated. A young unmarried woman of Caesarea in Palestine is found to be pregnant and is told by her lover to accuse a certain lector in the church. In an assembly of bishop and presbyters, the lector maintains his innocence until he is severely pressed by the bishop to admit his guilt. At that point, he still says it was not true, but since the bishop wanted to hear it, he would say that he did it. After he is deposed from office, he suggests that the girl be given to him in marriage.

So the bishop gave her over to the lector, thinking that the young man would stay with her and would not be able to relinquish his union with her. Instead, the young man took her from the bishop and her father to a women's monastery and asked the deacon of the sisterhood (*hē diakonos tēs adelphotēs*) to look after her until it was time for the birth.

As the story continues, the woman is in labor for many days and cannot deliver the child. She interprets this as punishment because she has denounced an innocent man and confesses her lie. When the lector and the bishop then pray together for her, the child is immediately delivered.

Texts like this one are often interpreted to mean that the title of deacon or deaconess by this time was simply used for the superior of a monastery. Some monastic superiors such as Olympias were deacons, but others were not. In this text, the deacon is not necessarily the superior. It was a woman deacon's role to give pastoral care and shelter to women in need, and this may have been the role of the deacon in the monastery with regard to women from the outside (for another such text, see Romana). Women's monasteries were probably havens for unwed mothers.

Unnamed female deacons

Pseudo-Ignatius, *To the Antiochenes* 12[74]

Ignatius, bishop of Antioch in Syria, was arrested and brought under guard to Rome to be martyred about 110 CE. On the way, he wrote a number of letters to communities who sent delegates to visit him as he was brought through western Asia Minor, and he sent a letter to the Roman community asking that they not try to obtain his release. The letters are rich sources of information about the church at the time and about Ignatius' own theology. Later, a number of other letters were written under his name and combined into a collection of thirteen that circulated throughout the early church and medieval period. In the nineteenth century, the careful work of scholars, notably J. B. Lightfoot, succeeded in establishing a "short recension" of seven original letters. The Letter to the Antiochenes belongs to the "long recension" and is not from Ignatius himself. Lightfoot argued that this group of letters was written in the late fourth century, possibly by a compiler of the AC, since they seem to reflect a similar church organization and thinking. After greeting presbyters and deacons, the text takes up as follows.

Greet the subdeacons, lectors, psalmists, doorkeepers, the laborers [grave diggers], exorcists, and preachers. Greet the guardians of the holy gates, the [female] deacons (*tas diakonous*) in Christ. Greet the Christ-imbued virgins, in whom I take delight in the Lord Jesus. Greet the distinguished widows. Greet the people of the Lord from least to greatest, and all my sisters in the Lord.

Presumably all the offices first listed are occupied by men. The author then begins a new list for women, listing first deacons, then virgins and widows, then finally a greeting to all the laity, but especially to the women. This is in keeping with Ignatius' own affectionate greetings to women he knew (e.g., Tavia and "the virgins called widows" [*Smyrnaeans* 13.1–2] and Alce [*Polycarp* 8.2]). But the elaboration of multiple church offices dates from a later time. One of the duties of female deacons in the fourth-century East was to serve as ushers, guarding the women's entrance of the church, keeping watch over those who entered, and seeing that women were seated in an orderly fashion (see *AC* 2.57–58; 8.28).

Unnamed female deacons

John Moschus, *Pratum Spirituale* 3[75]

John Moschus, also known as Eucratas, was born about 550, probably in Damascus. He entered monastic life in the monastery of St. Theodosius southeast of Jerusalem, between Bethlehem and St. Saba. At some point either here or in seclusion in a more remote part of the Judean desert, he met Sophronius, who would be his closest companion and future patriarch of Jerusalem. Together they visited the monasteries of Egypt and Sinai to collect stories of the desert ascetics, then returned to Palestine with the same mission. In 602 they left Palestine and traveled west, arriving eventually in Rome, where John died in 619. His faithful companion brought his remains back to St. Theodosius for burial. His collection of ascetic lore, the "Spiritual Meadow," was very popular and underwent many editions after his death.

Chapter 3 is about Konon, a presbyter of the monastery of Penthoukla near the Jordan River. John attributes the story to a monk named Athanasius at St. Saba monastery. Konon, a Cilician by birth, was appointed to baptize those who came desiring it. He baptized and anointed everyone but found it acutely difficult to anoint a woman because he was not well established in his own chastity. He wanted therefore to withdraw into greater solitude, but whenever he thought about it, St. John the Baptist appeared to him urging him to remain and promising to help.

One day a Persian girl came to be baptized. She was very beautiful, so that the presbyter was not able to anoint her with oil. She waited two days, and then the archbishop Peter heard of it, was angry at what happened, and wanted a female deacon to do it. But he did not do this because it was not the received custom.

As the story continues, Konon takes off from the monastery but is confronted by John the Baptist, who reproaches him for promising and doing nothing. John makes the sign of the cross three times "below his navel" and Konon is never again troubled by sexual temptation when baptizing women!

Baptism by immersion necessitated the removal of most if not all clothing. The immersion was followed by anointing on various parts of the body. The predicament in which Konon found himself was precisely the reason that women deacons were employed in the baptism of women, as described in the *DA* 16 and *AC* 3.16.1–4, where a bishop or presbyter anoints only the head of a woman being baptized while the deaconess anoints the rest of her body. The line that "it was not the received custom" is therefore difficult if we interpret what needed to be done only as the anointing, not the whole baptism, since we know that in many parts of the Eastern Church it was the custom, and inscriptional evidence tells us that there were women deacons in Palestine. It is not clear in the story whether Konon had already performed the baptism but not finished the ritual with anointing, or whether he had not begun the rite at all. John Moschus may mean the latter, so that the archbishop wanted a woman deacon to respond to the immediate pastoral need and perform the whole baptism. Against this, there was always resistance, yet the very fact that it is discussed may mean that women deacons did perform baptisms of women by themselves (see *DA* 15 and *AC* 3.9.1). "It was not the custom" is a far lighter response to the idea of women baptizing than, for example, Tertullian, *On Baptism* 17.4 or *Remedy of Heretics* 41.5. See also the chronologically closer Justinian, *Novellae* 6.6, where the ambiguous language also seems to suggest that persons presented themselves to a deaconess for baptism.

INSCRIPTIONS

These sixty-one inscriptions, given in alphabetical order, range across the Eastern Mediterranean area and include women who are celibate ascetics and others who are deeply embedded in family structures. The inscriptions yield little information about what these women actually did, but they testify to the expansion of the office, especially during the fourth, fifth, and sixth centuries.

Aeria [76]

Inscription on a stone with cross in the middle, found originally in 1885 in the Armenian quarter of a village near Amisos.

Here rests the ever-remembered servant of Christ, Aeria, who was a deacon of the holy ones, friend of all. She came to rest in the tenth Indiction in the month of January, being thirty years old, in the year 594. God-bearer [help?]

Aeria was a *diakonos* about whom conventional but nonetheless beautiful things are said. An earlier editor had read the date 6594, which would correspond to 1086 CE, far too late a date for the particularities of this inscription. For example, the editor notes that "friend of all" (*pantōn philē*) is a common expression in the fifth–sixth centuries but not in the eleventh. The date is to be read as 594 of the era of Amisos, which corresponds to 562 CE. For more on Indictions, see note 86.

Agaliasis[77]

An early-fourth-century family funerary inscription from the island of Melos in the Cyclades, Aegean Sea.

In the Lord: the presbyters worthy of every commemoration, Asclepis and Elpizōn and Asklepiodotos and Agaliasis the deacon and Eutychia and Klaudianē, virgins, and Eutychia their mother lie here. Since this tomb is full, I adjure you by the angel located before it that no one dare bury anyone else here. Jesus Christ, help the one who writes this and his entire household.

Here an ecclesiastical family buries many of its members together. Three sons are presbyters, two daughters probably consecrated virgins, and another daughter a deacon (*diakonos*). The mixture of names in the family derived from those of a Greek god (Asclepis and Asklepiodotos) and others probably with Christian connotations (Elpizōn, "hoping," and Agaliasis, "rejoicing") suggests a date early in

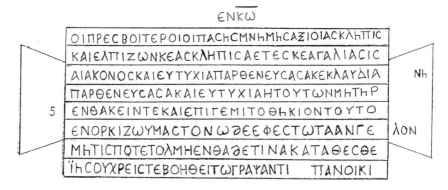

Figure 1. Agaliasis. Late third or early fourth century. *CIG* 4.9288

the development of Christian culture, when names derived from traditional gods were not yet thought to be out of place for Christians. The names Eutychia ("good luck") and Klaudianē (a common Roman-derived name) tell us nothing except the mixture of Greek and Roman nomenclature in the same family. The third name really reads in *CIG* "Asklēpisaetes," interpreted by the editor as Asklēpis *deuteros* (second time) or *heteros* (another). The uncertainty about this name of one of Agaliasis' brothers is not relevant here. Though the deacon's name is spelled with only one "l" in the inscription, the name is a common Greek word, *agalliasis* (see Luke 1:47). No mention is made of the father, who is probably still alive and is the most likely commemorator.

Guardian angels of tombs are known elsewhere in the Aegean area (see inscription of Epikto *presbytis*). Solemn warnings against tomb reuse and personal invocations of the inscriber are also known elsewhere. For the former, see the inscription of Athanasia of Delphi.

Agathē [78]

Funerary inscription from the graveyard of the "Extra-Muros" (outside the walls) fifth-century Christian basilica at Philippi in Macedonia.

Distinguished resting place of Agathē deacon and John treasurer and linen-weaver

This brief inscription probably records the burial of a wife and husband. Her title is *diakonos*. The terms used to describe her husband are disputed. He may have been treasurer or custodian of the church (*hypodektos*) as well as a worker or merchant in linen (*othōnētos*), but neither role is clear. He seems not to have been ordained. This inscription is a rare indication that not all women deacons were virgins or widows.

Agathokleia [79]

An inscription from Edessa in Macedonia, fifth to sixth centuries. The first word of the inscription is a Greek loanword from Latin, mēmorion. *For another funerary inscription from the same place using the same term, see that of Theodosia below.*

Memorial of Agathokleia, virgin and deacon

The *diakonos* Agathokleia is also called a virgin; she is undoubtedly a consecrated virgin. Both titles are also ascribed to Theoprepeia, also from Macedonia (see below). Eisen (*Women Officeholders,* 181) assumes that the order of titles here means

Figure 2. Agathokleia. Fifth-sixth centuries. Feissel, *Recueil* 21, p. 40

that the consecration to virginity preceded ordination as deacon, but this need not be the case. However, this inscription and that of Theoprepeia show that the two titles and thus the two functions, virgin and deacon, were considered distinct, yet could be combined.

Agrippianē [80]

A votary inscription in mosaic from Patras, Greece, early Byzantine period.

The deacon Agrippianē, most beloved of God, made the mosaic in fulfillment of her vow.

Agrippianē is a *diakonos* who exercised her patronage by paying for a mosaic floor after having made some kind of promise to God, the details of which are unknown. The usual pattern, often practiced by believers of the early Church, is to promise to do something specific if a request has been granted by God. Both clergy and laity could make such vows and were bound to fulfill them. The appellation "most beloved of God" (*theophilestatē*) is known in other contexts as a description of church officials.

Alexandra of Pontus [81]

A brief funerary inscription from Apollonia, Pontus (Thrace)

Alexandra subdeacon

The office of subdeacon is known for men, but is otherwise unknown for women. The title *hypodiakon* on the Greek inscription is an abbreviation either for *hypodiakonos* or *hypodiakonissa,* so her actual title could have been either term.

Alexandria of Elis [82]

This fourth-century inscription was first discovered in 1910 at Elis in the Peloponnesus. It is partially restored from the reassembling of eight fragments of a marble plaque that at some point was attached to a wall; still, the better part of the upper text is missing.

Here lies [———] only child, twenty-three years old, daughter of [———] and Alexandra deacon, raised and taken in by my father Erenianos in swaddling clothes, in distress and pleas, buried in hope by me. As God wished, I fulfilled this path for her in the fourteenth Indiction, September 13. [83]

The full meaning of the inscription is far from certain. Jeanne and Louis Robert emended an initial reading of *-driasdia[m]* at the end of the second line to a much more likely—*drias diak,* to identify the supposed mother of the deceased as a deacon or deaconess. [84] The beginning of her name is lost and could be something else, but Alexandra seems most likely. But if the deceased was a foster child, as the Roberts note, perhaps Alexandra is not her mother, but rather another, unknown party, perhaps a child of Erenianos who had taken in the deceased and thus foster sibling of the deceased. Unfortunately, it must all remain conjectural since the key parts of the inscription giving the relationship of the various persons to one another is missing.

Anastasia of Palestine [85]

A funerary inscription of the Byzantine period, from the burial caves at the St. George Choziba Monastery, Deir el Qilt in Wadi Kilt, between Jerusalem and Jericho.

Here lies Anastasia deacon, in the month of February 27, in the 11th Indiction [86]

After Anastasia's name is the abbreviation consisting of the four letters *diak,* so that it is not possible to know whether her title was deacon or deaconess. This inscription is one of at least two, and possibly four, women's burials out of a total of 211 burial inscriptions discovered in a famous desert monastery. It lies in the third of three burial caves, this one about 100 meters from the actual site of the monastery. Two of the other inscriptions were read as women's names by an earlier editor (Kleopas Koikylides in 1901) but are read differently as male names by Schneider. Only one other possible female commemoration (Basilis) contains a title of office. The monastery gave hospitality to travelers, including women. This hospitality to women was explained by a legend that the Virgin Mary Theotokos commanded that a wealthy woman from Byzantium should be brought there and so was healed. Anastasia must have died there while performing a pilgrimage.

Andromacha [87]

Sixth-century mosaic inscription on the left side of the main altar of the basilica of St. Leonidas, Klauseios, Achaia, between the two northern bases of the ciborium over the main altar. St. Leonidas was a popular local saint in the fifth and sixth centuries, with another shrine in Lechaion, north of Corinth.

Polygēros the most reverend lector and Andromacha the most beloved deacon[ess] of God, because of their vow, beautified [the place].

This is not a funerary inscription, but a dedicatory inscription set up by or in honor of the two patrons who did something considerable to adorn the church, probably a gift of the pavement. The titles of both persons are abbreviated. From Andromacha's title *diak,* her full title could be either deacon or deaconess. The relationship between the two donors is unspecified. Often when a gift is given to a church "because of a vow," it is a bargain made that if a certain favor is received, the recipient will dedicate something in the church.

Aretē [88]

A votary inscription of a female deacon somehow related to a certain Theodorus who is the major figure fulfilling the vow, from Aphrodisias in Caria, Asia Minor, on the column of a temple used as a church.

[In fulfillment of] a vow of Theodorus and Aretē [his]) daughter, deaconess

Only the last three letters of the woman's name are extant, with space for three letters before, thus the restoration Aretēs in the genitive case. The beginning of the name could be something else, however. The rest of the inscription is unambiguous, though the relationship of Aretē to Theodorus is not. Most likely it is as given in the translation, though it is also possible that it should read: ". . . Theodorus and Aretē, daughter of a deaconess." Her title *diakonissa* is preserved. The inscription as we have it is complete, with crosses marking the beginning and end.

Athanasia of Delphi [89]

Fifth-century tomb inscription from Delphi in Greece.

The devoted deaconess Athanasia, who lived a blameless life decorously, installed as deaconess by the most holy bishop Pantamianos, set up this memorial. Here lie her mortal remains. If anyone else dares to open this monument where the deaconess has been placed, may he share the lot of Judas the [betrayer] of our Lord Jesus Christ . . .

Athanasia's title appears three times in the inscription, once *diakonissa* and twice *diakonisa*. This is the only inscription of a female deacon that speaks of her installation as deaconess (*katastathisa*) and gives the name of the installing bishop, probably because of his importance. This verb (*kathistēmi*) is not normally used for ordination and is sometimes contrasted to ordination. It rather connotes official appointment to an office or function. The monument contains eight more lines whose meaning is uncertain. They make reference to a group of clergy, of uncertain sex.

Athanasia of Korykos [90]

From Korykos in Cilicia, site of several women deacon's commemorations (see Charitina, Theodora, and Theophila). Lines 3 and 4, which follow what is given here, are not legible. Line 3 contains philō . . . prikēs . . . , *both words surrounded by strikeouts. Line 4 contains a few letters completely struck through (see illustration).*

[Tomb] of Athanasia deacon and of Maria her foster-child . . .

This *diakonos* had adopted a foster-child (*threptē*) who is buried with her. Maria may have been an orphan or an abandoned child. This is one of several inscriptions that Elm assumes are of widows, but there is no evidence of Athanasia's marital status, other than that she is buried without any other kin; nor do we know the age of Maria. The commemorator did not leave his or her name, or it has not been preserved in the two further lines that are not legible. The commemorator could be Athanasia herself, Maria her foster-child, or a third party. This and many other deacon inscriptions show that women deacons sometimes had normal family relations.

Aurelia Faustina [91]

Funerary commemoration from fourth-century Laodicea Combusta, Eastern Phyrgia, Asia Minor. In this case, the deacon is the commemorator of her son Appas.

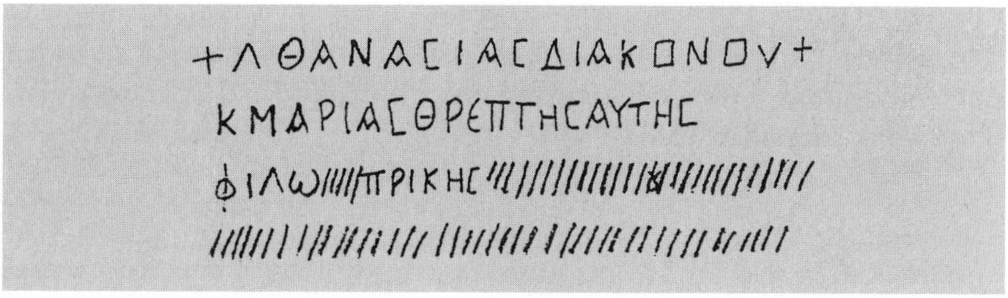

Figure 3. Athanasia of Korykos. *MAMA* 3.212b, p. 133; sketch, p. 135

Here lies Appas lector, the younger, well-raised son of Faustinus, to whom his mother Aurelia Faustina the deacon erected this monument to his memory.

This is one of the few inscriptions in which the deacon (*diakonos*) is the commemorator, in this case of her deceased son. His father has no title and so is not a cleric. He is probably previously deceased, or he would presumably be a co-commemorator. Thus Aurelia Faustina is probably a widow whose son has predeceased her.

Basilikē [92]

From the region of Neoclaudiopolis in Pontus, a marble plaque embedded into a wall of the church. The top of the inscription is broken off. The drawing and description indicate that the bottom of the stone contains two arched niches for oil lamps or offerings, called loculi *by the editors. They are, however, taller than they are wide, according to the illustration, and the total size of the stone (60 cm by 35 cm) does not allow them to be very big.*

[Deaco]ness Basilikē lies here.

Of her title, only the last four letters, *nisa* remain. It is possible but unlikely that they are the end of the first part of her name rather than her title.

Basilis [93]

From the burial caves of the Monastery of St. George Choziba, between Jerusalem and Jericho. For the history of the monastery, see Anastasia.

Basilis deacon, who died the third of March in the fifteenth Indiction[94]

This sixth-century inscription is not read as female by Schneider (no. 78, p. 321) for reasons that are not clear. He is aware of four other female burials in this men's monastery graveyard (nos. 16, 39, 103, and 197, the deacon Anastasia). Basilis is a feminine noun or adjective similar to Basilissa, meaning "queen" or "royal." Her title is abbreviated *diako,* which could be read as either *diakonos* or *diakonissa.* Another deceased of the same name without title of office in the same graveyard (no. 177) is also read as male.

Basilissa [95]

Funerary inscription of uncertain date from Iconium in Lycaonia, Asia Minor.

Quintus, son of Heraclius, first man of the village, with his wife Matrona and children Anicetus and Catilla, lie here in the tomb. The wife of Anicetus, the deacon Basilissa, erected the pleasant tomb with her only son Numitorius, still a child.

Basilissa's title has the unusual spelling variant *deiakonos.* She erected the tomb for her in-laws and husband, so she was clearly a widow with a small child at the time that the tomb was set up, which was probably the same time that her husband died. We do not know if she was a deacon during her husband's life. She seems to be the only one in the family group who holds a church office.

Celerina of Novae [96]

Dedicatory inscription on the lower part of a marble column in the episcopal basilica of Svištov, ancient Novae, probably from the time of the reconstruction of the basilica under Justinian (527–565).

Of Celerina deaconess

This is not a funerary inscription, but commemoration of the donor of the column. Celerina was therefore sufficiently wealthy, in independent control of her resources, and probably without immediate family at the time of the dedication.

Celsa (?) [97]

Funerary inscription from Tyriaion, about 45 miles northeast of Pisidian Antioch in eastern Phrygia.

[Ce]lsa deaconess to Septimius Pomponius Mnēsitheus [her] husband and Septimius Pomponius Mnēsitheus [her] father and Septimius Trophimus and . . . . and for herself while still living, for a memorial.

The first two letters of the name of the *diakonissa* are missing. Celsa is a likely reconstruction. She set up the memorial for her husband and two or three others while she was still living. The second man, whom she calls father, was most likely her father-in-law. If not, then her husband had been adopted by her own father and had thus taken his name, a familiar pattern for adoptions. The names of the men are familiar Roman names with the exception of Mnēsitheus, which could also be, instead of a proper name, an epithet: "one who remembers God." However, its repetition for both men makes it more likely a cognomen, or familiar man's name. Her relationship to Septimius Trophimus is unknown. The name

Trophimus is partially reconstructed. There are several unclear letters and spaces after his name, so there was probably one more name on the inscription that is now lost. The woman was a widow at the time of the erection of the monument. Whether she was a deaconess while married is not known.

Charitina[98]

Funerary inscription on a sarcophagus lid, from Korykos, Cilicia, in Asia Minor.

Tomb of Charitina deacon[ess?], Samaritan, daughter of Epiphanius

Charitina's title is simply abbreviated *di*, and it is at the end of a line, so we cannot tell whether it was *diakonos* or *diakonissa*. Since her filiation is given, she was probably not married. She is called a *Samarissa* (misspelled Sanarissa) instead of the more correct *Samaritis*. The date of the inscription is unknown, but it has been suggested that she was among those who fled Samaria at Justinian's suppression of the Samaritan revolt in 529. For a similar inscription from the same place, see Theophila.

Dipha[99]

Inscription on the edge of a cornice slab of polished white marble, beneath which is a sharply angled receding surface, creating a trapezoidal shape. From the village of Kuyucak, between Dorylaeum and Nacolea, about 200 miles northwest of Iconium in eastern Phrygia. The date of the inscription is likely fourth–sixth century.

[For a vo]w and salvation of Dipha deacon

This is not a funerary inscription but rather a dedication of a monument, perhaps originally in a church.

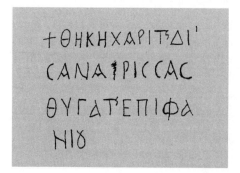

Figure 4. Charitina. *MAMA* 3.758, p. 209; sketch, p. 207

Domna [100]

Funerary inscription on rough stone from Bulduk in Asia Minor, date unknown.

Domna deacon, daughter of Theophilos the presbyter set up the memorial to her own father-in-law Miros and to her husband Patroklos.

This *diakonos* was a widow at the time of the commemoration. It is unusual that her husband is not named before her father-in-law, who may therefore have been of more significant status. Her filiation is given perhaps because of her clerical connection through her father, who was either still living at the time of the commemoration or had been commemorated elsewhere. In such inscriptions, in which the deacon was a widow at the time, the theory that only virgins and widows were ordained presupposes an ordination between the death of her husband and the funerary commemoration.

Eirēnē [101]

Recorded in 1910 at the coastal town of Nea Ankhialos, near Volos, Thebes, Thessaly, in the home of Constantine Daskalopoulos, a white stone in the wall on the right side of the entrance, broken off at top and bottom. The inscription possibly dates to the fourth century.

[Burial place of] Eirēnē deacon and Zoē my slave whom the L[ord took up]

The beginning and end of the inscription are lost. As the editor says, the first line could also have read shrine (*oikētērion*) or memorial (*mnēmorion*) or something with similar meaning. Eirēnē is a *diakonos* who has chosen to have her slave not only buried but commemorated with her, an unusual practice in surviving Christian inscriptions. Slaves were usually buried in family vaults or burial plots but seldom commemorated as such.

There is ample evidence of Christian ownership of slaves that extends well into the fifth and sixth centuries and beyond.

Eistrategis [102]

Inscribed stone found in the wall of a mosque in Goslu (Axylos), eastern Phrygia. The text is contained in a frame with arched top and surmounted by an ornamental cross in a circle.

Eistrategis deacon with my son Pancratius erected [the monument] to the memory of my husband Menneas, my sister-in-law Alexandria, and my son Domnus.

Eistrategis' title is abbreviated *diako,* so it is unknown whether her title was *diakonos* or *diakonissa.* Elm assumes in such texts that the deacon was a widow, that is, that she could not have become a deacon while married. This woman was certainly a widow, for she was burying her husband. But it is not clear when she became a deacon. As with other commemorations by female deacons of their husbands, this must presuppose diaconal ordination between the death of the husband and the dedication of the memorial, presumably a rather short time.

Elaphia [103]

Late-fourth-century limestone inscription in two parts from Nevinne, Laodicea Combusta, Phrygia in Asia Minor. The two parts are side by side, framed on each side of the whole by triangular marks that make the whole tablet into a tabula ansata.
On the left side:

Aurelius Antonius, son of Miros, together with his aunt Elaphia deaconess of the Encratites . . . [the text is broken off]

On the right side:

I Elaphia, deaconess of the Encratites, have set up this monument as memorial to the presbyter Peter together with his brother Polychronios.

We do not know if the inscription on the left is a funerary commemoration or something else. The text could have continued another three or four lines, where a few letters are preserved, but not enough to reconstruct the text. In both texts, however, Elaphia the *diakonissa* is an active agent. In the right inscription, she alone makes the commemoration, to a presybter and his brother, both of whose relationship to her is unknown. Since no relationship is stated, it is possible that she was acting as a church official to commemorate two brothers, one a cleric, who had no surviving family to do it for them. Elaphia's nephew Miros carries a name known elsewhere in Asia Minor (see Domna).

There is another inscription from the same vicinity involving a woman named Elaphia, dedicated by one Sisinnus presbyter for himself and his wife Elaphia (*MAMA* 1.xxv). There is no way to know if this is the same woman, but the three inscriptions do not contradict each other. This second Elaphia is not given a title. The Encratites were a sect of ascetics known from the second century on in the East. Celibacy was an important part of their practice, which makes it unlikely that this second, married Elaphia is the same. If she is, however, she was a deaconess while being married, since she predeceased her husband.

Elladis[104]

Undated sarcophagus inscription from Umm Qeis, Jordan.

Deaconess Elladis

No social information is forthcoming from this brief inscription. The title of Elladis is abbreviated *diaknisa.*

Eneon[105]

Fragmentary inscription above the entrance of a burial chamber in the village of Silwan (Siloam), south of ancient Jerusalem, an undated inscription in a stone reused in a wall. The inscription is difficult, and each reader reads it differently. The first reading, by J. Germer Durand, features a female deacon with an unusual name.

. . . Tomb of Eneon, daughter of Neoiketes, deaconess in this hospital . . .

The reconstruction is possible but not certain. The names Eneon and Neoiketis are not attested in the standard prosopographies.[106] The beginning and end of the inscription are incomplete. Without a photograph of the stone, it is not possible to know if there is room for other letters on the sides, which could lead to other possible configurations of letters. Surely present are the words *nosokomeion* (hospital) in the dative case, followed by *diakonis,* possibly meant to be *diakonissa,* probably in the genitive case.

Germer Durand suggests that the name of the *diakonissa* may be a feminine version of Aeneas, in which case it should be written Aineōn. Other examples of the substitution of "e" for "ai" are known. Just as male deacons were largely responsible for carrying out the bishop's charitable programs, so too were the women. This could be why she was commemorated in this way. Perhaps she also had some kind of liturgical role in the hospice.

It was customary for country monasteries to have houses in the city that functioned as shelters for pilgrims and the sick, especially at Jerusalem. Such hospices for pilgrims in the Holy Land began in the early Byzantine era. Nursing the sick was also an important work there, so that hospice and hospital were not clearly distinguishable. Many desert monasteries had them at the monastery site in connection with their guesthouses, and some of the Palestinian monasteries ran hospitals in Jerusalem at their city center. The role of deaconess in such a hospital is not clear. Perhaps she ministered spiritually to sick women inmates. The position of the inscription above a tomb chamber, probably with other names than hers, suggests that the chamber was used for a number of persons from the hospital.

The above reading was accepted by J. Leclercq in 1920,[107] but it was repudiated seven years later in the same publication by F.-M. Abel,[108] who claims that Germer

Durand's reading was faulty. Abel's translation is entirely different: "tombeau de la nouvelle grotte (?) et de l'hôpital qui s'y trouve du diacre Philète" (tomb of the new grotto and of the hospice there, of the Deacon Philetus). J. T. Milik offered a slight emendation of this reading.[109] This inscription is a real case of everyone seeing something different.

Epiphaneia (?)[110]

A marble plaque broken off on both sides, from Daldis in Lydia, Asia Minor, probably fourth century.

Vow of Asterius the devoted deacon . . . [and] of his mother [Epipha]n[e]ia deaconess of Christ and of his son Asterius and of all his household. Fulfilled . . .

Three generations of a family—mother, son, and grandson—together erected a dedicatory plaque, probably originally on a public building or some part of a church. Mother and son were both members of the clergy: she a *diakonesē* (a variant spelling of *diakonissa*), he a presbyter. Together they had made a vow to erect some monument or building and fulfilled it with this commemoration. Unfortunately, damage to the stone makes the text break off just at the point where the inscription probably gave the date. The name of the deaconess is reconstructed from four letters in the Greek text and could have been something else. Her title, however, is clear. She is probably a widow since no husband is mentioned.

Epiphania [111]

From the area between Philadelphia and Magnesia in Lydia. There are several spelling errors in the inscription, which breaks off at the end after five letters of the name that is most likely Marcellus or Marcella. The date is 507, 518, or 591.[112]

In memory and for a resting place of the most blessed Epiphania deaconess. This work was done with the assistance of all in the first Indiction, year 518, by vow of Marcell[us/a].

The relationship of Epiphania, *diakonissa*, to Marcellus/a is unknown. Nor is it clear who is involved in the "all" who assisted (*synhypourgēsantōn pantōn*).

Eugenia of Bithynia [113]

Inscription on a marble sarcophagus from Topallar, near Nicomedia in Bithynia, north-central Asia Minor, reused as a water trough in a nearby village. Date unknown.

In memory of Eugenia deacon we, the poor people of Geragathis, restored the sarcophagus that we decorated.

The burial place of this *diakonos* seems to have been held in veneration by this unknown group of people who identify themselves as "the poor of Geragathis." This proper name is known in another inscription as the name of a person (whether male or female is unknown). The group could be of a particular place or belonging in some way to a person. Eisen suggests the leader of a house for the poor where Eugenia had worked.

Eugenia of Nicopolis [114]

A beautifully carved marble monument from Nicopolis in Thrace, broken off on the top right. At the bottom, two peacocks facing each other, their beaks holding together a palmette. It is dated June 12, 538 CE.

Here lies Eugenia of praiseworthy memory, d . . . [stone broken off], who built the house (*domo[n]*, i.e., shrine) of the glorious apostle Andrew in a holy manner, and ended life on June 12 in the first Indiction, in the reign of our godly and reverend ruler (*despo[tou]*) Flavius Justinianus, eternal Augustus and Emperor, in the twelfth year of the consulship (*hypatia*) of the noble Flavius John.

The lady or her dedicator is more concerned with the correct political references than about her own life, except to say that she was patron for the construction of a memorial center to St. Andrew. Only the first letter of her title is preserved.

Goulasis [115]

A richly decorated block with inscription of unknown date, from Çeşme in ancient Lycaonia, central Asia Minor, within a tabula ansata, *vine, garlands, birds, and Latin cross.*

Aurelius Loukios and Aurelia Vaca in memory of their sweetest sister Goulasis deaconess

A brother and sister commemorate their deceased sister who was a *diakonissa*. The unusual names Vaca and Goulasis are known elsewhere in Asia Minor.

Lampadia of Smyrna [116]

Inscription on a marble block found in a garden in a village near Smyrna, reused as a stepping stone to a house.

Of Lampadia virgin, daughter of Pactolius, deacon. Hello, hello—you, too.

Lampadia is a *diakonos*. There are four words to the first part of the inscription, all in the genitive case: Lampadia, virgin, Pactolius, deacon. The relationship among the words is thus ambiguous. Normally the grammatical structure naming a woman with a man's name following in the genitive would mean that she is the wife of Pactolius, but this is obviously not the case here since she is called "virgin" (*parthenos*). It is also possible that Lampadia is not a deacon, but her father, Pactolius, is. But placement of a title of the deceased after filiation is not unknown and is so interpreted by Elm.[117]

The second part of the inscription is typical of satirical remarks frequently found on tombstones: *chere, chere* (usually spelled *chaire*) *kai su,* meaning you, the passerby will one day be in the same situation.

Magna of Laodicea Combusta[118]

A limestone funerary monument from eastern Phrygia containing a Latin cross. Both text and relationships of persons named are obscure.

Aurelia Nestorianē with my son Domnus set up this inscription to my sweetest husband, Euethios as a memorial. Magna the most pious deacon. Now I also signify death; swallowed up along with Paulos and Chrysanthos, I left behind the end of life.

The relationship of sentences to each other in this inscription is quite difficult. The first sentence is clear: a widow and her son set up a memorial for their husband/father. But how Magna is related to them is not said. The meaning of the first part of the third sentence is obscure: *sēmenō de kai ton thanaton eisphagis* (-eis). It could also read "By [this] sign, I am swallowed up." But the speaker in this final sentence is masculine, so it cannot be Magna. It must be Euethios. The relationship of Paulos and Chrysanthos to the others also remains unexplained.

It is possible that Magna is not buried here at all but was the representative of the church in the burial.

Maria of Archelais[119]

An inscription on grey marble stone, with cross and ivy decoration in the center, the inscription written below the arms of the cross. From Cappadocia, sixth century.

Here lies Maria the deacon of pious and blessed memory who, according to the saying of the Apostle, raised children, exercised hospitality, washed the

feet of the saints, and distributed her bread to the needy. Remember her, Lord, when she enters into your kingdom.

The inscription contains biblical allusions to 1 Tim 5:10 in the middle and Luke 23:42 at the end. The allusion to the work of widows in 1 Tim 5:10 makes it almost certain that Maria was a widow at the time of her death. The title "the Apostle" is frequently used of Paul by writers of this period. Everyone would know to whom it referred. Her title is *diakonos,* and the total lack of mention of any relatives is unusual. It may mean that she had no surviving relatives, or it may indicate her level of importance to her church community. Perhaps the community erected her memorial.

From the earliest Christian period, widows are known to have gathered in social groups and to have been a kind of service organization for the church. The description given here from 1 Timothy lists typical works that would be theirs. Raising children may mean not only their own but the neglected or orphaned children of others. Hospitality involved the washing of feet as a sign of welcome and was not understood only as slaves' work.[120] Feeding the poor was a necessary work of charity that was expected of all. The mention of these specific activities is a biblical allusion and does not necessarily mean that Maria excelled only at these functions.

The allusion to Luke 23:42 has an unexpected twist. Originally spoken to the dying Jesus who will enter into *his* kingdom, it now refers to the other who enters it.

Maria of Moab [121]

A stone inscription from Mahaiy, Moab, in present-day central Jordan, area near Kerak.

Here lies Maria daughter of Valens, deacon, who lived thirty-eight years and died in the year 538 [643–44 CE]

The date of death is given as 538.[122] Canova gives the corresponding date of 643/44 CE. The date on the inscription is that of the era of the Roman province of Arabia, erected the twenty-second of March, 105.[123] Maria's title is abbreviated *dk,* so we cannot know whether it was *diakonos* or *diakonissa.* She was already a deacon at the age of thirty-eight, despite the lower age limit of forty set at the Council of Chalcedon for ordination of a woman deacon (see also Olympias). These frequent discrepancies show that legislation may have been enacted, but wide observance was another thing.

Masa [124]

Inscription from the area of ancient Laodicea Combusta, Phrygia, Asia Minor, on bluish limestone, found in secondary use in the steps of a house. The stone has a fin-

ished top that included a Latin cross. The top was broken off so that only the bottom of the cross survives.

> Frontinos presbyter, Masa deacon, [and] Aurelios Mamas, children of Rhodon, presbyter, we erected this monument for ourselves while living and with purpose. In memory.

Masa's title is abbreviated *diak,* so we do not know if she was deacon or deaconess. She was sister and daughter of presbyters. The inscription they erected is called a *titlos,* a transliteration of the Latin *titulus,* a sign or notice. They erected the monument while alive (*zōntes*), a not unusual expression on tombstones, but also *phronountes,* which usually carries the meaning of intentionality or awareness. Perhaps it is the equivalent of the modern "of sound mind." The word for children is generic, masculine, and misspelled (*huiu*), so it is not certain that it is in the plural, but it would have been pronounced like the plural word, so that most probably Frontinos, Masa, and Aurelios Mamas were all siblings, children of a deceased father.

Matrona of Axylos [125]

A slab of limestone or coarse marble found in secondary use in the wall of a mosque in eastern Phrygia.

> Eugenis deacon with my son Menneas, we erected [the monument] to my wife Thekla and my mother Matrona, deaconess, and my sister Leontiana, and my children Matrona and Epiktēthe, in memory.

Here the *diakonissa* Matrona is also mother of a deacon. She may be widowed, since her husband is not mentioned. The wife's name, Thekla, was very popular in the Byzantine period, since St. Thekla was the most popular female saint.

Matrona of Stobi [126]

Inscription in a paved public area in Stobi, Macedonia, and likely dating to the fourth or fifth century. An exedra *is a small public rest area with seats.*

> In fulfillment of a vow of Matrona, the most reverend deaconess paved the exedra.

Identification of the woman is uncertain, since the word *matrona* can be a personal name or simply the word "matron." Thus the text could refer to one or even two unnamed women, a matron who wished to fulfill a vow and a deaconess who carried it out. Probably, though, both the fulfiller of the vow and the deaconess are the same woman, who may or may not have been named Matrona. Her title is sure, and is abbreviated *diak,* but there is enough room after it for the full title *diakonissa* on the damaged right side of the stone. Her title may also have been the shorter *diakonos.*

Mesalina [127]

A plain funerary monument from about 80 miles northeast of Pisidian Antioch in eastern Phrygia. The person commemorated is not Mesalina but a woman named Nexis, who is praised for her wisdom and good life in the first six lines. The top right side of the stone is missing and heavily reconstructed by the editor. Beginning at the seventh line is the inscription given below. The word diakonissa *is completely preserved.*

> Diotrephes, stepson [?] and priest, constructed this as a memorial, with [his?] sister the deaconess Mesalina and [his? her?] lawful children, and set it up.

The word "stepson" (*progonos*) is reconstructed from the first three letters. Mesalina was a *diakonissa* and sister of a *hiereus* (priest). The children probably belonged to Diotrephes, so Mesalina's marital status is unknown.

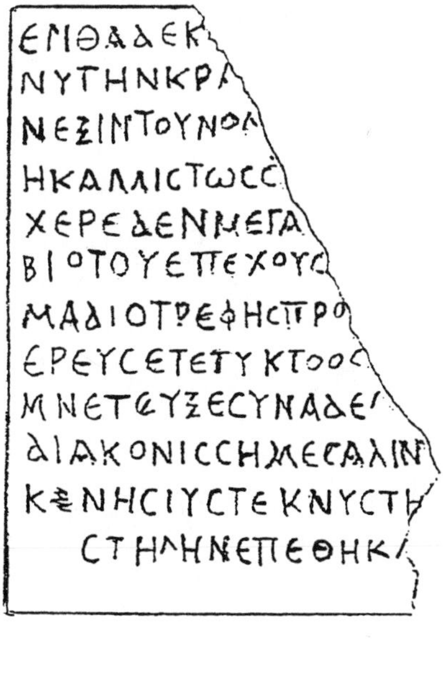

Figure 5. Mesalina. *MAMA* 7.585, p. 122; sketch, p.146

Nikagora[128]

From the monastery of Karea at Mount Hymettus, Athens.

I Neikagorē deaconess lie here.

Nikagorē (with alternate spelling Nei- on the tombstone) was a *diakonissa* who erected her own memorial for herself alone before her death.

Nonna of Galatia[129]

Inscription in a longitudinal rectangular framed panel.

Alexander presbyter erected [this monument] to the memory of his dearest mother Nonna deaconess.

Again, we see more than one member of the clergy in two generations of a family. Nonna's title is a variant spelling, *diakonēsa*. She was probably widowed, since there is no mention of her husband, Alexander's father.

Figure 6. Nonna of Galatia. *MAMA* 7.539, p.113; sketch, p. 143

Nonna of Palestine [130]

From a collection of inscriptions from the west side of the Jordan River in the Byzantine province of Palaestina Tertia, the southernmost section of Palestine.

Here was placed the blessed Nonna deacon, the twenty-third of the month of Daisius, in the first Indiction.

Nonna was a *diakonos* who died in Palestine in the Byzantine period. For information about Indiction dating, see note 86.

Nunē [131]

Fifth- or sixth-century inscription copied by William M. Calder in Karadilli, Axylos, ancient eastern Phrygia, in 1911 and included in a note about another inscription.

Because of a vow and the salvation of Kastor presbyter who erected [the monument?] [to] St. Cyrikos, and of Nunē deaconess, daughter of Kastor, and of Demetrius Bousios

This is not a funerary monument but a commemorative one that was perhaps originally in a church or some public building. It was done in fulfillment of a vow made by three people to a local saint: a presbyter and his deaconess daughter, and a third man, Demetrius Bousios, whose relationship to the other two is unknown. This is another example of church offices in the same family, in two generations. Nunē's title is a variant spelling, *dēakonnusē*. Her name may also be Nunes.

Paula [132]

Beautifully carved framed rectangular inscription, in poetic hexameters, from Laodicea Combusta, Phrygia. The stone is speaking.

Paula, deacon most blessed of Christ. She built me as tomb of her beloved brother Helladius, outside the homeland, constructed of stones as guardian of the body until the terrible sound of the trumpet wakes the dead as God has promised.

The inscription is not for the burial of Paula but for her brother, and it says little about Paula the *diakonos,* but one can infer her high level of education and family loyalty, and her sufficient wealth to afford an expensive memorial. Her deceased brother was away from home, so she probably was, too, the two of them traveling together when he was unexpectedly overtaken by death. The last line recalls 1 Cor 15:52.

Philogonis[133]

An inscription from Galatia near Ankara, possibly of the sixth century, with six lines at the top and eleven at the bottom, separated in the middle by a cross and two different birds in a rather careless design (according to the editor). There are many irregular spellings and omissions of letters. As restored by Jerphanion:

> Here lies the honorable (*timeios?*) and reverend (*geraros?*), most pious presbyter Joulianos, whose memorial his own wife Agousta erected, and the presbyter Hypatis and the deacon Philogonis erected to their own father, in loving memory.

Here an ecclesiastical family is revealed: the father and son were presbyters, the daughter a deacon (*hē diakonos* is very clear in the editor's transcription). Only the mother seems not to have had ecclesiastical rank.

Posidonia[134]

Marble stele from fourth–fifth century Philippi, Macedonia; first recorded in 1889, copied, and the original subsequently lost.

> Illustrious graves of Posidonia deacon and Panchareia, least of the canonesses

This burial includes two women with different ecclesiastical titles. Posidonia's is abbreviated *diak,* thus either deacon or deaconess. Her companion Panchareia

Figure 7. Posidonia. Fourth-fifth centuries. Feissel, *Recueil* 241, p. 204. (The acute accents over the *M* in line 1 and the *X* in line 4, as well as the dot over the *K* in line 3, seem to be signs of abbreviation.)

Figure 8. Pribis. *MAMA* 1.326, p.172

was a *kanonikē,* one of a group of women who lived together in community and engaged in the ascetic life and works of charity, apparently without formal vows or ordination.[135]

The intriguing question is why these two women with different ecclesiastical functions were buried together. Deacons, like presbyters, were often buried with their own families. We do not have enough evidence about *kanonikai* to know what the custom was for their burials. Perhaps these two women were friends, or perhaps Posidonia served some kind of ministerial function for the group of *kanonikai.*

Pribis [136]

Inscription in grey limestone surmounted by a cross. The stone breaks off in the fourth line. From Axylos, eastern Phrygia.

Aurelia Leontianē with my mother Pribis deacon and my son Anenclētus erected [the monument] . . .

Three generations joined to erect this memorial. The principal dedicator was the daughter, Aurelia Leontianē, but she was joined by her mother Pribis the *diakonos* and her son. Pribis could have been a widow, since there is no mention of her husband in the text that survives. The text breaks off in such a way that it is not known whether the memorial is for themselves or for someone else, possibly the father and husband. The unusual name Pribis also appears in MAMA 1.376, from the same area.

Calder, editor of the inscription, takes Pribis to be the deacon, "in spite of grammar." The words *diakonos ousa* are in the nominative case after the name of Pribis and should be in the dative to refer to Pribis. Eisen therefore interprets that the deacon is Aurelia Leontianē, since her name as chief dedicator is in the nominative case. Either is possible.

Figure 9. Inscription of Sophia "the second Phoebe," found in 1904 on the Mount of Olives, now at the Church of St. Anne, Jerusalem. Photo courtesy of William Tabbernee.

Severa [137]

From Hadrianopolis, eastern Phrygia, found in the village of Urus, twenty miles southeast of Pisidian Antioch.

> . . . to the deaconess Severa, mother . . .

This is a very fragmentary inscription, with seven letters on the second line that cannot be reconstructed.[138] Only the first three letters of the name are extant. Severa was a *diakonissa*; this word is perfectly clear. Nothing more can be known about her, except that she was a mother to at least one child. She was therefore either married or widowed.

Sophia, "the second Phoebe" [139]

Cré (1904) records that the stone was found by workers below the Tomb of the Prophets on the Mount of Olives in Jerusalem on December 8, 1903, in five pieces, with the bottom missing. It is now in the museum of St. Anne's Church, Jerusalem. It probably dates from the fourth century. The first six lines are well preserved.

> Here lies the slave and bride of Christ Sophia, deacon, the second Phoebe, who slept in peace the twenty-first of the month of March in the eleventh Indiction . . . the Lord God . . .

Calling oneself slave or servant of Christ or God was common early Christian language (see, for example, Rom 1:1; 1 Cor 4:5; Phil 1:1; Gal 1:10), and the use of bridal imagery, previously applied only to the church, for consecrated virgins was also beginning at this period. Sophia was a *diakonos* of a Jerusalem church. The most surprising part of the description is her appellation as "second Phoebe," a reference to Rom 16:1–2, where Phoebe, bearer of Paul's letter to Rome, is recommended to the recipients as *diakonos*—the earliest use of that term, with Phil 1:1, for an officer of a particular church—and *prostatis,* patron or benefactor (see Phoebe). The comparison to Phoebe is probably not only to her diaconate, which was common to many women of the period, but to her position as patron and benefactor.

G. H. R. Horsley proposes a comparison with several other inscriptions in which men are acclaimed as "new Homer," "new Themistokles," "new Theophanes," and "new Dionysios." In every instance, the reason for the title is major benefactions to their own or their adopted city. The titles may have begun as popular acclamation that stuck so well it accompanied them in death.[140] So it may have been with Sophia as well.

Tetradia of Volos [141]

*A complete white marble plaque discovered in 1935 in the south end of the citadel of Volos in Thessaly, in the factory of the Thessaly Distillery Association (*Panthessalikē Hetaireia Oinopneumatopoiia*). The inscription is beautifully lettered but contains many spelling discrepancies. There are two or three crosses at the top and one at bottom center.*

Tomb of Tetradia deacon. If anyone opens it except me, it will cost him the punishment of eternal fire.

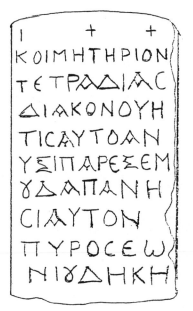

Figure 10. Tetradia. N.I. Giannapoulous, *"Palaiochristianikē epigraphē," Epetērias etaireias Byzantinōn spoudōn* 12 (1935): 26.

Threats against tomb robbers are common, usually, however, threatening the legal punishment of a large fine. Tetradia takes the threat quite a bit further, into eschatological damnation. Her comment that no one else can open it besides herself (*pareks emou*) may be a humorous comment, or an expression of faith in her coming resurrection, but it may also mean that the tomb was set up long before her death, and she wants it ready when she comes.

Theodora of Korykos[142]

A sarcophagus from Korykos in Cilicia with altar relief. Others similar also occur. In the opinion of the editor, these are reused, pre-Christian sarcophagi, so that the altar relief has no Christian meaning.[143] It cannot therefore be assumed to imply altar service in the case of Theodora.[144]

Cleansing [?] of Theodora . . . deacon

The first word, *loutra*, is ambiguous. The singular *loutron* ("washing") was commonly used as a reference to baptism in many different contexts. Since this is a funerary inscription, perhaps it is using baptism as an allusion to death. Theodora was a *diakonos*. Between her name and the word *diakonos* is a long erasure that extends far out to the right of the surviving three words, which are vertically aligned. The erasure could be from earlier use of the sarcophagus.

Theodosia[145]

Three women dedicated to divine service are buried together in one of the graves of a large cemetery at the fifth–sixth-century monastery of Hagia Triada (Holy Trinity), in Edessa, Macedonia, discovered in 1865. Of twenty-eight inscriptions recorded, nineteen were Christian, closely grouped around the church. A good number of these inscriptions are of persons holding church positions: presbyters, deacons, virgins, a lector, a cantor. Another inscription from the same place commemorates Theodosia and Aspilias, virgins. Apparently these were popular local names.

Figure 11. Theodora of Korykos. *MAMA* 3.395, p. 158; sketch, p.157

Figure 12. Theodosia of Macedonia. Fifth-sixth centuries. Feissel, *Recueil* 20, pp. 39–40

Memorial of Theodosia deacon and Aspilia and Agathokleia, virgins

Theodosia was a *diakonos* and the other two were undoubtedly consecrated virgins. Theodosia's marital status is unknown, but it is likely that she too was a virgin, since she was not commemorated by husband or children.

Theophila[146]

A brief inscription on a sarcophagus lid from Korykos, Cilicia.

Of Theophila deacon

Theophila was a *diakonos*. Nothing more can be known about her.

Theoprep(e)ia[147]

From Bonitsa, Macedonia, late fourth century.

Here lies the slave of the Lord, Theoprepeia, perpetual virgin and deacon[ess?] of Christ, who has completed a life ascetic, zealous, and distinguished in the Lord God

A great deal of information is contained in this inscription. The name on the inscription is Theoprepia, but the spelling Theoprepeia is a known name. The title "slave of the Lord" is traditional (see Sophia). Theoprepeia was *aeiparthenos,* a term that usually refers to a consecrated virgin, and is hailed for her ascetic life. She was also a *diak,* a common abbreviation that could be for *diakonos* or *diakonissa.* The combination of asceticism, which always includes celibacy, and the ecclesiastical role of deacon is not unusual. Others include Agathokleia and Sophia and those deacons who are superiors or members of monasteries.

Timothea[148]

Inscription over the entrance of a tomb chamber in Korykos, Cilicia.

Burial chamber of Timothea deacon of the holy monastery . . .

Timothea seems to have been important enough—or wealthy enough—to have her own tomb chamber. Her title is abbreviated *diak*, so it is impossible to know whether she was *diakonos* or *diakonissa*. The two words that follow (*monēs a*) could simply mean something about a "holy dwelling" but more likely refer to a monastery of which she may have been a superior or liturgical leader.

Zᶜôrtâ[149]

In a destroyed early Christian basilica in Zebed, north-central Syria, a series of inscriptions was found on the chancel screen panels, some in Greek, some in Syriac. This one is a Greek transliteration from Syriac: Zaōrtha samastha. It is thought to be contemporary with another similar inscription of one Rabūlā, placed two panels to the left. This may be Bishop Rabūlā of Edessa,[150] who was native to the area of Zebed. About 385, he distributed his goods and retired to the desert of Palestine, later to become bishop in Edessa (412–35). This inscription could commemorate his gift to the church of Zebed. If our inscription is contemporaneous, it is late fourth century and evidence of early interaction between Christian Greek and Syriac.

The letters go across the top and three letters down the right side of the frame of a central X-shaped design.

Zaōrtha deaconess

The word for deaconess that is transliterated into Greek as *samastha* is Syriac *shamāshtâ*, not the usual Syriac word, which is *mshamshānitâ*. The root meaning of the term is the same, "servant" or "minister." Whether this is a regional or some other variation is not known. Nor is anything further known about the deaconess Zᶜôrtâ. This is not a funerary commemoration but her dedication of a piece of the chancel screen as a pious offering to the church. She was therefore a person of means, probably a patron in the community. Together with the deaconesses to whom Severus wrote, she is evidence of the use of the office in the Syriac-speaking churches.[151]

Zoe[152]

From Rihab, Transjordan, in the province of Arabia, diocese of Bostra, under the patriarch of Antioch, two mosaic inscriptions from a church, dated to 594 CE.
In front of the altar:

For the salvation of Zoe, deac . . .

On the floor in front of the altar, below the step and chancel screen:

. . . Of Zoe deac . . .

In the first inscription, Zoe's office is abbreviated *dik* followed by illegible space. In the second, the title is *diako*. Either could have been an abbreviation for *diakonos* or *diakonissa*. Zoe was obviously a woman of some means to have been able to dedicate two mosaic inscriptions, which probably means that she paid for the mosaic pavement around the altar and below the step. Nothing more is known about her.

Unnamed deaconess [153]

A very fragmentary inscription from Asia Minor, 50 miles northeast of Iconium in eastern Phrygia:

. . . [an]d the [. . . dea]cones[s . . .]

The word "the" is clear, in feminine singular accusative (*tēn*), so that the word following is probably deaconess. Nothing more can be said about the inscription.

Unnamed deaconess of Thasos [154]

At the fifth–sixth-century basilica of the agora, a tomb composed of three recesses discovered in 1950 against the foundations of the north wall of the narthex. The inscriptions are painted in black paint on brown background near each burial. The tomb in the center is that of a martyr named Akakios, that to the north of the deaconess, and that to the south is no longer legible. Some think that this Akakios was a martyr of Constantinople, and that instead of a tomb, there was a reliquary in the center. The state of the remains does not allow a definitive answer.
    The north tomb inscription reads:

. . . anē..is + diakonis . . .

The word to the right of the cross in the center is the beginning of *diakonissa*, a deaconess buried next to one who must have been a renowned local martyr. The word to the left is probably her name, but not enough of it is extant to know what it was.

Unnamed female deacon, relative of Simplicius, from Iconium [155]

A highly reconstructed text with at least three lines missing at the beginning, and probably more missing at the end. The translation is therefore very loose.

... [if you want to know] who lies here peacefully, of distinguished life and shining ways, who lived a long time [or, who lived fully], unstained in judgment, dripping divine grace, completely reverent, of honored habits, who obtained the honor of the diaconate (*diakonia*), with brilliantly shining reputation. Simplicius is the name [of the one who placed her here], with [his] sister and children much loved in many ways. We rejoice eternally ...

Much of the construction is hypothetical, and the relationship of this unnamed woman to Simplicius and the rest of his family is unspecified, but she must surely have been his mother or wife. The statement of the woman's diaconate is clear.

CONCLUSION

This extensive presentation of material on female deacons in the East has shown that they appear in all kinds of contexts: funerary, dedicatory, as recipients of letters and subjects of letters, guardians of shrines, heroines of ecclesiastical conflicts, monastic superiors and followers, choir leaders, those who take care of others' concerns and those who cause concern to others—and more. They came from the nobility and the common population. Some were very much under ecclesiastical authority, others more independent, like the determined relic guardian Matrona of Cosila who retained her ecclesiastical allegiance even resisting pressure from the Emperor Theodosius, and Olympias, who in her devotion to John Chrysostom defied the authority of his episcopal successor. As we shall see in the next chapter, legislation about them was not lacking.

Notes

1. *Shepherd of Hermas,* ed. Molly Whittaker, GCS Apostolischen Väter (Berlin: Akademie-Verlag, 1967), 7; Carolyn Osiek, *The Shepherd of Hermas,* Hermeneia (Minneapolis: Fortress, 1999), 58–59.

2. See R. C. Kukula, ed., *C. Plini Caecili Secundi. Epistularum Libri Novem, Epistularum ad Traianum Liber Panegyricus* (Leipzig: Teubner, 1912), 317; *Pliny, Letters and Panegyricus,* trans. Betty Radice, LCL (Cambridge, MA: Harvard University Press, 1969), 2. 284–91; Mayer, *Monumenta,* 5.

3. Eisen is persuaded by the argument of A. N. Sherwin-White, an expert on Pliny's letters, that *ministra* represents a literal translation of the Greek *diakonos.* See Sherwin-White, *The Letters of Pliny: Historical and Social Commentary,* rev. ed. (Oxford: Clarendon Press, 1985), 691ff. Eisen also argues that this translation is confirmed by Ambrosiaster's commentary on Romans 16.1 (*CSEL* 83.476–77). But surely we should not rely on a text written more than two cen-

turies after Pliny to confirm the meaning of second-century usage. Eisen, *Women Officeholders* (173), also observes a "Greek formula parallel to Pliny's Latin" in Justin's *Apology* 1.65.5 (c. 150). In Justin the deacons (presumably both male and female) administer Eucharist. Eisen concludes: "The deacons thus clearly exercised sacramental functions. There is no reason to think that this service was not performed by both women and men" (173). However, this describes a situation some forty years after Pliny was writing and in the West; thus it would be dangerous to say that the situation described by Justin is mirrored in Asia Minor around 110. Much closer to the truth here is Martimort, *Deaconesses,* who observes, "We know absolutely nothing from Pliny or any other witness about what the role or function might have been of these *ministrae* in the community of Bithynia" and "to translate the word simply as 'deaconess' is certainly to force the sense of the text unduly and to get caught in a plain anachronism" (26). Therefore, we cannot quite agree with Eisen when she states, "Pliny's letter is an early witness to women deacons in northwestern Asia Minor," for the truth of this could only be assessed if we knew exactly what she means by "deacons." Thus, she may be caught in the very anachronism against which Martimort warns. As we shall see, particularly in the exegete Ambrosiaster (whose writings emphatically do not, as Eisen contends, argue for the translation "deacon" here), the Latin word *ministra* will pose a continuing difficulty for translation and interpretation because it is not as precise as the Greek words for "deacon" or "deaconess."

4. Texts: PG 52.659–660; 662–663; 718–719; discussed in Martimort, *Deaconesses,* 137.

5. Syriac text and translation: *A Collection of the Letters of Severus of Antioch,* ed. E. W. Brooks, PO 14.1 (Paris: Firmin-Didot, 1920), 75–118; M. Chaine, *Une lettre de Sévère d'Antioche à la diaconesse Anastasie* (Oriens Christianus n.s. 3 [1913], 36); discussed in Martimort, *Deaconesses,* 135.

6. The Syriac translation, though not the Greek original, of the story of Anastasia, abbess in Tabennesi in Middle Egypt in the cycle of stories about Abba Daniel, identifies this Anastasia as the same person, but "This is probably no more than a piece of guesswork" according to Sebastian P. Brock and Susan Ashbrook Harvey, *Holy Women of the Syrian Orient* (Berkeley and Los Angeles: University of California Press, 1987), 143.

7. We are grateful to Richard McCarron for assistance with the Syriac text.

8. Text: *Theodoret de Cyr: Correspondance,* ed. Yvan Azema, SC 40 (1955): 118; discussed in Gryson, *Ministry of Women,* 89, 153 n.140. The letters of Theodoret are in three different collections, all edited by Azema in SC, vols. 40, 98, and 111. This letter comes from a collection of forty-seven published in 1885 by Sakkelion from a manuscript on Patmos. Hence, letters in this collection are usually identified by that name.

9. Text: Eduard Schwartz, *Kyrillos von Skythopolis* (Leipzig: Hinrichs, 1939). The page references in the title are to this edition. An available translation of the whole is R. M. Price and John Binns, *Cyril of Scythopolis: The Lives of the Monks of Palestine* (Kalamazoo: Cistercian Publications, 1991), 237–39.

10. Text: *Theodoret de Cyr: Correspondance,* ed. Yvan Azema, SC 98 (1964): 62–64; discussed in Gryson, *Ministry of Women,* 89, 153 n.140. The 232 extant letters of Theodoret are in three collections; 142 of them were first edited and published by Jacques Sirmond, S.J., in Paris in 1642. Both this letter and that to Celerina come from that collection, which has its own numbering, usually preceded by the abbreviation "Sirm." The letter to Axia is from another collection, called "Patmos."

11. Text: *Theodoret de Cyr: Correspondance,* ed. Ivan Azema, SC 111 (1965): 18–20; discussed in Gryson, *Ministry of Women,* 9, 153 n. 140.

12. Text: Eduard Schwartz, ed., *Kyrillos von Skythopolis,* TU 49.2 (Leipzig: Hinrichs, 1939), 8.20–9.9; 10.5–14; 10.22–11.2; full English translation: R. M. Price, *Cyril of Scythopolis: The*

Lives of the Monks of Palestine (Kalamazoo: Cistercian Publications, 1991) 4, 6; discussed in Gryson, *Ministry of Women,* 153 n. 138.

13. L. Surius, *De Probatis Sanctorum historiis,* Col. Agrippinae 1570, 1:454; Mayer, *Monumenta,* 11.

14. Text: Anne-Marie Malingrey, *Vie anonyme d'Olympias, SC* 13bis (1968): 420; Mayer, *Monumenta,* 28; Martimort, *Deaconesses,* 137 n. 99; discussion in Malingrey, 421–22, and Martimort, 137.

15. Syriac text and translation: *A Collection of the Letters of Severus of Antioch,* ed. E. W. Brooks, PO 14.1 (Paris: Firmin-Didot, 1920) 273–74.

16. We are grateful to Richard McCarron for assistance with the Syriac.

17. Mayer, *Monumenta,* 28. A full translation of Sozomen is available in *Ecclesiastical History of Sozomen,* trans. Edward Walford (London: Henry G. Bohn, 1855).

18. *Vita sanctae Eusebiae seu Xenae,* ed. T. Nissen, *Analecta Bollandiana* 56 (1938): 111–12, no. 11; *PG* 114.981–1000, col. 989, no. 8; Latin translation in *AASS* 3.212–216; discussed in Martimort, *Deaconesses,* 124.

19. Syriac text and full English translation: *The Sixth Book of the Select Letters of Severus Patriarch of Antioch, in the Syriac Version of Athanasius of Nisibis,* ed. E. W. Brooks, Text and Translation Society (London: Williams and Norgate, 1904), 1.2.415–18; 2.2.368–71; discussed in Elm, *Virgins of God,* 178 n. 124; Martimort, *Deaconesses,* 135.

20. We are grateful to Richard McCarron for assistance with the Syriac.

21. *PG* 115.868; Martimort, *Deaconesses,* 135–36; *Dictionary of Christian Biography: Literature, Sects, and Doctrines,* ed. William Smith and Henry Wace (London: John Murray, 1877; reprint, n.d.) 1.755; 3.536.

22. *Vie de Sainte Macrine,* ed. Pierre Marval, *SC* 178 (1971): 236; ; English translation of whole text in *Fathers of the Church* (Washington, DC: Catholic University Press, 1967) 58.161–97.

23. *PG* 79.968–1060.

24. *LH* 163.

25. Text: Henri Grégoire and M.-A. Kugener, *Marc le Diacre, Vie de Porphyre Évêque de Gaza* (Paris: Société d'Édition "Les Belles Lettres," 1930), 78–79, with French translation. A very arcane English translation is that of G. F. Hill, *The Life of Porphyry Bishop of Gaza by Mark the Deacon* (Oxford: Clarendon, 1913), discussed in Gryson, *Ministry of Women,* 90, 153 n. 145.

26. See Grégoire and Kugener, *Marc le Diacre,* 78 n. 1.

27. Very little is known of the role of the *kanonikai* in this period; see Eisen, *Women Officeholders,* 179–80, for some brief discussion.

28. Text: Pierre Maraval, *Journal de voyage: Itinéraire/Egérie, SC* 296 (1982): 226–28.

29. *PG* 85.618; G. Dagron and M. Dupré la Tour, *Vie et miracles de sainte Thècle,* Text, translation, and commentary, Subsidia Hagiographica 62 (Brussels: Société des Bollandistes, 1978).

30. See A. Lambert, "Apotactices et Apotaxamenes," in *DACL* 1.2604–26.

31. Text: *PG* 67.1482–85.

32. Text: *PG* 67.1193; GCS 50.181.16–18; *Ecclesiastica Historia,* ed. Robert Hussey (Oxford: Oxford University Press, 1860), 1.411; discussed in Gryson, *Ministry of Women,* 89, 153 n. 135.

33. Mayer, *Monumenta,* 27; *PG* 67.1576.

34. Introduction and translation in Elizabeth A. Clark, *Jerome, Chrysostom, and Friends: Essays and Translations,* (New York: Edwin Mellen, 1979), 117–19, 145–57.

35. Text: Anne-Marie Malingrey, *Vie anonyme d'Olympias, SC* 13 (1968): 418–20. Full translation and discussion in Clark, *Jerome, Chrysostom, and Friends,* 117–19, 145–57; Kraemer, *Women's Religions,* 227–36.

36. *Dialogue sur la Vie de Saint Jean Chrysostome,* ed. Anne-Marie Malingrey *SC* 341 (1988): 2.206–7.

37. Luke 22:37; 2 Tim 4:7; Acts 20:25.

38. *SC* 341 (1988): 2.318–20.

39. Much has been written about this phenomenon in early Christianity. See, for example, Elizabeth A. Clark, "Ideology, History, and the Construction of 'Woman' in Late Ancient Christianity," *JECS* 2 (1994): 155–84; Gillian Cloke, *This Female Man of God: Women and Spiritual Power in the Patristic Age AD 350–450* (London: Routledge, 1995).

40. *SC* 341 (1988): 2.342–44.

41. GCS 50.361; Mayer, *Monumenta,* 27; *PG* 67.1537, 1540.

42. Mayer, *Monumenta,* 28; *PG* 67.1577, 1580.

43. Texts: *PG* 52.657–59, 663–64, 716; discussed in Martimort, *Deaconesses,* 137, and Gryson, *Ministry of Women,* 89, 153 n. 133.

44. Text: *PG* 82.1109–12; Latin translation in *AASS* 52.995–96, October 9.

45. I.e., to be bishop of Antioch, the first "see" of the apostle Peter. It has been suggested that this son was John Chrysostom, who certainly was a leading presbyter of Antioch for some years, but other sources give Chrysostom's mother's name as Anthusa. Theodoret, writing after 428, would surely have mentioned if he thought this was Chrysostom, that he went on to be bishop of Constantinople. Chrysostom died in 407.

46. Psalm 135:15.

47. Psalm 135:18.

48. Psalm 67:2.

49. 1 Sam 16:14–23.

50. Laura Swan, *The Forgotten Desert Mothers: Sayings, Lives, and Stories of Early Christian Women* (Mahwah, NJ: Paulist, 2001) 123. We have found no indication of this in Theodoret or in any of the sources we have consulted. Swan offers no documentation, but perhaps there is a source of which we are unaware. There is no doubt that there were many other illustrious deaconesses in the church of Antioch in the late fourth century; what is in question is whether others lived in Publia's community.

51. *PG* 68.636–37.

52. For a full translation of the Syriac version, see Sebastian P. Brock and Susan Ashbrook Harvey, *Holy Women of the Syrian Orient* (Berkeley: University of California Press, 1987), 40–62.

53. Text: *SC* 13bis (1968): 130.

54. Text: *LH* 41, 129. See also ACW 34.118; Gryson, *Ministry of Women,* 89, 153 n. 134.

55. Edmund Venables, *Dictionary of Christian Biography, Literature, Sects, and Doctrines,* ed. William Smith and Henry Wace, 4 vols. (London: John Murray, 1911; reprint New York: AMS Press, 1984) 4.573.

56. Text: *Evagrius Pontikus,* ed. W. Frankenberg (Abhandlung der Königlichen Gesellschaft der Wissenschaften zu Göttingen. Philologisch-historische Klasse n.s. 13.2, 1912–1914; Berlin: Weidemann, 1914) 573, 579; German translation by Gabriel Bunge, *Evagrios Pontikos: Briefe aus der Wüste* (Trier: Paulinus, 1986), 220–21, 232–33; discussion and partial translation in Elm, *Virgins of God,* 277–79.

57. The Gihon Spring lay to the south of Jerusalem. Apparently the expression was symbolic of crossing over into the world (Bunge, *Evagrios Pontikos,* 336).

58. So interpreted in Bunge's translation, but Frankenberg's critical text actually says "sons" (*huious*), which could extend as well to the male members of Melania's monastery.

59. 2 Tim 4:7–8.

60. Matt 7:14.

61. Text: *AASS* 46.151–60, esp. 157, chaps. 9 and 10, September 19; discussed in Swan, *Forgotten Desert Mothers,* 125.

62. Eleutheropolis was the Byzantine name for Beth Guvrin in the south Judean hills. It had its own bishopric.

63. Text: *AASS* 8.261–70, March 2; discussed in Gryson, *Ministry of Women,* 90, 153 n. 143.

64. *PG* 114.1357, no. 8; Latin translation also in *AASS* 5.37–42, text at no. 17, p. 40; discussed in Martimort, *Deaconesses,* 124.

65. Syriac text and translation: *The Sixth Book of the Select Letters of Severus Patriarch of Antioch, in the Syriac Version of Athanasius of Nisibis,* ed. E. W. Brooks, Text and Translation Society (London: Williams and Norgate, 1904) 1.2.411–13; 2.2.364–68; mentioned in Elm, *Virgins of God,* 178 n. 124; Martimort, *Deaconesses,* 135.

66. Text: *Saint Basil: The Letters,* ed. Roy J. Deferrari, LCL (London: Heinemann, 1930), 2.199; discussed in Gryson, *Ministry of Women,* 889, 153 n.137.

67. Callinicos, *Vie d'Hypatios,* trans. and ed. G. J. M. Bartelink, *SC* 177 (1971): 102–4.

68. Ibid., 9–19.

69. Text: GCS 19.190–92; discussed in Gryson, *Ministry of Women,* 89, 153 n. 136. An English translation of the whole is available: *History of the Church, from A.D. 322 to the Death of Theodore of Mopsuestia, A.D. 427, by Theodoret, Bishop of Cyrus, and from A.D. 431 to A.D. 594, by Evagrius,* Bohn's Ecclesiastical Library (London: Henry G Bohn, 1854); no translator given.

70. Mss. vary on the possessive adjective: "them" and "you" are other variants, but "her" seems correct.

71. This is not the only known reference to a woman as teacher. Eisen, *Women Officeholders,* 89–100, presents the teacher Kyria from a fourth-century papyrus; the title applied to Amma Syncletica, a Desert Mother; a funerary inscription of the teacher Theodora from Rome, dated 382; Marcella and Melania the Younger from fourth-century Rome; an inscription of another Theodora teacher in Beroea, Macedonia from the fifth or sixth century, and others, along with discussion. From the funerary inscriptions, little can be known of the scope of their teaching, but from the literary texts we know that women like Syncletica, Marcella, and Melania taught both men and women.

72. See discussion in Eisen, *Women Officeholders,* 100–103. This passage is still a flashpoint in conservative church circles.

73. Text: *LH* 165–67.

74. Mayer, *Monumenta,* 33, in part; James Barbour Lightfoot, *The Apostolic Fathers,* 2nd ed. (New York: Macmillan, 1889–90; reprint, Grand Rapids: Baker, 1981) part two, 3.241–42.

75. Text: *PG* 87.2853; Mayer, *Monumenta,* 40. Available in English translation by John Wortley, *The Spiritual Meadow of John Moschus,* Cistercian Studies 139 (Kalamazoo, MI: Cistercian Publications, 1992).

76. J. G. C. Anderson, Franz Cumont, and Henri Grégoire, eds., *Recueil des Inscriptions grecques et latines du Pont et de l'Arménie,* Studia Pontica 3.1 (Brussels: H. Lamertin, 1910), 22; discussed in Martimort, *Deaconesses,* 144.

77. Text: *CIG* 4.9288; Grégoire, *Recueil,* 1.209; *EG* 4.368–70, no. 2; Eisen, *Women Officeholders,* 174–75; mentioned in *NewDocs* 4.122.3, p. 240; Gryson 91, *Ministry of Women,* 153 n. 157.

78. Text: Charalambos Bakirtzis, "Exposition des Antiquités Paléochrétiennes au Musée des Philippies," *Athens Annals of Archaeology* 13 (1980): 90–98, at 95; Valerie Abrahamsen, "Women at Philippi: The Pagan and Christian Evidence," *JFSR* 3 (1987): 17–30, at 23 n. 22; partial text and discussion in Eisen, *Women Officeholders,* 180; discussion in Abrahamsen.

79. Text: J. H. Mordtmann, "Inschriften aus Edessa," *AM* 18 (1893): 415–19, at 416–17, no. 3; Feissel, *Recueil,* 21, p. 40.

80. Text: *BCH* 98 (1974): 625–26, fig. 116; *BE* 89 (1976): 288; *NewDocs* 4.122, p. 239 n. 2; Eisen, *Women Officeholders,* 175–76; translation, Kraemer, *Women's Religions,* 259; discussed in *NewDocs* 1.79, p. 121.

81. Text: *BE* (1963): 152; discussed in *NewDocs* 1.79, p. 121.

82. First published by R. Fleischer, "Epigraphisches aus Elis," *Jahreshefte des Österreichischen Archäologischen Instituts* 46 (1961–63; Beiblatt, 1965), 76–94, at col. 87–88, with photo; further comments and correction by Jeanne and Louis Robert, *Bulletin Épigraphique, Revue des études grecques* 79 (1966): 381–82 n. 213; discussed in Martimort, *Deaconesses,* 145.

83. For more on Indictions, see n. 86. The Greek text is very fragmentary at the top but relatively intact for the final three lines:

ΕΝΘΑ[―――――――――]ΝΟΓΕΝ[―]
ΕΤ(ΩΝ) ΚΓ ΘΥΓΑ[―――――――]ΔΡΙΑΣ ΔΙΑ[Κ]
ΑΝΑΘΡΕΨΑΜΕΝΗ Σ[―――――]ΑΛΙΦΘΙΣΑ[―]ΠΟ ΤΟΥ ΕΜΟΥ
Π(ΑΤ)Ρ(Ο)Σ ΕΡΕΝΙΑΝΟΥ ΕΝ ΤΟΙΣ ΣΠΑΡΓ ΑΝΟΙΣ ΜΟΧΘΩ ΚΑΙ
ΕΥΧΕΣ ΕΛΠΙΔΙ ΤΟΥ ΥΠ'ΕΜΟΥ ΤΑΦΗΝΕ ΩΣ ΔΕ Ο Θ(ΕΟ)Σ ΗΘΕ
ΛΗΣΕΝ ΤΗΝ ΟΔΟΝ ΤΑΥΤΗΝ ΠΡΟ ΑΥΤΗΣ ΕΠΛΗΡΩΣΑ ΙΝΔ ΙΔ ΣΕΠΤΕΜΒΡΊΟΥ
ΙΓ

84. Commenting that Fleischer had published the group of inscriptions *avec une grande incompétence.*

85. Text: Alfons Maria Schneider, "Das Kloster der Theotokos zu Choziba im Wadi el Kelt," *Römische Quartalschrift* 39 (1931): 297–332, at 328 n. 197; partial, Meimaris, *Sacred Names,* 177–78 n. 886; Eisen, *Women Officeholders,* 161.

86. The Indiction was a series of years calculated for the purpose of tax cycles. Begun in 287 CE in five-year cycles, they became fifteen-year cycles from 312 and were of obligatory use from 537. The "eleventh Indiction" really means the eleventh year of an unspecified Indiction, or cycle of fifteen years. There are nineteen possible years between 312 and the end of the sixth century. For precise dating, one would have to know not only the date of the month but also the day of the week, which is missing here. The particular use of the genitive here can be dated to the late fifth century. For more information on dating, see William Tabbernee, *Montanist Inscriptions and Testimonia: Epigraphic Sources Illustrating the History of Montanism* (Macon, GA: Mercer University Press, 1997), 495–96; Wilhelm Kubitschek, "Aera," *PW* 1.606–52; Elias J. Bickerman, *Chronology of the Ancient World,* 2nd ed. (Ithaca, NY: Cornell University Press, 1980). We are grateful to William Tabbernee for help with the dating system.

87. ΠΟΛΥΓΗΡΟΣ Ο | ΕΥΛΒΕΣΤΑΤ(Ο)Σ | ΑΝΑΓ(ΝΩΣΤΗΣ) ΚΕ ΑΝΔΡΟ|ΜΑΧΑ Η ΘΕΟΦΙΛ(Ε)Σ|Τ(ΑΤΗ) ΔΙΑΚ ΥΠΕΡ ΕΥ|ΧΗΣ ΑΥΤΩΝ Ε|ΚΑΛΙΕΡΓΗΡΑΝ, as published by Emmanuel Hatzidakis, *Praktika tēs Archaiologikēs Hetaireias* 1958 (1965): 61; reported by Jeanne Robert and Louis Robert, *Bulletin épigraphique, Revue des études grecques* 79 (1966): 386 no. 229.2; discussed in Martimort, *Deaconesses,* 143–44.

88. Text: Grégoire, *Recueil* 1.258; discussed in Gryson, *Ministry of Women,* 90–91, 153 n. 155.

89. Text: *EG* 4.345–47 no. 4 (fig. 99); J. Laurent, "Delphes chrétien," *BCH* 23 (1899): 206–79, at 272–78; Feissel, *BCH* 104 (1980): 469–70; *NewDocs* 4.122.3, p. 240; Eisen, *Women Officeholders,* 176–77; discussed in Gryson, *Ministry of Women,* 90, 153 n. 150; Kraemer, *Women's Religions,* 258.

90. Text: *MAMA* 3.212b, p. 133; Eisen, *Women Officeholders,* 163; discussed in Elm, *Virgins of God,* 176 n. 115.

91. Text: *MAMA* 1.194, p. 104; Eisen, *Women Officeholders,* 168–69; discussed in Gryson, *Ministry of Women,* 90, 153 n. 152; Elm, *Virgins of God,* 176 n. 115.

92. J. G. C. Anderson, Franz Cumont, and Henri Grégoire, eds., *Recueil des inscriptions grecques et latines du Pont et de l'Arménie, Studia Pontica* 3 (Brussels: H. Lamertin, 1910) 57 n. 44. The editors note that the inscription was copied by F. Cumont on April 17, 1900, and again by H. Grégoire in 1907. Discussed in Martimort, *Deaconesses,* 144.

93. Alfons Maria Schneider, "Das Kloster der Theotokos zu Choziba im Wadi el Kelt," *Römische Quartalschrift* 39 (1931): 297–332, at 321 n. 78.

94. For interpretation of the chronological system of Indictions, see n. 86.

95. Text: *MAMA* 8.318, p. 56; Eisen, *Women Officeholders,* 167–68; discussed in Elm, *Virgins of God,* 176 n. 115.

96. Text: *SEG* 45 (1995): 945; *AE* 1977.1311, p. 439.

97. Text: *MAMA* 7.120, p. 23; discussed in Elm, *Virgins of God,* 176 n. 115.

98. Text: *MAMA* 3.758, p. 209, with sketch, p. 207; Eisen, *Women Officeholders,* 164; discussed in Elm, *Virgins of God,* 176 n. 115.

99. *MAMA* 5.191, p. 89.

100. Text: *MAMA* 7.471, p. 102; translation in Kraemer, *Women's Religions,* 259; discussed in Elm, *Virgins of God,* 176 n. 115.

101. [KOIMHTHPION] | E]IPHNHC ΔIA|KONON KAI ZΩH|C THC ΔOYΛH|C MOY HN K[YPIOC] | ΠAPEΛABETO], N. I. Giannapoulos, "Chistianikai Epigraphai Thessalias," *Byzantinische Zeitschrift* 21 (1912): 152; discussed in Martimort, *Deaconesses,* 144. The editor estimates that the Christian inscriptions published in this collection date from third to sixth centuries. He assigns this one to the fourth century, mostly on the basis of the flourishing of women deacons at this time.

102. Text: *MAMA* 1.324, p. 171; Eisen, *Women Officeholders,* 168, 191 n. 74; discussed in Gryson, *Ministry of Women,* 90, 153 n. 151; Elm, *Virgins of God,* 176 n. 115.

103. Text: *MAMA* 7.69, pp. 12–13; Eisen, *Women Officeholders,* 170–72; discussed in Gryson, *Ministry of Women,* 90, 153 n. 153.

104. Text: *SEG* 32 (1983): 1504; Meimaris, *Sacred Names,* 178 n. 891; Michele Picirillo, *Chiese e Mosaici della Giordania Settentrionale* (Jerusalem: Franciscan Printing Press, 1981), 31 (plate 19, photo 24); Eisen, *Women Officeholders,* 161.

105. Text: J. Germer Durand, "Epigraphie chrétienne de Jérusalem," *Revue Biblique* 1 (1892): 560–88, at 566 n. 10; Peter Thomsen, *Die lateinischen und griechischen Inschriften der Stadt Jerusalem und ihrer nächsten Umgebung* (Leipzig: Hinrichs, 1922), 79–80 n. 119; Meimaris, *Sacred Names,* 178 n. 887 (partial transcription of seventeen letters); discussed in Gryson, *Ministry of Women,* 90, 153 n. 149.

106. Three names of similar but different spelling are attested: Eniōn in Hellenistic Crete, Enniōn in first-century CE Cyprus, and Enneōn in fourth-century BCE Arcadia, but all appear to be masculine names; see P. M. Fraser and E. Matthews, *A Lexicon of Greek Personal Names* (Oxford: Clarendon, 1987), vol. 1, *s.v.*

107. "Diaconesses," *DACL* 4.733.

108. "Jérusalem," *DACL* 7.2363.

109. "Tombeau du Nouvel-Eléona et de l'hôpital qui s'y trouve" (tomb of the New Eleona and of the hospice there), the New Eleona being those monasteries rebuilt on the Mount of Olives after the Persian invasion of 613; "La topographie de Jérusalem vers la fin de l'époque byzantine," *Mélanges de l'Université Saint-Joseph* 37 (1961): 149. Martimort, *Deaconesses,* 145, excludes the name from the list of deaconesses, following Abel and Milik. Milik includes two drawings of possible reconstruction, one much sketchier than the other (plate 3).

110. Text: *TAM* 5.643; Grégoire, *Recueil* 1.341; Eisen, *Women Officeholders,* 169, 191–92 n. 80 with some discussion.

111. ΥΠΕΡ ΜΝΗΜΗС Κ[Ε | ΑΝΑΠΑΥСΕΩС [Τ|ΗС ΜΑΚΑΡΙΟΤΑΤΗ[Σ | ΕΠΙΦΑ-ΝΙΑC ΔΙΑΟΚΟ|ΝΙССΗС ΕΓΕΝΕΤΟ | ΤΟ ΕΡΓΟΝ ΤΟΥΤΟ | ΣΥΝΥΠΟΥΡΓΗСΑΝ|ΤΩΝ ΠΑΝΤΩΝ | ΙΕΝΔ(ΙΚΤΙΩΝΟΣ) Α' ΕΤΟΥС ΦΙΗ' | ΥΠΕΡ ΕΥΧΗС ΜΑΡΚΕ-, as given in *BCH* 7 (1883): 502; defective reading in *SIG* 4.293, no. 8624, corrected in *BCH*.

112. See discussion in *BCH* and *SIG* published texts.

113. Text: *TAM* 4/1.355; *BE* 684 (1976); Eisen, *Women Officeholders,* 172–74 with discussion, and Sencer Şahin, "Neue Inschriften von der bithynischen Halbinsel," *ZPE* 18 (1975): 27–48, at 46 no. 141; discussed in *NewDocs* 1.79, p. 121.

114. +Ενθαδε κατκ[ιτε] | Ευγενια η της ευ[λαβους] | μνημης γεναμενη δ[ιακονισσα] | οκοδομησσα δομο[ν του] | ενδοξου αποστολου Α[νδρε]|ου κ(ε) εν σεμνη πολιτια [τε]| λεσασα τον βιον μ(ηνι) Ιουνιω βι' ινδ(ικτιωνι) α' βα[σλι]ας του θιοτ(ατου) κε ευσεβ(εστατου) η[μων] | δεσπο(του) Φλ(αβιου) Ιουστινιαν[ου] | του αιωνιου Αγ(ουστου) κ(ε) Αυτοκρ[α]|τορος ετους βι' υπατιας Φλ(αβιου) | Ιωαννου του λαμπρ(οτατου)+, as read by V. Beševliev, *Spätgriechische und spätlateinische Inschriften aus Bulgarien* (Berlin: Akademie Verlag, 1964), 164–66 no. 231, photo Table 99; discussed in Martimort, *Deaconness,* 144. No. 1510 in the Sophia Archaeological Museum.

115. Text: *MAMA* 8.64, pp.12–13, and plate 4; Eisen, *Women Officeholders,* 170, 192 n. 88, with brief discussion.

116. Grégoire, *Recueil,* 1.67; Elm, *Virgins of God,* 178 n. 125.

117. *Virgins of God,* 178 n. 125.

118. Text: *MAMA* 7.75, p. 14. We are grateful to Edward Krentz for help with this difficult inscription.

119. Text: *SEG* (1977): 948 A; *BE* (1939): 451, (1978): 498; text and discussion, *New Docs* 2.109 pp. 193–94; Eisen, *Women Officeholders,* 164–67; discussion, Gryson, *Ministry of Women,* 90; translation; Kraemer, *Women's Religions,* 258.

120. See references in Eisen, *Women Officeholders,* 166

121. Text: D. Geninetta Canova, *Iscrizioni e monumenti protocristiani del paese di Moab,* Sussidi allo Studio dell' Antichità Cristiana 4 (Vatican City: Pontificio Istituto di Archeologia Cristiana, 1954), 383 no. 391 (fig. 426); Meimaris, *Sacred Names,* 178 no. 888; Eisen, *Women Officeholders,* 160–61.

122. Incorrectly given as 548 in Eisen, *Women Officeholders,* 161.

123. Canova, *Iscrizioni e monumenti,* xciv–xcv.

124. Text: *MAMA* 1.178, p. 96; Eisen, *Women Officeholders,* 170; mentioned in Gryson, *Ministry of Women,* 90, 153 n. 152; Elm, *Virgins of God,* 176 n. 115.

125. Text: *MAMA* 1.383, p. 199; Eisen, *Women Officeholders,* 169, 191 n. 78; mentioned in Gryson, *Ministry of Women,* 90, 153 n. 151; Elm, *Virgins of God,* 176 n. 115.

126. Text: Feissel, *Recueil,* 275, p. 231; James Wiseman, *Stobi: A Guide to the Excavations* (Belgrade: National Museum of Titov Veles; Austin: University of Texas Press, 1973), 59–61; *New Docs* 2.194–95 no. 109; Eisen, *Women Officeholders,* 176; English translation in Kraemer, *Women's Religions,* 259.

127. Text: *MAMA* 7.585, p. 122; discussed in Elm, *Virgins of God,* 176 n. 115.

128. Text: *IG* 3.2.3527; *CIG* 4.9318; Eisen, *Women Officeholders,* 177; Charles Bayet, "De titulis Atticae christianis antiquissimis commentatio historica et epigraphica" (Ph.D. thesis, University of Paris, 1878), n. 105; mentioned in Gryson, *Ministry of Women,* 91, 153 n. 156; *New Docs* 4.239 n. 122.

129. Text: J. G. C. Anderson, "Exploration in Galatia Cis Halym," *Journal of Hellenic Stud-*

ies 19 (1899): 52–134, at 130 no. 155; *MAMA* 7.539, p. 113, illustration p. 143; Eisen, *Women Officeholders,* 191 n. 79; discussed in Elm, *Virgins of God,* 176 n. 115.

130. Albrecht Alt, *Die Griechischen Inschriften des Palaestina tertia westlich der 'Araba* (Berlin: de Gruyter, 1921), 23 no. 37; Eisen, *Women Officeholders,* 161.

131. Text: *MAMA* 1.323b, p. 170; also *MAMA* 4.120b, p. 38; discussed in Gryson, *Ministry of Women,* 90, 153 n. 151; Eisen, *Women Officeholders,* 193 n. 112; Elm, *Virgins of God,* 176 n. 115, dating it without explanation to early fourth century.

132. Text: *MAMA* 1.226, p. 120 with photo; Eisen, *Women Officeholders,* 169–70; mentioned in Gryson, *Ministry of Women,* 90, 153 n. 152; Elm, *Virgins of God,* 176 n. 115.

133. ΕΝΘΑΔΕ Κ[Α]∥ΤΑΚΙΤΕ Ο Τ[Ι]Μ[ΕΙΟ] (Γ)ΕΡΑ[Ρ]ΟC | ΕΥΛΑΒΕ(C)ΤΑ∥ΤΟC ΠΡ(Ε)CΒΥΤΕ∣Ρ(ΟC) ΙΟΥΛΙΑΝΟC ∣ΟΝΠΕΡ ΑΝΕCΤΗ∣CΕΝ Η ΙΔΙΑ ΓΥ∣ΝΗ ΑΓΟΥCΤΑ ∥ΚΕ Ο ΠΡΕ(C)ΒΥΤΕ∣ΡΟC ΥΠΑΤΙC ΚΕ | Η ΔΙΑΚΟΝΟC | ΦΙΛΟΓΟΝΙC Α∣ΝΕCΤΗCΑΝ ∥ ΤΩ ΙΔΙΩ ΠΑ∣ΤΡΙ ΜΝΗΜΗC | ΧΑΡΙΝ, as read and grammatically corrected by P. G. Jerphanion, "Inscriptions grecques de la région d'Alishar," *Mélanges de l'Université Saint-Joseph* (Beirut) 19 (1935): 94–95 no. 25; discussed in Martimort, *Deaconesses,* 143.

134. Text: Feissel, *Recueil,* 241, p. 204; Louis Jalabert and René Mouterde, "Inscriptions Grecques Chrétiennes," *DACL* 7.1 (1926): 623–94, at 652; reference there to L. Heuzey and H. Daumas, *Mission Archéologique de Macédoine,* 95 no. 50; Eisen, *Women Officeholders,* 179–80.

135. See discussion and references in Eisen, *Women Officeholders,* 179–80. Letters 52 and 173 of Basil are addressed to women with this title but yield no information about their role. One source indicates responsibility for burials (Grégoire, *Recueil,* 1.108).

136. Text: *MAMA* 1.326, p. 172; Eisen, *Women Officeholders,* 191 n. 77; mentioned in Gryson, *Ministry of Women,* 90, 153 n. 151; Elm, *Virgins of God,* 176 n. 115.

137. Text: *MAMA* 7.186, p. 37; discussed in Elm, *Virgins of God,* 176 n. 115.

138. The letters are PROHKOU. The editor suggests the emendation PROOIKOU.

139. Text: L. Cré, *RB* 13 (1904): 260–62, with photo; Alt, *Griechische Inschriften,* 18 no. 17; *EG* 4.445, fig. 132; *NewDocs* 4.122, pp. 239–44; Eisen, *Women Officeholders,* 158–60; discussed in Gryson, *Ministry of Women,* 90, 153 n. 148; Kraemer, *Women's Religions,* 257–58.

140. *NewDocs* 4.241.

141. ΚΟΙΜΗΤΗΡΙΟΝ | ΤΕΤΡΑΔΙΑC | ΔΙΑΚΟΝΟΥ Η∣ΤΙC ΑΥΤΟ ΑΝ∣ΥΞΙ ΠΑΡΕΞ ΕΜ∣ΟΥ ΔΑΠΑΝΥ∣CΙ ΑΥΤΟΝ | ΠΥΡΟC ΕΩ∣ΝΙΟΥ ΔΗΚΗ, N. I. Giannapoulos, *"Palaiochristianikē epigraphē,"* *Epetērias etaireias Byzantinōn spoudōn* 12 (1935): 26 with photo; discussed in Martimort, *Deaconesses,* 144.

142. Text: *MAMA* 3.39, p. 158; Eisen, *Women Officeholders,* 163–64, 189 n. 45; discussed in Elm, *Virgins of God,* 176 n. 115.

143. *MAMA* 3, p. 121.

144. See discussion in Eisen, *Women Officeholders,* 163–64.

145. Text: Feissel, *Recueil* 20, pp. 39–40; Eisen, *Women Officeholders,* 181–82.

146. Text: *MAMA* 3.418, p. 161; discussed in Elm, *Virgins of God,* 176 n. 115; Eisen, *Women Officeholders,* 164, 189 n. 47.

147. Text: E. Mastrocostas, "Palaiochristianikai basilikai Drumou Bovitsēs," *Athens Annals of Archaeology* 4 (1971) 185–95, at 188–89 (fig. 6); E. Popescu, "Griechische Inschritften," in *Quellen zur Geschichte des frühen Byzanz (4.-9. Jahrhundert). Bestand und Probleme,* ed. F. Winkelmann and W. Brandes (Amsterdam: Gieben, 1990), 81–105, at 95; Eisen, *Women Officeholders,* 178.

148. Text: *MAMA* 3.744, p. 208; Eisen, *Women Officeholders,* 163; discussed in Gryson, *Ministry of Women,* 90, 153 n. 154; Elm, *Virgins of God,* 176 n. 115.

149. Ζαωρθα σαμασθα, given by Enno Littmann, *Semitic Inscriptions,* Publications of the

American Archaeological Expedition to Syria in 1899–1900, Part Four (New York: Century, 1904) 55, drawing, 46; discussed in H. Leclercq, "Diaconesses," *DACL* 4 (1920): 734 n. 3.

150. The same name is often spelled Rabbūlā; the double consonant disappeared in Western Syriac (Littman, *Semitic Inscriptions,* 52).

151. We are grateful to Richard McCarron for assistance with this text.

152. Text: Michael Avi-Jonah, *Quarterly of the Department of Antiquities in Palestine* 13 (1947): 69 nos. 3–4; Meimaris, *Sacred Names,* 178, nos. 889–890; reference and sketch, Michele Piccirillo, *The Mosaics of Jordan,* American Center of Oriental Research Publications 1 (Amman: American Center of Oriental Research, 1992), 311.

153. Text: *MAMA* 8.91, p. 16.

154. Text: *BCH* 75 (1951): 158–60; Feissel, *Recueil,* 256B, p. 214; Eisen, *Women Office-holders,* 196 n. 149.

155. Text: *MAMA* 8.321, pp. 56–57.

Chapter Four

WOMEN DEACONS IN THE EAST

Canons and Comments on Church Practice

After having seen some of the real data about the lives and activities of female deacons, we turn to some of the prescriptive texts to compare images of their functions in the church. The *Didascalia Apostolorum* is the earliest church order text to describe the office of female deacons. The Council of Nicaea is the earliest church council to legislate about them, and its Canon 19 concerns only a particular problem, not deaconesses in general. The *Apostolic Constitutions* of the fourth century include the most complete description of deaconesses' activities before Justinian. Following that, Justinian's *Novellae* give us more enticing information at least about how deaconesses functioned in the Great Church, Hagia Sophia, of Constantinople, and that arrangement, while undoubtedly on a larger scale than anywhere else, was presumably the liturgical model to which other churches looked in the middle of the sixth century.

The Theodosian decree, Canon 15 of Chalcedon, the "Arabic Canons" of Nicaea, and Justinian's *Novellae* 6.6 all deal with the minimum age for diaconal ordination of women. Their disagreement indicates doubt and variable practice. Olympias and Maria of Moab (see chapter 3) are known exceptions to even the lowest minimum age of forty. Here, as in all legislation of the era, the reader should not presume that what is legislated is what was always done.

DIDASCALIA APOSTOLORUM AND
APOSTOLIC CONSTITUTIONS

DA 9 = *AC* 2.26.3, 5–8[1]

The Didascalia Apostolorum *is one of the more developed church order texts from the early church, written in Greek in Syria during the first half of the third century. Only a complete Syriac and a partial Latin translation survive. The* Apostolic Constitutions, *which survives in its original Greek, is a compilation and rough editing of several church orders including the* DA, *and dates from the late fourth century. Both texts reflect churches already strongly centered on episcopal authority and with a diversity of ministerial roles including widows and female deacons. The* AC *adds virgins as an identifiable group. The* DA *is incorporated into books 1–6 of the* AC. *In texts that follow, italicized words are not contained in the* DA *but are added to its edited version in the* AC.

3. For these [bishops] are your high priests and the presbyters are your priests, and your levites are the deacons and lectors and cantors and porters, *your female deacons,* your widows and *virgins* and orphans, but the high priest is *above all these . . .*

5. But let the deacon stand next to him [the bishop] as Christ to the Father . . .

6. Also let the female deacon be honored by you as the type of the Holy Spirit, doing or saying nothing apart from the deacon, *just as the Paraclete does or says nothing of himself but glorifying Christ, remains according to his will. And just as no one can believe in Christ without the teaching of the Spirit, so let no woman approach the male deacon or the bishop without the female deacon.*

7. And let the presbyters be deemed by you as a type of our apostles . . .

8. And let the widows and orphans be reckoned to you as a type of sacrificial offering.

The first sentence of this section of the *AC* reflects the early Church's conscious claims to replace the religious structures of Israel. Thus each group of ministers is assigned a correspondence with some aspect of Israelite Temple service. In the second part of the selection trinitarian theology comes to the fore: just as Christ is at the right hand of God, so the male deacon stands beside the bishop at the liturgy. The female deacon represents the Holy Spirit who, according to the theology presented here, acts in harmony with Christ. That the presbyters, the bishop's council, correspond to the apostles while the deacon represents Christ shows the primarily typological intent of the passage and perhaps also the growing importance of deacons as personal agents of the bishop. The typology of deacons and presbyters (without female deacons) was first used by Ignatius in *Magnesians* 6, and expanded here. In this church, women deacons are present along with widows and consecrated virgins. That only the women deacons are singled out as participants in the trinitarian typology, while widows are relegated to the offering, indicates an official role for the deacons of both sexes. In both references to them the male word *diakonos* is used along with the feminine article. The later word for "deaconess" has not yet been introduced (see *AC* 3.11.3 below). The careful procedure of having a female deacon accompany any woman who approaches a male deacon or bishop, presumably for confidential conversation, is in keeping with eastern Mediterranean propriety and signals an additional role for the female deacon as a kind of chaperone.

DA 12 = *AC* 2.57.10, 12[2]

10. *And let the porters stand in the entrances of the men in order to guard* **them** *and let the female deacons stand at those of the women* . . .
12. **And let** *the virgins and* **the widows and the older women be the first of all to stand or sit.**

The mention of separate entrances to the place of assembly for men and women follows the description of separate seating (paragraph 5 of the same chapter). Male porters monitor the men's entrance because the male deacons are occupied with liturgical ministry, while the female deacons guard the women's doors. In both cases they see that those entering are in proper attire and good order. The female deacons are again designated with the masculine term and feminine articles as in 26.3.5–8. The context of v. 12 is seating and standing arrangements in the assembly. While children and younger women will either stand or sit depending on available space, seating priority will be given to older women. The *AC* adds virgins to this group, presumably because of the honor given to consecrated virgins. The term for "older women" (*presbytides*) is a feminine form of the presbyter or elder and can sometimes possibly refer to female presbyters. That is unlikely in this case given their listing behind virgins and widows (but see Canon 11 of the Council of Laodicea).

DA 12 = *AC* 2.58.6[3]

If any poor person should come [into the assembly], either local or visitor, whether elderly or young in age, and there is no room, let *the deacon* **with all his heart find room for such as these, so that his regard be not merely human, but that his ministry might be pleasing to God.** *And let the female deacons do the same thing for the women as they come forward, whether they be poor or rich.*

Special regard for the poor is traditional (see James 2:1–4, which probably inspired this passage). There is a significant difference between the *DA* and *AC* besides the addition of women in the *AC*: The *DA* directs the *bishop*, not the deacon, to see to the seating of the poor person even if the bishop has to sit on the floor!

DA 15=*AC* 3.6.1–2[4]

It is not fitting nor is it necessary for women to teach, above all concerning the name of Christ and the redemption of his passion. For you have not been appointed (*constitutae***) to teach, you women, and especially you widows, but instead to pray (***ut oretis***) and to supplicate the Lord God.**

The AC *text is shorter here:*

> We do not allow women to teach in church, but only to pray and hear the teachers.

Both texts then go on to name Mary Magdalene; Mary, wife (daughter, *DA*!) of James; and the other Mary in order to use them as examples of women who could have been, but were not, sent out to teach by Jesus. The *AC* adds the mother and sisters of Jesus, Martha and Mary sisters of Lazarus, and Salome. The *Didascalia* seems to leave open the possibility of women teaching at least the "rudiments" of faith, as suggested by Gryson,[5] though the teaching of deeper dogmatic matters is proscribed. The *AC* also goes on to quote 1 Cor 11:3, "The head of the woman is the man," concluding that it is not right for the rest of the body to rule the head. The use of this quotation shows the close connection made in the early Church between teaching and ruling. The context is the suppression of teaching activity of widows, who are told that they should not move from house to house. The amount of care given to the discussion indicates that some women, especially widows, were exercising a teaching ministry in private houses.

The Latin *constituo*—"appoint"—can also carry the meaning of endowed with a nature. Thus, the second sentence here can be construed as suggesting that women are not capable by nature of teaching, an idea that would not be inconsistent with ideas that were becoming increasingly widespread in the ever more clearly defined orthodox Christian communities. The only role left them would be to pray (for almsgivers and for the universal church). On the other hand, and more positively, it could suggest that being "appointed," they constituted a distinct ecclesiastical order, an order recognized and cherished by their having a specific place in liturgical gatherings. While this text does not specifically mention women in church office, it shows the sensitivity of the issue of women's leadership in the churches of third- and fourth-century Syria.

DA 15 = *AC* 3.8.1–3[6]

> 1. Therefore, the widows must be serious, obeying the bishops and the presbyters and the deacons, and *even more the female deacons* with piety, reverence, and fear, neither usurping authority nor desiring to do anything concerning the instruction apart from the counsel of the (male) *deacon* [*DA*: bishop], as for example desiring to go to someone's house to eat or drink with him or to receive something from anyone. But if she does any of these things without being commanded, let her be punished *with fasting or with separation* as one who is rash.
>
> 2. For what does she know, from what sort of woman she is receiving or from what ministry she is setting aside food? . . .

3. Also, let the widows be prepared to obey what is ordered to them by the superiors and let them obey the teachings of the bishop as if to God.

Again the masculine word *diakonos* with feminine article is used. The subject of the passage is submission of widows to the four groups who exercise authority in the church: bishops, presbyters, male deacons, and female deacons. The problem seems to be abuse in the practice of widows accepting charitable dinner invitations without proper supervision. From other texts we know of this practice of charity and some of the resulting problems (e.g., Hippolytus, *Apostolic Tradition* 30).[7]

The parallel text in the *DA* places more centralized authority in the hands of the bishop as the ordinary superior to whom widows are accountable rather than the deacon.

DA 15 = *AC* 3.9.1[8]

AC: Now as for women performing baptism, we assure you that it is no small risk for those undertaking this. Therefore, we do not advise it, for it is perilous, rather uncustomary, and irreverent.

DA: We do not approve of women baptizing or of being baptized by a woman because this is unlawful and a great danger both to those who baptize and those who are baptized.

Already at the end of the second century Tertullian had spoken out against the practice of women performing baptism among groups he considers heretical (*On the Remedy of Heretics* 41.5). Here a century and more later the question arises again, which can only mean that the custom has continued in some places and circumstances. The two texts are so different that both translations are given here. The *DA* warns of danger to both parties, the *AC* only to the baptizer, and the *AC*, over a century later than the *DA*, discourages but does not prohibit the practice as does the *DA*. From what we know of the official customs of baptism throughout this period, the ritual took place only in the presence of the bishop as principal presider and administrator. The objection to women baptizing seems to belong within these churches; it is not a problem of outside, heterodox groups as with Tertullian. What then is being spoken of, and what is the perceived danger? Elsewhere in the *AC* 3.16.4 the bishop baptizes and then the deacon or deaconess anoints the naked body according to the respective sex. Perhaps what is alluded to in this objection is mixing the sexes so that a deaconess would anoint the body of a male neophyte.

There is also the likelihood that baptism created some kind of patronal relationship, in which the baptizer held a kind of superior and responsible position with regard to the one baptized. That too would have been discouraged for women.

AC 3.11.3 [9]

But we do not permit presbyters to ordain deacons, deaconesses, lectors, assistants, cantors, or doorkeepers, but rather only the bishop. This is the church order and harmony.

This passage has no parallel in the *DA*, but is completely inserted into it by the *AC*. Here for the first time the word "deaconess" (*diakonissa*) appears in the text of the *AC* as a specific term for female deacons. Bishops alone are to ordain to church offices and functions. The term for "ordain" (*cheirotonein*), literally, to lay on hands, earlier meant simply "to elect" or "appoint." By this time it can refer to imperial or divine appointment (e.g., *AC* 5.20.11), but it is coming more to have the specific meaning of ordination to ministry as membership in the clergy. This passage is one of the clearest indications that deaconesses or female deacons were ordained members of the clergy.

AC 3.15.5 [10]

For the bishop ought to be concerned for all, for *the clergy, virgins, widows and the laity.*

The bishop is chief pastor of the church and his pastoral concern extends to all. Since we know from previous *AC* texts that there are women deacons or deaconesses in the church, the lack of a specific mention of them along with virgins and widows can only mean that they are included among the clergy (klērikoi).

DA 16 = *AC* 3.16.1–2, 4 [11]

1. Therefore, O bishop, appoint your co-workers of life and righteousness, such deacons as are *well pleasing to God,* whom you approve to be worthy out of all the people and well equipped for service as deacons. And also appoint a *trustworthy and pure* female deacon for services to the women. For sometimes in certain houses, you are not able to send a male deacon to the women because of the unbelievers. Therefore, send a woman deacon *on account of the attitudes of the wicked.*

2. For we stand in need of a woman deacon for many reasons, first in the baptism of women, *the male deacon* will anoint *only their foreheads* with *holy oil and after him,* the female deacon *shall anoint* them; for there is no necessity for the women to be seen by the men . . .

4. You therefore, O bishop anoint the head of those who are to be baptized, whether men or women, *with holy oil as a type of the spiritual baptism.*

> Then, either you, *the bishop* or the presbyter under you say the sacred formula upon them invoking *Father, Son, and Holy Spirit,* and baptize them *in the water.* And *let the male deacon* receive *the man* and the female deacon the women, so that the distribution of the benefits of the seal of baptism may be done with sobriety. *And after this, let the bishop anoint with ointment those who have been baptized.*

While the Latin translation of the *DA* gives the word *diakonissa,* the Greek *AC* here retains *diakonos* with feminine grammatical attributes. The *DA* envisions a possible case where there is no woman of any kind qualified to anoint the body of a female baptizand. The *AC* assumes the presence of a female deacon. This text illustrates the two major functions of female deacons in the church of the *AC*: pastoral visits to women in their homes and anointing of women in the baptismal ritual. While the *AC* text limits her role to these two functions, the *DA* adds a post-baptismal instructional role for the maintenance of the holiness of baptism in ongoing life. Both the pastoral visitation and instruction presuppose a considerable mobility and responsibility of the female deacon toward women in the community.

AC 6.17.4[12]

> And let the deaconess be a pure virgin; but if not, then at least a widow married only once, faithful and honorable.

This text and its context have no parallel in the *DA.* Here the word *diakonissa* is used in the Greek text as in *AC* 3.2.3. The preference for virginity for female ministers blurs the distinction between them and consecrated virgins, another group in the church, but is not surprising given the growing esteem for virginity at this time. The *univira,* a woman married only once, was already an ideal in imperial Roman family life. She epitomized fidelity and respectability (see 1 Tim 5:9).[13] The interest in the sexual status of the female ministers and the rejection of the idea of married women performing such duties was to be persistent in the church. The context is very interesting. The ideal of the once-married bishop in 1 Tim 3:2 has been extended by now: in the previous passage (17.1–3), a bishop, presbyter, or deacon can be married only once, whether their wives are living or dead, and if they are ordained unmarried, they may not marry afterward (v. 1). Assistants, cantors, readers, and doorkeepers must also marry only once, but that one marriage can take place even after they have entered the clergy (*eis klēron parelthōsin,* v. 2). But no one in the clergy (*en tō klērō*) can have a concubine, a slave mistress, a widow, or a divorced woman (v. 3). The passage about the deaconess follows immediately as the last verse of the paragraph, indicating that she too is a member of the clergy.

DA 19 = *AC* 3.19.1–2[14]

And let the deacons be blameless in all things as the bishop is, but even more active, in proportion to the size of the church, in order that they may be able to serve the powerless as "unashamed workers" (2 Tim 2:15). And let the woman in charge of the women hasten to give care, both of them by proclamation, travel, ministry (*hypēresia*), service (*douleia*), as Isaiah also spoke concerning the Lord saying "To justify the just one who serves many" (Isa 53:11).
2. Therefore, let each one understand one's own place and discharge it properly, with consensus, with one mind, knowing the reward of ministry (*diakonia*).

The tasks of male and female deacons in pastoral care under the supervision of the bishop are stressed here. Deacons are the extension of the bishop's ministry. The women are strangely without title here, being literally "the woman of the women" in the *AC*, even less specific in the *DA*. While the *DA* stresses at the end of the passage the harmony that should characterize the interaction of male and female minister, the *AC* envisions active ministry for both that includes preaching and travel to reach those in need of their ministrations.

AC 8.13.14[15]

And after this, let the bishop receive his share, then the presbyters and the deacons and the subdeacons and the readers and the singers and the ascetics and among the women, the female deacons and the virgins and the widows, then the children, and then all the people according to a fixed order with reverence and discretion without fear.

The reference is to the order of reception of communion at the liturgy. The listing is that of the recognizable ecclesiastical groups, beginning on both male and female sides with those elsewhere assigned ministerial responsibilities. The male "ascetics" probably correspond to the female "virgins" as those consecrated to prayer and ascesis but not ministry. The placement of children after widows probably refers to their own children, not to children in general since widows and orphans (i.e., the widows' children) were together supported by the church. Another term is introduced here for the female deacons: *diakonē*, a female form of *diakonos*.

AC 8.19–20: Ordination of the Deaconess[16]

19.1 But now concerning a deaconess, I Bartholomew make this teaching.
19.2 O bishop, you will lay your hands on her in the presence of the presbyters and the deacons and the deaconesses and you will say:

20.1 "O Eternal God, the father of our Lord, Jesus Christ, Creator of man and woman, who filled with the Spirit Miriam and Deborah and Anna and Huldah, who did not disdain that your only begotten son should be born of a woman, who also in the tabernacle of testimony and in the Temple appointed the guardians of the holy gates (Ex 38:8; 1 Sam 2:22),

20.2 now also, look upon your servant who is to be appointed to the diaconate and give to her the holy Spirit and cleanse her from all filthiness of flesh and spirit that she may worthily perform the work which is entrusted to your glory and the praise of your Christ, with whom glory and worship be to you and to the holy Spirit for ever. Amen."

The prayer for the ordination of the deaconess (*diakonissa*) parallels and follows that for the deacon (chaps. 17–18), which begins "Concerning the ordination (*cheirotonia*) of deacons." The opening of the prayer for the deaconess does not repeat the term ordination, but its parallel placement with that of the deacon implies that it too is an ordination. The later summary of the *AC*, the *Epitome* 19–20,[17] uses the chapter heading "About the Ordination (*cheirotonia*) of the Deaconess." Similarly, Canon 14 of the Trullan Council of 692 specifies age limits for the *cheirotonia* of deacons (twenty-five) and deaconesses (forty).[18] The deaconess is seen as serving in the line of biblical prophetesses, and as such the Holy Spirit is invoked over her. The prayer for cleansing and allusion to flesh and spirit is typical of the preoccupation with and high level of ambiguity about female sexual functions (see *AC* 6.17.4).

AC 8.24.2; *AC* 8.25.2–3[19]

24.2 A virgin is not to be ordained, for we have no command of the Lord . . .

25.2 A widow is not to be ordained, but if she lost her husband many years ago and she has lived moderately and above reproach taking good care of her household, like the distinguished Judith and Anna, let her be chosen into the order of widows.

25.3 But if she has lost her husband recently, let her not be trusted.

In both passages the term for "ordained" (*cheirotoneitai*) is probably a technical term in this document, though many other similar terms are used loosely, all meaning generally to elect or appoint by laying on of hands. Neither virgins nor widows perform ministerial duties, as do deaconesses, so their ritual of election is different. The hesitation about accepting recent widows echoes the suspicion in 1 Tim 5:11–12 that they will not remain firm in their resolve not to remarry. The fact that it is clearly stated that virgins and widows, as well as exorcists (26.2) are not ordained, further clarifies that those who precede them in the text, namely, bishops, presbyters (8.16), deacons (8.17–18), and deaconesses (8.19–20) *are* ordained.

AC 8.28.4–8[20]

4. A deacon does not bless or give a blessing but receives it from a bishop or presbyter. He does not baptize or make the offering, but when the bishop or presbyter makes the offering, he gives it to the people, not as a priest but as one who ministers to the priests.

5. It is not permitted to the rest of the clergy to do as the work of the deacon.

6. A deaconess does not bless, nor does she perform anything that the presbyters or the deacons do but rather she is to watch the doors and to assist the presbyters in the baptism of women for the sake of decency.

7. A deacon can separate a subdeacon, a lector, cantor, or a deaconess, if the situation calls for it and a presbyter is not available.

8. It is not lawful for a subdeacon to separate anyone, nor a lector, a cantor, or a deaconess, either to separate a cleric or a lay person, for they are assistants of the deacons.

Only bishop and presbyters can pronounce blessings over offerings and people, and make the eucharistic offering. Verse 6 makes it clear that the deaconess (*diakonissa*) has no liturgical role at the altar as does the deacon. As in *DA* 16/*AC* 3.16.1–4 the primary role of the deaconess is that of supervision of women at the assembly and assistance in the baptism of women. The deacon, in virtue of his direct representative role for the bishop, has the authority to impose certain penalties on those in other ministerial roles, including the deaconess. The word here translated "separate" (*aphoridzein*) probably means in this context a temporary exclusion from the assembly as a penance. However, v. 5 makes it clear that deaconesses and possibly also subdeacons, readers, and cantors (v.7–8) are members of the clergy (*klēros*).

AC 8.31.2[21]

According to the judgment of the bishop or the presbyters, let the deacons distribute the offerings left over from the mysteries among the clergy: to the bishop, four parts; to the presbyter, three parts; to the deacon, two parts; and to the others, the subdeacons or lectors or cantors or deaconesses, one part.

The portions of distribution obviously represent degrees of honor, not of need.

The placement of the deaconesses (*diakonissai*) at the end as in *AC* 8.28.7 may be in order of gender rather than rank, since elsewhere they are listed before lectors and cantors.

Excerpt 1 from the *AC* 19–22[22]

19. So that the bishop anoints only the head of the woman who is being baptized, but the deacon anoints the mouth and chest, and the deaconess anoints the whole body.

20. With regard to baptism, the deacons should receive the men and the deaconesses should receive the women.

21. The laity may not baptize, offer sacrifice, ordain, or bless.

22. The women should not do anything, neither to baptize nor to teach.

This text of uncertain provenance and dating (anytime between the fourth and eleventh centuries!)[23] repeats liturgical customs and regulations already present in earlier texts. The deaconess has a role to play in the baptism of women, both during the ceremony and in "receiving" women, which probably includes instruction both before and after baptism, a function evidenced for women leaders in many other contexts. In view of v. 21 that intervenes between the role of deaconess and that of women, the women in v. 22 should be understood as lay women, not deaconesses, a further specification by gender of the immediately preceding statement (compare the description of deacons in 1 Tim 3:8–13, in which "the women" of v. 11 are not women in general but either female deacons or possibly wives of deacons). This and similar prohibitions of women teaching refer to public teaching in mixed groups, not to women instructing other women.

OTHERS SOURCES BEFORE THE SIXTH CENTURY,
IN CHRONOLOGICAL ORDER

Clement of Alexandria, *Stromata* 3.6.53[24]

Titus Flavius Clemens was a prolific teacher and writer, who was born about 150 and died by about 215 CE. His search for right teaching began in Greece and led him finally to the "catechetical" school of Pantaenus in Alexandria, which he later headed for many years. According to Eusebius, Clement was an erudite Christian scholar, a married man and probably not a presbyter but a lay scholar. His three major works are the Protreptikos *or "Exhortation," The* Paidagōgos *or "Teacher," and the* Stromata *or "Miscellany."*

But on the other hand, these [i.e., the apostles], appropriately to the ministry, devoted themselves to preaching without distraction; they took women not as wives but as sisters, fellow ministers to the households of women. Through them, the Lord's teaching came also into the women's quarters without scandal. For we also know much concerning the ministry of women which the noble Paul himself taught in the other letter to Timothy.

In a context in which Clement defends the good of marriage, he notes that the male apostles were accompanied by female companions (cf. 1 Cor 9:5). Paul's expression "a sister woman" or "a sister wife," which probably means a wife who is a believer, Clement interprets as a celibate relationship, a sort of male-female ministry team (*diakonia*), in which the women are co-ministers (*syndiakonoi*) of the men for the ministry of women. This need for gender separation in ministry reflects more the expectations of the time and place of Clement than those of Paul. Though Clement's Alexandrian church does not seem to have had deaconesses, he extrapolates the need for them from the Pauline churches. The passage from Timothy to which Clement must be referring is not from the "other" (i.e., second) letter, but in 1 Tim 3:11.

Council of Nicaea Canon 19[25]

The Council of Nicaea was held in 325 CE at the behest of Constantine to settle the Arian controversy. In addition to its historic Trinitarian pronouncement, it issued twenty disciplinary decrees, or canons.

The Paulianists spoken of here are probably followers of Paul of Samosata, bishop of Antioch (260–68). His heterodox Trinitarian teaching led to his deposition by an episcopal synod in 268, but he refused to leave the episcopal church (the building complex of the bishop) until, under appeal by the bishops to the emperor Aurelian, he was expelled by imperial troops, the first use of imperial force against one Christian group at the request of another. Because there was doubt whether his baptism was fully Trinitarian, rebaptism was decreed to be sure of validity.

Concerning the Paulianists, who have fled for refuge to the Catholic Church, it has been decreed that they must all be rebaptized, but if any have formerly been numbered among the clergy, if in fact they seem blameless and without reproach, when they have been rebaptized, let them be ordained by the bishop of the Catholic Church; but if the examination discovers them to be unfit, then they should be rejected. And likewise, concerning the deaconesses and all those who have been examined in the rule of faith, the same pattern should be observed. But we mean by deaconesses those who have been formally selected, since they do not have any laying on of hands. For this reason, they are to be entirely numbered among the laity.

The Paulianist church had deaconesses (*diakonissai*), but they were seen by the council fathers to have no ordination (*cheirothesia*) and therefore to belong with the laity. It is important to note that the council did not reject the ordination of deaconesses by this canon, but legislated a specific case of those coming from a schismatic church that apparently did not ordain them. The Nicene legislators were familiar with deaconesses and did not know what else to call these female ministers. By implication, if they had received the formal laying on of hands (*cheirothesia*), they would be considered among the clergy. Yet we know that other female deacons did receive it (e.g., *AC* 8.19–20).

Basil of Caesarea, *Letter* 199.44 [26]

For background on Basil, see chapter 3, unnamed daughters of Count Terentius.

> The female deacon who committed fornication with the Greek should be admitted to penance. Let her be admitted to communion in the offering in the seventh year, provided she remains pure. But the Greek who returns to the sacrilege after having once accepted the faith returns to the vomit (Prov 26:11). The body of the female deacon, because it is consecrated, we no longer allow to have fleshly use.

This pronouncement belongs to a series of church regulations on various cases known as the Canons of Basil. As is usual in the time and place and elsewhere in Basil's regulations, punishment for sexual sin falls more heavily on the woman than the man. Here it seems to have been the case of a pagan man having sexual relations with a female deacon (*diakonos*), then entering the faith and renouncing the relationship, then at least trying to return to it. Nothing more is known about the situation. This text is another witness to the expected celibacy of female deacons (see *AC* 6.17.4) and perhaps to the ignoring of a minimum age for consecration as female deacon (see Sozomen on the ordination of Olympias in chapter 3), a minimum that gradually slid from sixty to forty. Gryson thinks that the seven-year penance imposed on the female deacon indicates that those in the order in Basil's church were not considered members of the clergy, since members of the clergy were deposed but not excommunicated for the sin of fornication. [27]

Theodosius, *Codex* 16.2.27 [28]

The code of law promulgated by the Eastern emperor Theodosius (379–95) reveals how intimately united were imperial and ecclesiastical spheres, how interested the emperor was in the health of the church, and how unafraid he was to intervene directly in ecclesiastical affairs. The Codex *includes a number of laws regarding widows and deaconesses, of which the following, dated June 21, 390, is an example.*

According to the precept of the Apostle, no woman may be transferred to the association of deaconesses (*diaconissarum consortium*) unless she has lived for sixty years, and whose wished-for progeny (*votiva proles*) be at home.

According to Sozomen (next entry), this law was enacted in order that women not be admitted to the diaconate until age sixty in order to prevent scandal, indeed to prevent a recurrence of a scandal like one that had occurred in Constantinople, where an aristocratic woman praying in church was violated by a cleric.[29] Note that the requirements for admission to widowhood enumerated in 1 Timothy are made here to pertain as well to deaconesses. But there may be another reason for the law, which goes on to demand that deaconesses not be allowed to name as heir of their property any church, cleric, or poor person (*nullam ecclesiam, nullum clericum, nullum pauperem*). Thus the law may well have been motivated by the desire to prevent scandal only secondarily, and primarily to prevent diaconal wealth, as Gryson has suggested, "from falling too easily into the hands of ecclesiastics."[30] (The law was later rescinded by the emperor Marcian.) In any case, the law represents a nonecclesiastical witness to the existence of deaconesses, and to imperial recognition of the legitimacy of their status, functions, and prerogatives, as well as the limits of their freedom.

Sozomen, *Church History* 7.16 [31]

For Sozomen, see Olympias in chapter 3.

This reference to a regulation of the age of diaconal ordination for women from the Theodosian Code 16.2.27 comes at the end of a fascinating chapter in which Sozomen recounts his version—though he admits that there are other versions in circulation—of the reason for the cessation of individual confession and penance in the church at Constantinople. He implies that it was previously an established custom, by which a presbyter of unquestionable virtue and wisdom was assigned by the bishop to stay in the church to hear the confessions of penitents privately. But under bishop Nectarius, predecessor of John Chrysostom, a distinguished woman who remained in the church afterward to pray attested that she had been raped by a deacon. The deacon was promptly deposed, and the practice of private confession discontinued. Sozomen laments that under the old system, people sinned less because of their fear of having to confess their sins! Then he suggests that the emperor Theodosius had the same kind of thing in mind when he enacted the following. Presumably this means that Theodosius was tightening the rules.

It was for this reason, I think, that the emperor Theodosius, wanting to promote the renown and distinction of the church, decreed that women were not to be allowed into the diaconal ministry of God unless they had produced children and were more than sixty years old, according to the precept of the apostle Paul. He also decreed that women who had shaved their heads should be cast out of the church, and the bishops who had admitted them should be deposed from the episcopate.

Women childless and younger than sixty were not to be admitted to *diakonia*. This of course is good evidence that in many places and times, virginity was not requisite for ordination. Here it seems to be even excluded, but that is doubtful; it is probably taken for granted that virgins can be deacons. Given average age expectancy, many women would not survive to age sixty. Perhaps because of this, both the Council of Chalcedon (451) and Justinian (mid-sixth century, *Novellae* 123.13) would reduce the age requirement to forty. The allusion to Paul is to 1 Tim 5:9, where a widow to be enrolled for church support must be at least sixty, married only once, have given proof of raising her children well, and be of proven virtue. It is interesting that Sozomen and the Theodosian legislators conflate widows in 1 Timothy with deacons in their own church.

The cryptic allusion to women with shaved heads is unclear. Perhaps it was monastic tonsure or some other ascetical practice. For a similar prohibition, see the Council of Gangra (340s or 360s in Paphlagonia) Canon 17.

Epiphanius, Bishop of Salamis, to Bishop John of Jerusalem, *Letter* 51, translated by St. Jerome[32]

The bishops Epiphanius and John had been estranged by a number of sources of conflict, both theological and canonical in nature. Among other things, they were leading antagonists in the Origenist controversy.[33] In this letter, dated 394, Epiphanius explains why he had irregularly ordained, first as deacon and then as priest, Jerome's brother Paulinian, a monk whom John thought to be under his jurisdiction. Epiphanius explains that, as a monk, Paulinian was not within the limits of John's jurisdiction. He goes on to assert in his own defense:

I have never ordained (*ordinavi*) deaconesses (*diaconissas*) to send to the provinces of others.

This letter survives only in Jerome's Latin translation from the Greek.[34] Epiphanius does not mean to suggest that he does not ordain deaconesses. Indeed, the practice of ordaining them was widespread in the East in the late fourth century. Rather, he insists that he has not ordained them for the purpose of allowing them to exercise ministries in dioceses other than his own (*alienas provincias*). The text suggests that Epiphanius, as bishop, was following the common oriental practice at the time of ordaining deaconesses in his own province. (It may also suggest that Epiphanius

believed John to have ordained ministers for ministry in dioceses other than his own.)
In any event, this text suggests that Epiphanius regarded deaconesses as part of the
clergy, and that their clerical status was signified by induction in a rite of ordination.
Such an interpretation cannot be certain, given that we only have a translation.

Bishop of Edessa, Canon of Rabbula

*The following canon was preserved in an eighteenth-century volume on the writings of
the Syrian Monophysite church by the distinguished Vatican librarian and orientalist
Joseph Simeon Assemani (1687–1768).*[35] *It was then reprinted in the mid-eighteenth
century by John Pinius (fl. 1740) in a treatise on deaconesses.*[36] *The canon itself was
issued early in the fifth century by Bishop Rabbula of Edessa (412–35), dubbed by his
local clergy "the tyrant of Edessa."*[37] *Heavily involved in the christological controversy
of the fifth century, he fervently supported Cyril of Alexandria, who addressed his treatise "On the Orthodox Faith" to him. Sometime early in the fifth century, in a Synod
of Edessa, he ratified the following decree on the relationship in the Divine Office of
what we should call the regular and secular clergy.*

> Let the monks not proceed to vigils without the presbyter, nor nuns without
> the deaconess (*diaconissa*), so that the presbyter may thus be before (*praeest*)
> the monks and the deaconess before the nuns in the divine office.

In this text, we see that the function and status of the deaconess, and even the
meaning of the word, were different in this part of the empire in the early fifth century. The deaconess stood in the same relationship to the nuns as the presbyter did
to the monks, in an exercise of liturgical leadership in the recitation of the Divine
Office. She also may have been head of a community of nuns (as, indeed, the deaconess Marthana seemed to be in Egeria's travelogue). Indeed, "deaconess" here
may be synonymous with the term "abbess." No mention is made of a sacramental role in eucharist or in baptism. Martimort is thus correct to observe that "she
was a woman exercising a function of authority in a religious community,"[38] but
such authority also included a form of liturgical, though not sacramental, leadership. In this particular role in the divine office, what the presbyter was to the
monks, the deaconess was to the nuns. Such a connection between being a deaconess and being head of a religious community began no later than the late fourth
century, with Olympias in Constantinople. However, such a connection was not
everywhere observed then or later.

Council of Chalcedon Canon 15 [39]

*The Council of Chalcedon in 451 produced the major christological formula of the full
and uncompromised humanity and divinity of Christ that has dominated in the East-*

ern and Western churches ever since, and which caused the great Eastern schism of the Copts, Syrians, and Armenians in the fifth and sixth centuries. Bishops assembled in council to debate theological questions always used the opportunity to decide also on some disciplinary issues. One of them is given here.

> A woman shall not be ordained as a deaconess before the age of forty, and this only after strict examination. But if after receiving ordination and having persevered for a certain time in ministry (*leitourgia*), she gives herself in marriage, she is then spurning the grace of God. Let her be anathematized with the man united with her.

In spite of several conciliar pronouncements that suggested the deaconess was not really ordained, the Council of Chalcedon assumed the ordination (*cheirotonia*) of deaconesses (*diakonissai*), but set a lower age limit for the ordination (cf. 1 Tim 5:9, where a widow is not to be enrolled in the church's service organization of widows before the age of sixty). The minimum age for deaconesses also differed in different times and places. According to *AC* 6.17.4, deaconesses were to be either virgins or widows. This is the situation presumed here. The word for ministry, *leitourgia*, is not often used in women's ministry as it usually connotes by this time altar ministry, which may be envisioned here, contrary to the *AC*, which excluded women from such ministry. But the Divine Office is also *leitourgia*, and there is ample evidence of women's leadership there. The way in which the deaconess's possible marriage is spoken of suggests a fait accompli, perhaps a secret marriage without the knowledge of the bishop. The anathema as punishment is probably excommunication from the Church.

Didascalia Arabica 38.21[40]

This document, likely from the fourth–fifth century, exists in both Arabic and Ethiopic versions. The Ethiopic document draws heavily on the AC; the Arabic, here, on the TD.

> Thus let the bishop perform the liturgy with the veil drawn. Within are the presbyters, deacons, subdeacons, readers, and widows, who are called deaconesses (*diaconissae*), and those who have spiritual gifts.

This liturgical arrangement bears a remarkable resemblance to that imagined in *TD* 1.23, on which it depends. In both texts, a veil is drawn and the clergy are enclosed by it. Here, unlike in the *TD*, widows and deaconesses are identified. The author of this *Didascalia* certainly imagined such women as part of the clergy. Much more problematic is the question of whether this text reflects actual practice in Egypt or Ethiopia. The dependence of the text on the *TD* and the lack of other evidence leads us to agree with the conclusion of Martimort: "this kind of text . . . has led some historians to believe that the institution of deaconesses did, after all, exist in Egypt. However, this kind of text was an importation from the East and, in fact, had no practical influence on the local institutions, either in Egypt or in Ethiopia."[41]

Arabic Canons of Nicaea 74/79 [42]

The eighty "Arabic Canons of Nicaea" were not produced by the fathers at the first ecumenical council of Nicaea (325); scholars generally agree that that council produced only twenty canons. Nonetheless, the time and place of these "Arabic Canons" remains unclear, though they postdate Nicaea (some of the canons were taken from the later Theodosian or Justinian codes). Gryson has suggested they were produced in or around Antioch in the fifth century.[43] In any case, they have been known in two Latin versions since the second half of the sixteenth century. The first was translated by the Jesuit Francisco Torres, who also attempted to prove that the Nicene Canons far exceeded twenty in number; the second by the Maronite Abraham of Hekel, who had eighty-four canons in his collection and Latin translation, though he did not suppose they were Nicene in origin. The two canons under consideration here both deal with deaconesses.

Canon 74 (Torres)
These [deaconesses] (*diaconissae*) . . . must be sixty years of age, as blessed Paul ordained. Let deaconesses of this kind be prepared for this alone: to receive women in baptism.

Canon 79 (Hekel)
Let these [widows] be appointed who have proven to be beyond reproach . . . at least sixty years of age, as blessed Paul ordained, especially in order to assist deaconesses in baptism.

In whatever ways they differ, both canons agree that deaconesses must have achieved the age of sixty and that their sole role is to assist in the baptism of women.

JUSTINIAN, *NOVELLAE* [44]

After his military career, Justininian (482–565 CE, Byzantine emperor 527–565) succeeded his uncle Justin (518–27) to the throne in Constantinople. Under him, the golden age of Byzantine power and culture flourished. Following the Nika riots against him in the capital city (532), he rebuilt the imperial palace and the great church of Hagia Sophia that still stands. Other surviving buildings are the Church of St. Catherine at Mount Sinai and the Church of the Nativity in Bethlehem. One of his lasting

*achievements was the codification of all previous Roman law along with his own leg-
islation into his* Codex, Digest, Institutes, *and the new laws, or* Novellae. *The following articles of legislation about female deacons in the context of clerical regulations
are drawn from the last collection. It is known that his empress Theodora exercised a
profound effect on him and was responsible for the improved legal status of women in
the legislation.*

Novellae 3.1

In some articles, female deacons are not among the clergy (klērikoi*), but in others the distinction is not clear. In the following article, aimed at controlling the number of church
personnel dependent on the church, we see the ambiguity. In the first sentence, there are
three classifications: clerics, women deacons, and porters. But in the second paragraph,
women deacons are included among the clergy, with only porters being excluded.*

> We decree that those who are now at the most holy great church [Hagia
> Sophia in Constantinople] and the rest in all the other [religious] houses, and
> the most pious clerics and women deacons (*gynaikas diakonous*) and porters
> should remain where they are assigned. We do not reduce what is the present
> arrangement but are providing for the future. In the future, let there be no
> ordination (*cheirotonia*) until the number of reverend clergy established at
> the beginning by those who founded the churches is reached.
>
> We decree that no more than sixty presbyters be assigned to the most holy
> great church, one hundred male deacons, forty female, ninety subdeacons,
> one hundred ten lectors, and twenty-five cantors, so that the total number of
> reverend clergy of the most holy great church not exceed four hundred twenty-
> five, plus one hundred of those called porters.

The list of functionaries assigned gives an idea of the massive operations at the
great church of Hagia Sophia during the time of Justinian. The great disparity in
numbers of male (one hundred) and female (forty) deacons indicates that as in
most cases, so too here male deacons had a wider range of responsibilities.

Novellae 3.2

*The next article forbids movement of clergy from one church to another and repeats
that there are to be no new ordinations until they fall below the established number (set
in 3.1); it specifies that this is in regard to the great church.*

> With regard to all the other churches which are financially supported by the
> great church, we decree that those who are there should remain as established,

and let no one else be ordained until the statute[45] determined for each church by its founders is attained, of presbyters and deacons, male and female, subdeacons, lectors, cantors, and porters, and not a single one shall be added.

The same decree goes on to say that those to be ordained will be sent to the bishop by the emperor himself. The patriarch of Constantinople is to refuse all requests, even if they come from the palace, under penalty of a fine. This is an interesting insight into the degree to which imperial authority controlled ecclesiastical activities, as well as the extent to which various persons in high places tried to influence ordinations.

Novellae 6.6

Article 6.6 is entirely about female deacons, called deaconesses (diakonissai) in the first part of the article but diakonoi later. It legislates age and qualifications for ordination and penalties for neglect of duty. Again here, deaconesses seem not to be included among the clergy.

Everything said by us about the reverend clergy (*klērikoi*) we wish also to be done with regard to the God-beloved deaconesses, so that they shall do nothing outside the appropriate regulations.

First, they should be of right age, neither too young at the fullness of passion, vulnerable to making false steps, but already well into life, about fifty years old, according to the sacred canons. Thus they can arrive at sacred ordination (*cheirotonia*), whether they are virgins or have been married to one man. We do not allow those married twice or those of notorious life or under any suspicion to approach the sacred diaconate (*tēn hieran . . . diakonian*), to administer (*hypēretein*) baptism to those who present themselves (masculine plural) and to participate (*pareinai*) in other secret rites (*aporrētoi*) and most sacred mysteries (*sebasmiōtatois mystēriois*) that they are accustomed to practice.

But if it is necessary to ordain someone deacon below the age we said, let her be ordained in some monastery in which she should live, for she cannot mingle with men or choose her own way of life, but by a withdrawn and moderate life she will give good witness. We desire that those ordained as deacons either from widowhood or from virginity should not live with "brothers" or relatives or those called *agapētoi*.[46] With such as these, their life will be filled with suspicion. Let them live alone or only with parents or children, or true brothers or uncles, about whom if anyone dares to suggest evil, that one will be judged impious and irreverent.

If anything is said about anyone wishing to enter into ordination as a deaconess, that she has lived disguised under good appearance and thus falls under suspicion of evil, in no way should such a woman approach diaconal ordination. If she has been ordained and then does such a thing and lives with someone under a false name or disguise, let her be expelled from the diaconate, and both she and the man involved shall be liable to our laws and punished in the same way as others who commit the crime of seduction (cf. *Novellae* 123.43).

All the reverend ordained deaconesses at the time of their ordination must be admonished and should hear the sacred instructions in the presence of the other reverend deaconesses so that they might reverence God and be confident in the sacred instructions, ashamed to fall from the sacred order (*hiera taxis*), knowing that if they dare to shame their ordination or leave the sacred order to pursue marriage or choose any way of evil life, they will be liable to the death penalty and their property confiscated to the holy churches or to the monasteries in which they have been. Those who dare to corrupt or marry them will be liable to the sword, their property confiscated to the public treasury. For indeed, if in the ancient laws for those called virgins death was the result of their error when they were corrupted, how much more those truly dedicated to God ought to see that modesty should be safeguarded in such a way that what is fitting to nature and to the priesthood (*hierosynē*) be kept.

The age for acceptance into the official association of widows was set in 1 Tim 5:9 at sixty. The canonical age for the ordination of a female deacon was set at forty by Canon 15 of Chalcedon, though it sometimes varied in other times and places. Here it is fifty. In article 123.13, the age has been lowered to forty, while the next paragraph of this very article envisions exceptions, of which there were probably many. (See in chapter 3 the case of Olympias, who was ordained in the late fourth century in Constantinople when she was well below the canonical age.) The prohibition of church leadership to those who have entered a second marriage begins already with 1 Tim 3:2 and 5:9. The previous article in the code (6.5) discourages second marriages for male clergy and eliminates those married a second time from consideration for the episcopate. But they are not penalized in so severe a manner as are the women.

The second paragraph comes closest to giving any details about the actual liturgical role of deaconesses. Along with the *DA/AC*, it specifies a role in baptism. But surprisingly, here it does not seem that that role is limited to assistance in the baptism of women. The language is more general and, surprisingly, undifferentiated with regard to gender. The rest of the description of their duties is general language about secret and sacred rites, intriguing and unspecified. Certainly it must mean some connection to Eucharistic celebration, and perhaps other sacramental or quasisacramental functions.

Why would it be *necessary* to ordain a woman deacon below the requisite age? This may tell us something about the function of social status. It may have been that this ordination was considered an honor that sometimes could not be denied to women of high status if they requested it. It could also refer to a situation of pastoral need.

The legislation in this article tells us quite a bit between the lines about the relative social freedom of women in general to choose how they would live—at the possible price of their reputation, of course. The ancient fixation on the chastity of women so common in Mediterranean cultures as sign of a well-ordered society is magnified in these pieces of legislation in the case of women publicly dedicated to celibacy or virginity. The "ancient laws" about death to virgins who violated their virginity in the last paragraph is a reference to the Vestal Virgins of ancient Rome, young women specially selected from prominent families to serve as priestesses in the temple of the goddess Vesta in the Roman Forum for thirty years, during which time violation of their virginity was punishable by death. It is an interesting allusion to the conscious continuity of the Byzantine empire with the legendary glory of ancient Rome.

Novellae 123.5

The following legislation allows presbyters, deacons, and subdeacons to accept family responsibilities as executors of estates. Since the gender of said deacons is not specified, and since it is known that women deacons possessed property and often had children, and that women had independent administration of their property under certain conditions, it is reasonable to assume that they are included here.

> We do not permit the God-loving bishops or monks by any law to be appointed guardians or curators of anyone whatsoever. But we do permit presbyters, deacons, and subdeacons to become guardians or curators of an estate if they are in the proper and necessary relationship, and we authorize them to undertake this responsibility (*leitourgia*).

Novellae 123.13

While earlier legislation quoted above specified the minimum age of fifty for ordination of women, here it is forty, perhaps evidence of the varied sources from which this legislation was drawn.

> We do not allow anyone to become a presbyter at less than thirty years of age, nor deacon or subdeacon at less than twenty-five, nor lector at less than

eighteen years. A deaconess is not to be ordained (*cheirotoneisthai*) who is less than forty or who has had a second marriage.

Novellae 123.21

If anyone brings a lawsuit[47] against a cleric or monk or deaconess (*diakonissa*) or nun (*monastria*) or female ascetic (*askētria*), let that person first inform the bishop to whom both parties are subject, and let the bishop decide the case between them.

The article goes on to specify that after ten days the aggrieved party, if not satisfied, can go to a magistrate, and from there to a higher court if the magistrate's decision is different from that of the bishop. The legislation shows that women, even those in ecclesiastical and ascetic lifestyles, were subject to legal proceedings. The one bringing the action could also, of course, be a woman.

Novellae 123.30

Deaconesses were strictly sworn to celibacy. The penalty for violation was deposition, relegation to a monastery, and confiscation of property. This legislation tells us that deaconesses in good standing were supported by the church but might live independently, have their own house, and bequeath their property to their children.

In no way do we permit a deaconess to live with a man in such a way as to produce suspicion of an unseemly life. If she disregards this, the bishop[48] to whom she is subject will notify her in no uncertain terms that she is to expel such a man from her house. If she hesitates to do it, she is to be removed from her charge (*hypēresia*) and her daily support and handed over to a monastery for the rest of her life. If she has children, her property shall be distributed evenly to them, with the monastery receiving her own share to pay for her support. If she does not have children, her property should be divided evenly between the monastery where she has been placed and the church to which she was previously assigned.

The "suspicion of unseemly life" may well be the institution of the *agapetae*. See the discussion under *Novellae* 6.6.

Novellae 123.43

If anyone rapes, seduces, or corrupts a female ascetic or deaconess or nun, or any other woman of pious life or wearing a religious habit (*schēma echousan*), we order that in punishment his property and that of the accomplices in his defilement be turned over to the holy place in which the woman lived, by the holy bishops and their stewards as well as by the governors of each province and their contingents. Both those who err this way and those who participate fall under sentence of death. The woman is to be completely investigated and placed with her own property in a monastery in which she can be securely guarded so that the same charge will not occur again. If such a deaconess should have legitimate children, the legally specified share is to be given to the children.

The opening statement assumes a wide variety of choices of lifestyle for women who want to practice asceticism or serve within the context of the church. The religious habit seems to have been quite distinguishable. The next article (123.44) forbids any in worldly occupations, especially actors and prostitutes, to use or imitate the habit of men or women under pain of corporeal punishment and exile. One can easily imagine how those in the comic theatre would have liked to make use of it!

No distinction seems to be made between rape and seduction. The punishment is the same, albeit certainly more severe for the man than for the woman. Even bishops are authorized to do the civil action of seizing property of offenders in order to give it to a monastery to which the woman will be assigned. The text seems to assume that such a rape or seduction could not be carried off by one man alone, but that he would need help. Only the deaconess is envisioned as having children, since she could be a widow, whereas it is assumed that other female ascetics will not have been married.

Novellae 131.13

Bishops were not allowed to give to family or otherwise alienate property that came to them after episcopal ordination, but they could use it for their own church and charitable works. Thus they had a financial responsibility to use their goods for their ministry. They could, however, give to their family property acquired before episcopal ordination. This also applied to administrators of orphanages, shelters for the poor, hospitals, homes for the aged, hospices for travelers, and other pious institutions, during the time of their administration. The mention of so many charitable works gives the impression of a quite well organized relief effort, at least in the capital. The clerical or social rank of such administrators is not specified. Presumably these could be members of the clergy, or deaconesses, or laity. (See Enneon, [if the correct reading] named as an administrator or liturgist of a hospital in Jerusalem in chapter 3.) The legislation then goes on to specify what happens when someone in church office died without a will.

If a bishop or cleric or ecclesiastic of any rank or deaconess of a church dies intestate and without a legal heir, the inheritance should go to the church in which he or she was ordained.

CONCLUSION

From the third-century *Didascalia* to the sixth-century legislation of Justinian, female deacons were objects of regulation alongside other members of the clergy. The discrepancies from one piece of legislation to another, albeit all in the Eastern Church, show the developing self-understanding of the various churches with regard to each other and to the living of faith in their assemblies and everyday life. Structures evolved in answer to changing needs, and the structure of the diaconate was part of that evolution.

Notes

1. Funk, *Didascalia,* 1.105; Mayer, *Monumenta,* 18.

2. Funk, *Didascalia,* 1.163; Mayer, *Monumenta,* 19.

3. Funk, *Didascalia,* 1.169–71; Mayer, *Monumenta,* 19.

4. Funk, *Didascalia,* 1.190; Mayer, *Monumenta,* 21.

5. *Ministry of Women,* 37.

6. Funk, *Didascalia,* 197–99; Mayer, *Monumenta,* 22.

7. For discussion, see Charles A. Bobertz, "The Role of Patron in the *Cena Dominica* of Hippolytus' *Apostolic Tradition,*" *JTS* 44 (1993): 170–84.

8. Funk, *Didascalia,* 1.199–201; Mayer, *Monumenta,* 22.

9. Funk, *Didascalia,* 1.201; Mayer, *Monumenta,* 23.

10. Funk, *Didascalia,* 1.209.

11. Ibid., 1.209–211; Mayer, *Monumenta,* 23.

12. Funk, *Didascalia,* 1.341; Mayer, *Monumenta,* 25.

13. M. Lightman and W. Zeisel, "*Univira:* An Example of Continuity and Change in Roman Society," *Church History* 46 (1977): 19–32; Suzanne Dixon, *The Roman Mother* (London: Routledge, 1988), 6, 22. Ironically, the ideal persisted while Augustan marriage legislation was strongly in favor of remarriage. See also 1 Tim 5:14 and the beginnings of the Christian extension of the ideal to men in 1 Tim 3:2.

14. Funk, *Didascalia,* 1.213–15; Mayer, *Monumenta,* 24.

15. Funk, *Didascalia,* 1.516; Mayer, *Monumenta,* 25.

16. Funk, *Didascalia,* 1.524.

17. Ibid., 2.81.

18. Mayer, *Monumenta,* 40.

19. Funk, *Didascalia,* 1.528; Mayer, *Monumenta,* 25.

20. Funk, *Didascalia,* 1.530; Mayer, *Monumenta,* 26.

21. Funk, *Didascalia,* 1.532–34; Mayer, *Monumenta,* 26.

22. Funk, *Didascalia,* 1.140; Mayer, *Monumenta,* p. 27.

23. Funk, *Didascalia,* 1.xxxiii–xxxiv.

24. *GCS* 15.220; Mayer, *Monumenta,* 7–8.

25. Text: Mansi, *Sacrorum Conciliorum,* 2.675–78; Mayer, *Monumenta,* 10–11; translation with comment, NPNF n.s. 14.40–42.

26. *PG* 32.730; Mayer, *Monumenta,* 14; *Saint Basil: The Letters,* ed. Roy J. Deferrari, LCL (London: Heinemann, 1930), 3.130.

27. Gryson, *Ministry of Women,* 51.

28. *Codex Theodosianus,* ed. Theodor Mommsen and Paul Meyer, 2 vols. (Berlin: Weidmans, 1905), 2.843.

29. See *Ecclesiastical History* 7.16.1–10.

30. Gryson, *Ministry of Women,* 70.

31. Text: *PG* 67.1457–64; *GCS,* 50, 322–24; full translation of chapter in *Ecclesiastical History of Sozomen,* trans. Edward Walford (London: Henry G. Bohn, 1855), 334–39.

32. I. Hilberg, ed., *Sancti Eusebii Hieronymi Epistulae,* Epistula 51 in *CSEL* 54 (1996): 395–412.

33. See J.N.D. Kelly, *Jerome* (New York: Harper and Row, 1975), 195–209 and 227–63 for good discussion of the controversy.

34. The accuracy of the translation has been questioned. See J. Labourt, trans., *Saint Jérôme: Lettres,* 8 vols. (Paris: Les Belles Lettres, 1951) 2.203.

35. *De syris monophysitis dissertatio* (Rome: Sacred Congregation Propaganda Fide, 1730); Mayer, *Monumenta,* 18.

36. *Tractatus de Ecclesiae Diaconissis,* in *AASS* September 1, v–vi.

37. Edessa is modern Urfa, Turkey.

38. *Deaconesses,* 139; also see the discussion of sixth-century texts from the same region, which presume that the deaconess leads a community of nuns (ibid.).

39. Text: Mansi, *Sacrorum Conciliorum,* 7.363–64; Mayer, *Monumenta,* 28; the whole English text with comment is in NPNF n.s. 14.279.

40. Funk, *Didascalia,* 2.132. There is not a little literature on the Arabic and Ethiopic manuscripts of this text. See also the introduction, 2.xxviii–xxxii. Funk preserves the only fragments of the Arabic version, translated into Latin, 2.120–36. See also F. Nau, *La Didascalie des douze Apôtres,* 2nd ed. (Paris: Lethielleux, 1912), ix–x, xxii–xxiii; J. M. Harden, *The Ethiopic Didascalia* (London: Macmillan, 1920); and T. Pell Platt, *The Ethiopic Didascalia* (London, 1834).

41. *Deaconesses,* 96.

42. Mansi, *Sacrorum Conciliorum,* 2.978, 1008. See discussion in Gryson, *Ministry of Women,* 63.

43. Gryson, *Ministry of Women,* 63.

44. Text: Mayer, *Monumenta,* 34–37; *Corpus Iuris Civilis,* vol. 3, *Novellae,* ed. Rudolf Schoell and William Kroll (Berlin: Weidmann, 1954), 18–23, 43–45, 604, 608–11, 616, 623–24, 661–62. An available English translation, *Enactments of Justinian,* ed. S. P. Scott, 17 vols. (Cincinnati, 1832; reprint, New York: AMS Press, 1973), is helpful but not reliable on technical terms.

45. The word in Greek is *statouton,* a loanword from Latin *statutus,* meaning "fixed" or "determined."

46. The reference is to the ascetic practice, well attested in the patristic church, of man and woman living together celibately. This may be already the reference in 1 Cor 7:36–38. It is difficult to know how widespread the custom was. It does not seem to have enjoyed official church support, since most references to it from bishops and church legislation are attempts to elimi-

nate it. On "spiritual marriage," see Elizabeth A. Clark, "John Chrysostom and the Subintro-ductae," *Church History* 46 (1977): 171–85; *Ascetic Piety and Women's Faith: Essays on Late Ancient Christianity* (Lewiston: Edwin Mellen, 1986), 265–90; and *Reading Renunciation: Asceticism and Scripture in Early Christianity* (Princeton: Princeton University Press, 1999).

47. *Agōgē,* a legal action.

48. The word here is *hiereus* ("priest") but should not be understood as presbyter, who is not called "priest" at this period. Rather, it is the bishop who exercises priestly office; see *Novellae* 131.13.

Chapter Five

WOMEN DEACONS IN THE EAST
Later Texts Bearing on Earlier Evidence

 The following discussions in the Eastern Church from the seventh century and later all shed light on further interpretation of some of the texts presented in the previous chapter. Several, for example, witness to the belief in their day that, though deaconesses no longer functioned liturgically, they were once fully ordained members of the clergy and even entrusted with some kind of altar ministry.

John of Damascus, *On Heresies* 49[1]

John of Damascus (c. 676–c. 749) is often regarded as the last of the Church fathers. A "doctor of the church," he is perhaps most celebrated for his defense of images in the iconoclastic controversy. His most famous work is The Fount of Wisdom, *the middle part of which is a treatise* On Heresies, *which is preserved. Making no claims to originality, John's book was encyclopedic in character. His treatment of known heresies is heavily dependent on Epiphanius' Panarion. Indeed, of the hundred or so heresies he discusses, eighty are copied verbatim from Epiphanius; the remaining material consists of discussion of new heresies (and Islam). While the work survives in its entirety in Syriac, only fragments remain in Greek, and the translation here comes from a Latin version. In the forty-ninth chapter of the treatise, he discusses the role of women in the Pepuzian heresy.*

The Pepuzians, who are also called Quintillians—who resemble the Artotyritae—are two different heresies. Although counted among the Cataphrygians, the Pepuzians believe several diverse things they do not.

They hold in divine honor Pepuza, an uninhabited town between Galatia and Cappadocia, and Phrygia they say to be Jerusalem . . . they allow women to be teachers and priests (*magistrates et sacerdotia deferent*). They celebrate sacred rites by piercing a child with brass needles—as the Cataphrygians customarily do. Once the flour is mixed with blood (*sanguini farina admista*), they confect the bread and share in the sacrifice.

Although John asserts that the Pepuzians constitute a distinct heresy, they seem almost entirely similar. All of the groups named have theological and disciplinary connections to Montanism. Like the Montanists, the Pepuzians allowed women significant functional roles, authority, and status, here explicitly sacerdotal. A work spuriously ascribed to Augustine named *Praedestinatus*[2] also refers in chapter 27 to the Cataphyrgians (whom he identifies with the Montanists) and distinguishes them from the Pepuzians, who, he says, think themselves better than the Cataphrygians. (Perhaps this is the only distinction of significance.) The latter, he also states, give leadership to women and honor some as priests. The confection of the eucharist from the blood of a child is, we recall, also attributed to the Cataphyrgians in Augustine, *On Heresies,* 27. The legends of similar practices were told earlier of Jews and Christians.

Trullan Synod Canons 14, 15, and 48[3]

The Trullan Council or Synod was held in 692 in the domed hall (trullus) of the imperial palace of Justinian II in Constantinople to complete the disciplinary work of two previous councils numbered fifth and sixth in 553 and 680–81, hence its secondary name of "Quinisext" or "fifth–sixth." Its canons largely concerned questions of clerical life and were not accepted in the West.

Canon 14
Let the canon of our holy God-bearing fathers be retained, namely, that a presbyter not be ordained before the age of thirty even though he be fully qualified, but let him be held back. For Our Lord Jesus Christ was baptized in the thirtieth year and began to preach. Likewise a deacon before the age of twenty-five, nor should a deaconess (*diakonissa*) be ordained (*cheirotonein*) before the age of forty.

The age limit for women's diaconal ordination that was set at Chalcedon is reaffirmed.

Canon 15
A subdeacon is not to be ordained before twenty years. If anyone in any priestly (*hieratikē*) rank is ordained before the established age, let that one be deposed.

The first part of this canon simply continues the age limitations for clergy. The summary that comprises the second part considers deaconesses to be part of the clergy, since they are included in the list above.

Canon 48
The wife of one who is raised to episcopal status, with common consent of the husband with whom she has been living, should be separated ahead of

time, and after his ordination let her enter a monastery far away from the episcopal residence, and let her benefit from episcopal providence. But if she seems worthy, she will be raised to the diaconal status (*diakonia*).

Here the celibacy of bishops, even previously married ones, is reinforced by involuntary separation of the spouses. The canon requires common consent, but the choice was probably to separate or renounce episcopal appointment. The former wife should leave his bed before the ordination but only afterward enter a monastery—perhaps so that she could be present at the ceremony? She will be supported from church funds there, but no other choices are offered her. The diaconal ordination comes as something of an afterthought and does not seem to be intimately related to her husband's new status.

Photius, *Canonical Collection* 1.30 [4]

The name of Photius (c. 810–895) is well known in the history of East-West relations and the deterioration thereof. He was appointed Patriarch of Constantinople in 858 upon the deposition of his predecessor, who refused to abdicate. The ensuing schism dragged the bishop of Rome and many others into the fray. At his rival's death in 877, Photius assumed his office as patriarch. Throughout the period, he was heavily involved in controversies of theology and discipline between East and West, and was a champion of the Eastern Church's autonomy over against Rome.

According to the model of Lord Heraclius, in the great church there were established eighty presbyters, fifty deacons, forty deaconesses (*diakonissai*), seventy subdeacons, one hundred sixty lectors, twenty-five cantors, and seventy-five porters.

Heraclius was Byzantine emperor 575–641, beginning ten years after the death of Justinian I, who built the new Hagia Sophia in Constantinople, the "great church" to which Photius refers, and which still stands in faded splendor. In every case, the number is reduced from those given in Justinian's *Novellae* 3.1, indicating something of a cutback from the golden age of the great Justinian. The issue is economic: all these clerics served full time in the church and were supported by imperial subvention (see Justinian). Even so, the numbers given here imply a major operation with abundant personnel.

Theodore Balsamon, Comment on Several Church Canons

Theodore Balsamon (c. 1140–95) was a Greek canonist who commented on ecclesiastical and civil law in Constantinople. Named Patriarch of Antioch, he was unable ever to occupy the position because the Latin Crusaders were in possession of the city and the region, so he remained in Constantinople.

On Canon 19 of the Council of Nicaea[5]

This is what happens with deaconesses (*diakonissai*). Virgins were coming to the church and with encouragement from the bishop, they were maintained as dedicated to God, but in the dress of the laity. This is the way it was arranged. Having attained forty years of age, they were worthy of ordination (*cheirotonia*) as deaconesses, if they were found to be completely deserving. If any were found to be among the Paulinists, they would be dealt with the same as the men.

Balsamon adds more than the Canon of Nicaea, for he goes on to specify age of ordination, bringing in this information from Canon 15 of Chalcedon. He implies that the office of deaconess began with consecrated virgins and arose from this group. As we will see with his further comments, he also assumes an original sacramental ministry for them. The final comment here relates to the integration of the followers of Paul of Samosata into the catholic church: their ordinations done before reconciliation and (re)baptism in the church were not considered valid (see Canon 19 of Nicaea).

On Canon 15 of the Council of Chalcedon[6]

Balsamon begins by quoting the canon, then:

The issues concerning the present canon have received wide attention [or, are completely outdated; *pantēescholasan*]. A deaconess (*diakonissa*) today is not ordained, even if some female ascetics are loosely referred to as deaconesses. For there is a canon that defines that women may not enter the sanctuary (*bēma*). How could one who cannot approach the altar (*thysiastērion*) perform the function of the deacons? Read canons fourteen and fifteen of the Trullan Synod, which depose a deaconess ordained before the age of forty. Doesn't the present canon anathematize one who marries after ordination? It offends the grace of God.

Balsamon mixes two things here. The first comment confirms that ordination of deaconesses is a thing of the past, though some monastic women may still bear the title in twelfth-century Constantinople, without ministerial function. The reason for women being excluded from the altar is given in his *Response to Mark's Questions* 35: "the monthly affliction." But the final comments refer to the Trullan Synod (692) and do presuppose the existence of deaconesses, remarking on the minimum age limit. The fifteenth canon in fact speaks only of subdeacons but then affirms that all the clergy mentioned above (presbyters, deacons, deaconesses, and subdeacons) should be deposed if ordained before the required age. Thus Balsamon witnesses to the interpretation that deaconesses were considered members of the clergy. (See text and comment on the Trullan Synod.)

On Canon 48 of the Trullan Synod [7]

It is not true that only laywomen are qualified for the diaconal office (*diakonikon*). Nuns (*monazousai*) are also qualified.

Canon 48 of the Trullan Synod (692) provides for the diaconal ordination of qualified former wives of bishops who have entered monasteries, and who were therefore previously married laywomen. Perhaps confusion arose from this canon that female monastics were not to be deaconesses. There is ample evidence from the earlier period of ascetic monastic women who are deaconesses. One wonders what is the connection between this comment and the previous one, in which Balsamon says that in his day *only* monastic women bore the title.

Responses to Mark's Questions, 35 [8]

The interrogator plays the role of posing a series of specific questions in this section regarding canonical rules for the clergy.

Question 35: The divine canons mention deaconesses (*diakonissai*). So we want to learn what were their liturgical roles (*leitourgēma*).

Response: In times past, orders (*tagmata*) of deaconesses were recognized, and they had access to the sanctuary (*bēma*). But the monthly affliction[9] banished them from the divine and holy sanctuary. In the holy church of the see of Constantinople, deaconesses were appointed to office, without any participation in the sanctuary, but attending to many church functions and directing the women's assembly according to church procedures.

Again Balsamon implies that ordination of deaconesses was once fully practiced and that at one time they exercised some kind of sacramental ministry, the meaning of access to the sanctuary. He thinks, however, that once the liturgy was established in Constantinople in the fourth century, this practice already had been terminated. One wonders if setting the minimum age of forty for ordination was not already an attempt to deal with the cultic problem of menstruation. Nevertheless, Balsamon attributes the restriction of women from the sanctuary not to any inherent inferiority but to cultic purity concerns.

Matthew Blastares, *Alphabetical Collection* 11[10]

Matthew Blastares was a monk and canonical compiler in Thessalonica in the early fourteenth century. His alphabetical collection of canons is thought to have been written in 1335. The text is important witness to later memories of female deacons in earlier centuries. Blastares obviously has no direct experience of them.

Previously there was an order (*tagma*) of female deacons (*diakonoi gynaikai*) and another of widows. The fathers ordained (*cheirotonein*) deacons those who chose the dignity of virginity and lived a chaste life, and who were at least forty years old. But out of suspicion of their tendency to be easily deceived and slide toward evil, they [the fathers] thought this age was necessary, for the apostle determined that those accepted into the order of widows should be not less than sixty,[11] reasonably so. For those who had not tasted worldly pleasure could not easily be dragged into it after so long a time. But widows, being used to the marriage bed, would rather be more inclined to passion, with their customary carnal attitudes stirred up. Therefore they delineated the age of sixty for the widow, so that since they are already growing old, the flame of passion should be extinguished.

But there were some who had not yet attained sixty years and who lived moderately, choosing lay dress. For the most part the fathers were concerned about them, deprived of husbands, and the church supported them, lest because of need, they would necessarily seek a second marriage when widowers proposed it, so as to provide in many ways a secure living. In the first letter of the great Paul to Timothy, it is clearly stated how much care widows deserve from the church.[12]

Women deacons then fulfilled a certain service among the clergy (*klēroi*), which is nearly unknown to everyone now. There are some who say that they baptized women because it was not proper for men to see undressed those being baptized who were of a certain age. Others say that they were allowed to approach the holy altar and perform nearly all the functions done by male deacons. They were forbidden access and performance of these services by later fathers because of their monthly flow that cannot be controlled. So it was legitimate in previous times for women to have access to the holy altar, and indeed for many others to seek after it, especially according to the funerary oration that the great Gregory did for his sister.

But for a woman to be deacon of the holy and unbloody sacrifice does not seem plausible to me. It is not a safe policy [literally: a saving word] that those to whom it is not conceded to teach publicly should be allowed the rank of deacon, whose work is to cleanse by their teaching the unbelievers who approach for baptism.

Like Balsamon, Blastares acknowledges that in the early church women deacons were among the clergy and that some say they exercised a sacramental ministry. He gives three reasons for the cessation of this practice, all stereotypical misogyny: women's inclination to evil and passion, menstruation, and the prohibition of women teaching publicly (see 1 Tim 2:11–12). The reference to women's attraction to evil was of course fed, if not originated, in interpretations of Genesis 3. The belief that women were more sexually passionate was commonplace and endured until the Victorian era. The idea that women baptized women may come from the *Didascalia* and *Apostolic Constitutions,* where a bishop or presbyter begins the baptism but the female deacon anoints the body of the woman being baptized.

The allusion to Gregory's sister is to Funerary Oration 8 of Gregory Nazianzen on his sister Gorgonia, a married mother who for Gregory exemplified the ideal of Christian womanhood in her virtue, asceticism, and learning. In paragraph 18, he relates that when she was afflicted with a disease of fever and paralysis, she went to the church at night, took the eucharist in her hand, demanded a cure—and got it!

The play on blood and cleanliness in the final paragraph implicitly puts women, blood, and impurity together on one side, male deacons and purity on the other, a not untypical way of thinking about women in this culture.

CONCLUSION

This brief selection of later texts is included to show the opinions of some later church authors that female deacons functioned in the church in its early centuries. In large measure, such comments were for these authors an exercise in "once upon a time." Nevertheless, they demonstrate the continuing memory in the church of what once was. The motif of blood as uncleanliness unworthy of the purity of the altar, as expressed by Matthew Blastares, was one of the most common reasons given for the exclusion of women from altar service, once the celebration of the Eucharist acquired the connections with cultic purity that accompanied the understanding that it replaced Temple sacrifice.

Notes

1. *PG* 94.707–9.
2. See *PL* 53.587ff. Some argue that the author was Arnobius the Younger. See, e.g., F. Gori, ed., *Il Praedestinatus di Arnobio il Giovane* (Rome: Institutum Patristicum Augustianum, 1999).
3. Text: Mansi, *Sacrorum Conciliorum,* 11.949, 965–66; Mayer, *Monumenta,* 40–41.

4. *PG* 104.556; Mayer, *Monumenta,* 63.

5. Text: *PG* 137.304; Mayer, *Monumenta,* 63 (partial).

6. Text: *PG* 137.441; Mayer, *Monumenta,* 64 (partial).

7. Text: *PG* 137.688; Mayer, *Monumenta,* 64.

8. Text: *PG* 138.988; Mayer, *Monumenta,* 4 (partial).

9. *Kakōsis,* a word that carried the connotation of evil done *to* someone, so it could be understood as "disaster" or "catastrophe."

10. Text: *PG* 104.1173; Mayer, *Monumenta,* 65.

11. 1 Tim 5:9.

12. 1 Tim 5:3–8.

Chapter Six

WOMEN DEACONS IN THE WEST

There is no evidence for female deacons in the West until the fifth century, about the same time, curiously, that the inscriptions about female presbyters appear. The objections to women serving at the altar, however, are from the previous century, probably under the influence of Priscillian (see chapter 8, First Synod of Saragossa).

LITERARY TEXTS

The two texts we have from the West both come from the end of the sixth century, and both refer to monastic women. From the fourth century, monasticism flourished in Gaul. In the course of the fifth and sixth centuries, distinguished and noble nunneries were established in the great Roman towns of Tours and Poitiers, as well as in or near other Frankish cities. The women who inhabited and presided over these houses were often aristocratic and accomplished. As a consequence, they often sought or were granted direct protection by the papacy, which left the local ordinary with only limited powers of oversight.

The Letter of Gregory the Great to Respecta does not specify a title of office, and the *Life of Saint Radegunda* is highly legendary. Considering known practice at the time and in the next centuries, it can be assumed that Respecta's ordination would be to the order of deaconesses, as specified in the *Life of Saint Radegunda*. This latter text needs to be compared carefully with the previous and contemporary condemnations of this practice by various councils and synods, given farther below.

Gregory to Abbess Respecta, November 15, 596[1]

One of the four "doctors of the church," Pope Gregory the Great (590–604) is often called, not without justice, "the father of the medieval papacy." His influence on the history of the medieval church—not least by the example of his own life—can be said, with no exaggeration, to have been enormous. Among the areas in which this influence was exercised most effectively and profoundly was in his promotion of monasticism. Besides having founded seven monasteries and having been a monk himself before becoming deacon, diplomat, and then pope, Gregory also wrote the Life of St. Benedict *and thus lent the saint and his* Rule *the considerable patronage of his name. Much of his voluminous correspondence is given over to the regulation of monastic life. As his letters indicate, Gregory was very active in granting certain* privilegia *to monasteries, both male and female. Here, in a letter to Abbess Respecta of the Monastery of Saint Cassian in Marseilles, Gregory, in the course of describing such privileges as he has granted to the monastery over which she presides, explains the process by which abbesses shall be selected and installed.*

> **Accordingly, to the monastery consecrated to the honor of Saint Cassian in which you are selected to preside . . . we have provided these privileges that, when the abbess of the above-mentioned monastery should die, not a stranger, but she whom the congregation has elected from its own numbers, shall be ordained (*ordinetur*). If she has been judged worthy of this ministry, the bishop of the same place shall ordain (*ordinet*) her.**

Some sixth century monasteries were exempt by papal action from the jurisdiction of the local ordinary. This is a case in point. Accordingly, the Saint Cassian monastery here referred to fell under the authority of Pope Gregory. Here, then, it is of interest not merely that the abbess is said to be "ordained" but that it is the pope himself who uses this language and that it is used as late as around 600.

Radegunda, Deacon, Venantius Fortunatus, *Life of St. Radegunda* [2]

Born around 540 in Treviso (near Venice), Venantius Fortunatus died around 600 in Poitiers, the city over which he had long presided as bishop. He was one of the last of the great Gallic poets and hymnists. In addition to leaving some eleven books of poetry, he provided some of the language and meter for the celebrated hymn, Pange Lingua. *In addition, he wrote a poetic life of St. Martin. He also wrote a* vita *to commemorate the life of Radegunda (born c. 536), whose holiness so impressed him that he resolved to become a priest. In the chapters preceding the twelfth, excerpted here, Radegunda was the official queen of Clothar I (511–58); their marriage had borne no children. At the beginning of the chapter, we learn that Radegunda's brother was killed in battle, a misfortune that, along with her marital circumstances, prompted her to "live in religion." In the episode that follows (c. 550–55), Radegunda, having left the King, approaches Médard, Bishop of Noyons and Tournai.*[3] *Frankish nobles attempt to frustrate him from veiling Radegunda, and the bishop hesitates, but Radegunda demands that he consecrate her.*

Coming to the blessed Médard at Noyon, she begged vehemently (*instanter*) that she might change her vestments and be consecrated (*consecraret*) to the Lord . . . The most holy woman, entering the sacristy and putting on monastic garb (*monachica veste*), proceeded to the altar and, speaking to the blessed Médard, said these words to him: "If you hesitate to consecrate (*consecrare*) me . . . Pastor, his sheep's soul will be required from your hand." Thunderstruck by that argument, he laid his hand on her and consecrated (*consecravit*) her a deaconess (*diaconam*).

As a piece of hagiography, this is a text not to be trusted in all its details. Nonetheless, this is likely an indication that earlier canonical prohibitions against consecrations and ordinations of deaconesses were, for a long time, simply a dead letter in Gaul and that, as late as the end of the sixth century, women were still put in office—despite the several canonical prohibitions we have considered—by a ritual act of consecration. This text is also good evidence for the powerful place held by some women in that Frankish society.[4] In addition, it suggests a connection, seen already in Constantinople at the end of the fourth century, between the status of deaconess and religious community. Note that it is said here explicitly of Radegunda that she dons monastic garb. Some of the details of her story, as well as the strong connection between her status and religious life, are strikingly paralleled in the life of Olympias of Constantinople.

INSCRIPTIONS

The Western epigraphical evidence for female deacons is slim, probably because of the vagaries of inscriptional survival, in view of the efforts of councils of the fifth and sixth centuries to eliminate them. The canons and episcopal letters below, on access of women to the altar, should also be compared. That so much effort was given to suppression has to indicate more of a custom than the few inscriptions and literary references reveal.

Accepta[5]

This inscription comes from Rukuma in Africa Proconsularis. It is carved into a slab of local limestone and is now broken.

Accepta the deacon[ess].

This tomb inscription dates from the late sixth or early seventh century. All we know of Accepta is her name and her title. This is the only female deacon attested to in Africa.

Anna [6]

The following is a sixth-century votive inscription from Rome describing a vow offered by a fairly high ranking papal official and his sister.

> By the gift of God and of the Blessed Apostle Paul, Dometius, the deacon and controller of the monies of the holy, apostolic and papal chair, together with Anna the deacon[ess], his sister offered this vow (*hoc votum*) to the blessed Paul.

Both Dometius and his sister Anna are described in this inscription using the same Latin abbreviation: DIAC. There is no question that Dometius was a deacon. About Anna's title, it is impossible to be sure. Eisen (*Women Officeholders,* 182–83) translates DIAC as "deacon." But she then acknowledges, correctly, that "Anna's title of office is abbreviated, so we cannot tell whether she was called *diacona* or *diaconissa.* Both titles are attested in the West cheek by jowl from the fifth century onward." The same ambiguity is seen in the sixth century inscription of Ausonia (see below) because the same abbreviation is used.

Ausonia [7]

This sixth-century inscription from Doclea, Dalmatia, is another of the few pieces of epigraphical evidence in Latin that has survived pointing to the existence of female deacons or deaconesses in the Latin-speaking Mediterranean world in late antiquity.

> Ausonia the deacon[ess] (*diac*) for her vow and that of her children (*filiorum*). [8]

The Latin abbreviation *diac* is, by itself, capable of two translations: deacon or deaconess. Eisen translates it "deacon"; Gryson, "deaconess." [9] In either case, the inscription "attests," as Gryson has observed, "to the deaconesses in this [i.e., Mediterranean] culture."

Theodora of Ticini [10]

This inscription comes from Ticini in St. Trinitas in Gaul.

> Here in peace rests the deaconess (*diaconissa*) Theodora of blessed memory, who lived in the world for about 48 years. She was buried here on July 22, 539.

Along with the several synodal and conciliar decrees from the fourth through sixth centuries, also translated in this collection, this inscription gives evidence for the existence and activity in Gaul of deaconesses, despite the attempts of the councils to eradicate them, limit their activities, or forbid their ordination. As this inscription demonstrates, these decrees remained at least to some degree a dead letter.

This inscription is interesting by comparison to that of Ausonia in that her title is not abbreviated. It is thus clear that Theodora held the title "deaconess," not "deacon."

CANONS AND COMMENTS ON CHURCH PRACTICE

The earliest references to female deacons in the West are in decrees of church councils trying to suppress the practice that had probably arrived from the East, where it was flourishing at this time. After two condemnations, the Second Council of Orleans (533) acknowledged the existence of female deacons but wanted to put a stop to the practice. Yet even by the eleventh century a pope not only acknowledged but confirmed the practice in Portugal!

Council of Orange Canon 26[11]

The Council of Orange was convoked in November 441. (It is not to be confused with the more famous Synod of Orange, which occurred in 529 and dealt almost exclusively with issues of free will and grace.) With seventeen bishops from three provinces in attendance, it produced thirty canons on a wide variety of matters. Several of these deal with the status and conduct of women in consecrated office. For example, one decreed that widows should make a profession of chastity and wear the proper dress. Another recommended that those who had broken their profession of virginity be compelled to do penance. Finally, Canon 26 deals with deaconesses, in particular the question of whether they should be ordained.

> Female deacons (*Diaconae*) are by no means (*omnimodis*) to be ordained (*ordinandae*). If there are any who have already been ordained (*si quae iam sunt*), let them submit their heads to the benediction (*benedictioni . . . capita submittant*) that is granted to the laity (*quae populo impenditur*).

This canon is both fascinating and frustratingly tantalizing. First of all, it, like other canons produced in the fourth and fifth centuries is not certain the irregularity it condemns is even occurring (*si . . .*). Still, it seems quite likely that the forbidden practice had been occurring in the early fifth century in Gaul. That would account both for the canon having been promulgated at all and for its force: women deacons are *by no means* to be ordained.[12] Quite obviously, the bishops assembled at Orange were anxious to preserve the distinction between the male clergy and the laity, of which, in their minds, the female deacons made up a part. The recommendation to receive the blessing given to the laity is thus intended as a ritual act intended to undo their elevation to the clergy and to resituate them with the people, where they belong. The text is wholly interested in the status of widows and how it is symbolized; it says nothing about function.

The forbidding of ordinations in this Western province is of special interest because it is unambiguously clear from several sources that, in the East, female deacons were being ordained publicly at the same time by imposition of hands and prayer of the bishop and using prayers similar to those used in other sorts of ordinations. In other words, in the East female deacons were considered wholly part of the clergy in the fifth century—probably the very understanding the fathers at Orange were at pains to avert in the West.

Council of Epaon Canon 21[13]

This Frankish council was convoked in 517 under the presidency of Bishop Avitus of Vienne (d. 520), just six years after the letter written by three Gallic bishops was written. It enacted a decree that forbade the consecration of altars made of any material except stone. This decree may have indicated new opposition to the ordination of female deacons. The council also forbade Christians to dine with Jews (again, an indication that this was probably taking place). In addition, it dealt with ways in which heretics were to be received back into the church, in which context it discussed the imposition of hands. For our purposes, it is this discussion that is of highest interest because it is only this form of blessing that the assembled bishops wished deaconesses to receive. As is apparent, the bishops were uncomfortable with the term "deaconess" itself.

> We wholly abolish throughout our region the consecration (*consecrationem*) of widows, who are called deacons (*diaconas*); if they wish to convert, let them receive only the penitential benediction.

This canon indicates that Canon 26 of the Council of Orange, which forbade the ordination of female deacons and required them to submit to the benediction given to the laity, was not wholly successful. Evidently, eight decades later women were still being ordained in Gaul, as the term *consecratio* used here is probably the equivalent of *ordinatio* used in Orange.[14] Both terms indicate blessing in a solemn ritual which made women part of the clergy and gave them recognition as deacons. The bishops here demand that they receive only the blessing given by those who wished publicly to embrace (or "convert to") the ascetic, or penitential, life and who received blessing by imposition of hands. In this way, they seem also to wish to abolish the female diaconate and thus to exclude women from the clergy.

Second Council of Orléans Canons 17 and 18[15]

This was the second of the six national councils in the Merovingian period held in Orléans. Twenty-five bishops attended in June 533 under the presidency of Childebert. This council, like others convoked in Gaul in the fifth and sixth centuries, dealt with a variety of matters. Among other things, it forbade the marriage of Jews and Christians (as always, an indication that such was likely taking place) and put outside ecclesiastical communion anyone who ate flesh sacrificed to idols. Two of the canons treated matters regarding women deacons.

Canon 17.

Women who, to this point, have, against its interdiction by the canons, received the benediction of the diaconate (*benedictionem diaconatus*), if they be proven to have again entered into marriage, are to be banished from communion.

Canon 18.

It has been decided that, from now on, no women may be given the diaconal benediction (*diaconalis benedictio*) on account of the fragility of their sex.

The "interdiction of the canons" refers presumably to the decrees of Orange and Epaon, which have clearly been ignored. The bishops assembled here are especially concerned about women who have been consecrated into the diaconate and left it for a second marriage; they are excommunicate. So seriously did the bishops regard the "fragile" female tendency to abscond from the diaconate for marriage that, in Canon 18, they did away with the diaconal benediction altogether. It is Gryson's opinion that it is not just a rite being eliminated here but that the bishops are attempting to abolish an entire ecclesiastical category or office.[16] The fragility to which they refer thus means the difficulty of living out consecrated life in the world rather than in a cloister, which would presumably protect them from the "temptation" of marriage.

Pope Benedict VIII to Benedict, Bishop of Porto[17]

This letter was written in 1017 by Pope Benedict VIII (1012–24) to the Bishop of Porto in northwest Portugal, the city renown for its red wine. The letter confirms certain possessions (e.g., two fishermen, an island with two churches, and so forth) and privileges to the bishop. Among these are the following:

In the same way, we concede and confirm to you and to your successors in perpetuity every episcopal ordination (*ordinationem episcopalem*), not only of presbyters but also of deacons or deaconesses (*diaconissis*) or subdeacons.

In spite of all the earlier efforts of Western councils to eliminate deaconesses, it is remarkable to find a pope, early in the eleventh century not only recognizing the office of deaconess but acknowledging that the rite of initiation is an ordination.

CONCLUSION

Though the evidence for female deacons in the West is little and late, it must represent only a small selection of what was really happening, as witnessed by the concerted efforts of councils to stop whatever practice there was. It does not seem that the female diaconate in the West took any clear shape. It probably consisted of local adaptations of what people in the time and place knew of the office in the East, sometimes being confused with an order of widows. Yet in the eleventh century, a pope could confirm the office with no hint of doubt as to its propriety. Apparently the office of the diaconate for women definitely existed in the West by the fifth century, but was not widely accepted.

Notes

1. Mayer, *Monumenta,* 49–50; *Gregorii I Papae Registrum epistolarum. Libri I–VII,* ed. C. Rodenburg *Monumenta Germaniae historica (MGH). Epistolae saeculi XIII e regestis,* (Berlin: Weidemanns, 1883–94), 1.454; *PL* 77.866.

2. *Venanti Honori Clementiani Fortunati presybteri italici Opera pedestria,* ed. Bruno Krusch, MGH Antiquissimi (Berlin: Weidemanns, 1885), 4.2, 41.

3. See Gregory of Tours, *History of the Franks,* 4.19.

4. For a learned treatment of that topic, see S. F. Wemple, *Women in Frankish Society* (Philadelphia: University of Pennsylvania Press, 1981). Wemple mentions Radegunda on p. 142.

5. *AE* 1981.881, p. 249.

6. Text in C.M. Kaufmann, *Handbuch der altchristlichen Epigraphik* (Freiburg, 1917) 294; Eisen, *Women Officeholders,* 192–83. See the brief, though unilluminating, discussion in Martimort, *Deaconesses,* 202.

7. Text in *CIL* 3.13845 and *ILCV* 1.1239, also with discussion and bibliography in Eisen, *Women Officeholders,* 183–84; Gryson, *Ministry of Women,* 91 and 153 n. 158; and brief allusion in Martimort, *Deaconesses,* 202.

8. +*Ausonia diac*

9. Gryson, *Ministry of Women,* 91; Eisen, *Women Officeholders,* 183.

10. *CIL* 5.6467; *ILCV* 1.1238. Discussion in Eisen, *Women Officeholders,* 184; Gryson, *Ministry of Women,* 91, 153 n. 158; and a brief allusion in Martimort, *Deaconesses,* 202.

11. *Concilia Galliae, 314–506,* in *CCL* 148 (1963): 84.

12. See Martimort's comment: "And while the Council of Nîmes seemed to be aiming at a practice proper to somewhere else and not very clearly spelled out, the bishops of the Council of Orange were reproving an abuse much closer to home and perhaps existing within their own

territory, an abuse, moreover, that involved a member of the hierarchy, since this was an ordination" (*Deaconesses,* 193–94).

13. *CCL* 148a (1963): 163–65.

14. Though Martimort disagrees, observing that the council avoided the term *ordinatio,* he thinks intentionally (*Deaconesses,* 198). Gryson is closer to the mark when he notes: "The terms *benedictio* and *consecratio,* and their corresponding verbs, appear frequently as synonyms of *ordinatio* and *ordinare* in texts of this period (*Ministry of Women,* 107).

15. *CCL* 148a (1963): 64–71.

16. *Ministry of Women,* 107.

17. *PL* 139.1921; Mayer, *Monumenta,* 52. The concession was confirmed by Pope Leo IX (1049–54) in virtually the same words. See *PL* 143.602.

Chapter Seven

WOMEN DEACONS

Testamentum Domini Nostri Jesu Christi and Related Texts

 The *TD* is an early Christian church order, depending literarily on some form of Hippolytus' *Apostolic Tradition,* as well as an apocalypse and other sources.[1] It purports to include the instructions Christ gave to the Twelve after the Resurrection, on issues of ecclesiastical order, architecture, daily prayer, and other matters. The date, occasion, authorship, and provenance of this text are all somewhat unclear. Probably written in Greek in the late fourth or (as Harnack suggested) the fifth century,[2] it survives today in Syriac, Ethiopic,[3] and Arabic. Where it was written is unclear, but scholars have proposed Syria, Egypt, and Asia Minor, with the last perhaps being the likeliest possibility. At the end of the nineteenth century, it was edited and translated into Latin by the distinguished Orientalist and Syrian Catholic patriarch Monsignor Ignatius Ephraem II Rahmani.[4] The nine texts from the *TD* presented here are translated from the Latin of this nineteenth-century edition.[5]

These texts do not fit into any other categories. The *TD* mentions deaconesses, widows, and female presbyters, and in it all three groups are clearly distinguished from one another. Unlike in any other church order, it gives the widows the greatest responsibility and honor. The other two texts included bear some relationship to the *TD.*

Testamentum Domini 1.19

In the following text, taken from the part of the first book treating the constitution of the church, is discussed the seating and placement of widows and of deaconesses in relation to other officials in the liturgy.

Let the position (*aedes*) of the bishop be near to the place that is called the front stage (*atrium*).

Likewise, let the place of the widows,[6] who are said to have precedence in sitting (*praecedentiam sessionis*) be in the same place (*ibidem*).

Let the place of the presbyters and deacons be behind the baptistry (*post bapisterium*).

Let the deaconesses,[7] however, remain near the main door of the church (*apud portam domus dominicae*).

In this text, as in others in the *TD,* widows enjoy a prominent role in the ecclesiastical community and, indeed, are venerated by it. Gryson has correctly observed that "no other document attributes to women a rank as high in the ecclesiastical hierarchy as that of the widows."[8] Here that rank is expressed by their physical location in the liturgical assembly. Unlike even the male presbyters, they stand and sit in the atrium of the church. Conversely, the deaconesses in the *TD* have almost no role. As Martimort has observed, "deaconesses occupied a very humble place in this scheme of things."[9] They place themselves at the main door of the church, and their functions seem to be limited to greeting and overseeing the entry into church of the female congregants. Thus, an overall comparison with the *AC* is quite instructive. Indeed, the situation imagined there, with respect to women and ministry, inverts the one described in the *TD.* The latter text gives far, far more attention to the functions, status, and qualities expected of a widow.

Testamentum Domini 1.23[10]

On the Sabbath let [the bishop] offer three breads as a symbol of the Trinity; on Sunday, four breads as an image of the Gospel.

When he offers the sacrifice, let the veil of the sanctuary be drawn closed, as a sign of the wandering of the ancient people, and let him offer it within the veil with the presbyters, deacons, canonical widows (*viduis canonicis*), subdeacons, deaconesses (*diaconissis*), readers, [and] those having spiritual gifts (*charismata*).

Let the bishop stand first in the middle, and the presbyters immediately behind him on both sides; the widows (*viduae*) behind the presbyters who are on the left side; the deacons behind the presbyters who are on the right side; and behind these the readers; and behind the readers the subdeacons; and behind the subdeacons, the deaconesses (*diaconissae*).

During the sacrifice of the eucharist, the *TD* imagines that a veil will be drawn. Included within the veil are all the categories and members of the clergy. Here widows and deaconesses are both mentioned, and, indeed, the *TD* considers both to be members of the clergy. There is, however, a strict vertical hierarchy in the oblation, and the widows seems to suffer a "slip." Whereas in 1.19 they occupy a position adjacent to the bishop, here they occupy a place behind the members of the three major male orders. That is, their place in the hierarchy seems to shift during the celebration of the eucharist. At the same time, the deaconess, who has almost no role beyond that of greeting women at the door of the church, is brought within the veil and, though mentioned last, she experiences an "upward" shift, so to speak, and is explicitly brought into the penumbra of the clergy. All are clearly separated from the laity.

Testamentum Domini 1.23 [2][11]

Let the clergy (*clerus*)[12] receive first in the following order:
Bishop, then presbyters, afterwards deacons, then widows, then readers, then subdeacons, then those who enjoy spiritual gifts, and the newly baptized and then children.
The laity (*populus*) in this order: the elderly, the male virgins, then the rest.[13]
The women: first the deaconesses, then the others.

Here the widows are again—and as explicitly as anywhere in the *TD*—included within the clergy (*clerus*). However, they receive only after the members of the three major male orders. But they are placed ahead of the readers, subdeacons, and charismatics. Oddly, this text seems to exclude the deaconesses from the clergy. Though they receive first among the women, they are placed with the laity. This is perhaps consistent with the generally diminished role they exercise in comparison with their counterparts in the *AC*. But it seems in tension with the decision to include them with the clergy in the oblation described in 1.23.

Testamentum Domini 1.34 [14]

In the church, let there be designated (*noti sint*) twelve presbyters, seven deacons, four subdeacons, and three widows having precedence of seating (*pracedentiam sessionis*).

The *TD* specifies the number of presbyters and deacons. It is a measure of their importance in the community that the number of widows is also indicated.

Testamentum Domini 1.35 (The Prayer of the Deacon)[15]

For the bishops let us pray . . .
For the presbyters we pray . . .
For the deacons we pray . . .

> For the female presbyters (*presbyteris* [*feminis*])[16] we pray, that the Lord may hear their supplications and, by the grace of the Spirit, perfectly keep their hearts and aid their work.
>
> For the subdeacons, readers, and deaconesses (*diaconissis*) we pray, that the Lord may allow them to receive the reward (*mercedem*) of their patience.

Eisen argues that the term presbyterae here is a reference to women presbyters.[17] It may be true, as Eisen suggests, that in the East in the fifth century, "women presided over communities as presbyters or presbytides." But neither this text, nor any text in the *TD*, lends support to such a conclusion. Both the entire context of the *TD* and the particular structure of the passage under consideration here suggest quite clearly that the *TD* was not imagining women with presbyteral status and powers (i.e., presidential and liturgical powers). However, the female presbyters are members of the clergy who rank (here as in *TD* 1.34) on the fourth rung of the clerical hierarchy (beneath the bishops, presbyters and deacons). Prayer is named everywhere in the *TD* as their primary work. They are to be distinguished from the widows in the congregation, as is especially clear in *TD* 2.19, where during the paschal feast they pray and rest with the bishop until dawn while the widows remain in the temple.

Testamentum Domini 1.40 (On Ordination of Widows)[18]

> Let a widow be ordained[19] (*ordinetur*) who is chosen (*eligitur*), who for a long time has been without a husband, and who has been induced by many men to be married; who nevertheless on account of her faith has not wished to be joined to a man. Otherwise, let her not yet be chosen (*nondum eligenda est*) but be proven for a time (*sed ad tempus probetur*), if she was pious, if she educated the children she had in holiness, if she has not taught them the wisdom of the world, if she has formed them in the love of the sacred law and the church, if she has been assiduous in prayer, if she has shown herself humble, if she has gladly aided the afflicted, if it has been revealed to the saints concerning her, if she has not neglected the saints, if she has ministered with all her power, if she is fit to bear and sustain the yoke (*iugum*). Next, let her be one who prays without ceasing and perfect in every way, fervid in spirit and having the eyes of her heart open to all things. Let her be kind at all times, loving simplicity, possessing nothing in this world, but continually bearing and carrying around the cross, which abolishes every evil, persevering at the altar night and day, gladly and secretly devoting herself to her work. If she has one or two or three associates of one mind in my name, I will be among them. Let her be perfect in the Lord, as one visited by the Spirit. Let her accomplish those things made known to her with fear and diligence. Let her exhort dis-

obedient women (*mulieres inobedientes*), let her instruct the ignorant,[20] convert the guilty, and let her teach those, that they be chaste, and let her examine carefully the deaconesses. Let her make known to those who enter how and who they ought to be, and let her exhort those who remain outside. To those who hear, let her patiently offer counsel concerning those things that are good. Let her not speak to the disobedient after three admonitions (*admonitiones*). Let her foster those who long to be in virginity or purity.

Let her correct modestly and peacefully those who are contrary. With everyone, let her be pacific. Let her reprehend privately those saying superfluous and vain things. If they refuse to listen, let her take with her a woman advanced in age, or let her take the matter to a hearing of the bishop (*ad aures episcopi*). Let her be silent in church and assiduous in prayer. Let her visit the sick women, every Sunday taking with her one or two deacons to help them.[21]

Her supplications to God will be accepted, and they will be the sacrifice (*holocaustum*) and altar[22] of God. For those who ministered rightly (*probe*) will be glorified by the archangels. But those who are intemperate, loquacious, curious, raging, inebriate, wicked, or too fond of pleasures (*vehementer diligentes delectationes*)—the likenesses (*simulacra*) of their souls, which abide in the presence of the Father of Light, will perish and be led away to dwell in darkness.

Their works, which indeed are visible, ascend to the highest, easily thrust them into the abyss, so that after the transformation and destruction of this world, the likeness of their souls will rise in testimony against them and impede them from gazing upward. Indeed, the image or type of every soul stands in the presence of God before the foundation of the world.

Therefore, let her be chosen who can go against the holy phials.[23] From them are the twelve presbyters (*presbyteri*) who praise my Father in Heaven, who receive the prayers of every pure soul and offer them to the Most High as a sweet aroma.

This is a complete chapter of the *TD*. It is dedicated solely to the criteria for ordination or appointment, and the contemplative and prayerful roles the widow is to assume and exemplify (some lifted from 1 Tim 5). First of all, the widow is explicitly said to be "ordained" to her office. As Gryson has pointed out, the *TD* does not distinguish (as does the *AC*) between "to ordain" and "to appoint." In addition, the widow is said to be "ordained" in precisely the same way as other major clerics. In the previous chapter, for example, the deacon is "ordained" in the same way as the widow.[24] As Gryson has pointed out, that the widow was "chosen" almost certainly implies (as it does with bishop, priest and deacon) "an election in good and due form, implying inquiry and examination."[25]

Second, the ideal of the once-married (*univiram*) is celebrated here as in other texts in this collection, with the codicil that the prospective widow is explicitly to have rejected offers of marriage "for the faith." In this way, she demonstrates her dedication to her pastoral ministry. Third, the text is unusually receptive to the notion of both the community and the widow herself functioning as bearers of revelation from the Holy Spirit. Indeed, revelation to "the saints" seems to be a criterion of appointment and a sign of community approval, and the widow herself is expected to be "visited" by the Holy Spirit, which, again, marks her as favored among the women in the community. Fourth, the text is unusually detailed about her duties, especially pedagogical and exhortatory ones regarding women in the community. Here her duties overlap with those imagined for deaconesses in the *AC*. She is, so to speak, an auxiliary bishop for women. Finally, the text is quite detailed on her exemplary role as an ascetic and contemplative and imagines that it will not be an easy one. She must be fit and capable of sustaining a heavy yoke, bearing constantly a cross of poverty and incessant prayer. In this latter connection, she is connected both physically and symbolically with the altar.

Testamentum Domini 1.41 (Prayer of the Widows Who Sit in Front)[26]

As already mentioned, the TD *includes prayers for the ordination of all the clergy, including women clergy. Following are the instructions for the ordination of a widow and the prayer the bishop says in ordaining her.*

The ordination (*ordinatio*)[27] of a widow should occur like this. While she is praying at the entrance of the altar and looking downward, let the bishop say quietly (*submisse*), so that only the priests may hear:

Holy and lofty God, who sees humble women, who has chosen the infirm and the powerful,[28] who has created, O honored one, even these who are scorned, impart, O Lord, a spirit of power upon this your servant,[29] and in your truth strengthen her so that, fulfilling your commandment and laboring in your sanctuary, she may be for you an honored vessel and may give glory on the day, O Lord, on which you will glorify your poor ones.

Give to her power of happily practicing the teachings prescribed by you in the rule of your handmaiden. Give to her, O Lord, a spirit of humility, of power and patience and kindness, so that she might, bearing your burden with ineffable joy, sustain her labors. Truly, Lord God, who knows our infirmity, perfect your handmaiden for the glory of your house; strengthen her for edification and as a shining example. God, sanctify her, make her wise and comfort her, because, God our Father, your kingdom is blessed and glorious . . .

The people: Amen.

The same Syriac word for ordination, *mettasrhanuta,* is used for bishops, presybters, deacons, and subdeacons. This is another piece of evidence of the exalted role the widow enjoys in the community. However, see the opinion of Martimort, who observes that it is an "error to speak of the ordination of widows," as the laying on of hands, in his view, is reserved only for the three sacerdotal orders.[30] The emphasis on "things scorned" seems in odd tension with the venerable role the widow elsewhere enjoys in the document. Here, her role and ideal are emphasized, as well as qualities we have already seen celebrated: her capacity for praying at the altar; bearing the burden of poverty, solitariness, and ceaseless prayer; and serving in an exemplary capacity for the community.

Testamentum Domini 1.42 [31]

This chapter, which follows the one furnishing instructions on the ordination of a widow, describes how she is to conduct herself as she enters her new life and ministry.

> After the widow has been instituted in this way, let her be solicitous of nothing: but let her be by herself (*solitaria*), and to occupy herself with the supplications of piety. For the foundation of sanctity and of life for the widow consists in solitude (*in solitudine*), so that she might love no others except the God of gods, the Father who is in Heaven.

> At the established hours, let her offer her praises by herself, at night and daybreak.

> If she is menstruating (*menstrua*), let her remain in the nave and not approach the altar, not as if she were polluted (*non quasi sit polluta*) but on account of the honor of the altar (*propter honorem altaris*); and after she has fasted and washed herself, let her persevere at the altar. In the days of Pentecost, let her not fast. In the paschal feast, let her give to the poor from those things that she possesses, and let her wash herself and pray thus.

> When she gives thanks or offers her praises, if she has friends who are virgins of one mind (*unanimes*) with her, it would be best if they prayed with her in responding, "Amen." If not, though, let her pray alone by herself either in church or at home, above all at midnight (*media nocte*).

> The times in which it is necessary for her to offer her praises are Saturday (*Sabbatum*), the Lord's Day, either Easter or Epiphany or Pentecost. For the remainder of the time, let her give thanks in humility with psalms, canticles and meditations; and let her labor in this way.

> The Most High will indeed sanctify them [the widows] and will remit all the sins imputed to them and their ignorance. My heavenly Father shall comfort them and shall enlighten their faces, as the faces of sacred vessels, and they will shine in my glory on the day of reward.

From this text it is clear that the main function of the widow is solitary prayer, for which she needs the capacity of perseverance at the altar. Rahmani observes that this section on the menstruant is absent from the Copto-Arabic version.[32] While concerns for the purity of the altar precincts prevail here, it is notable that the menstruating widow is not regarded as polluted. More importantly, this text seems to indicate that the canonical age of sixty was moot, and that there were younger once-married widows imagined for this community. This text is one of the few in the *TD* that enumerates the rewards to be showered on the widows, which include (despite the unkind reference to ignorance, again oddly in tension with the pedagogical role widows are expected to assume with women) remission of sin and the promise of eternal glory. Again, these are vivid indicators of the exalted status of these women in the community.

Testamentum Domini 2.4 [33]

This text comes from a chapter on the instruction and conduct of catechumens about to be baptized.

> Let women not ornament themselves . . . lest the young men and church be snared; but let them behave with modesty and with knowledge (*scienter*): otherwise, let them be admonished by the widows who sit in front (*a viduis habentibus praecedentiam sessionis*).

The pedagogical and exhortatory role exercised by the widows that we have seen elsewhere (e.g., 1.40) is re-emphasized here. This text, too, witnesses to the powerful respect with which these ordained women were regarded and their particular role with women congregants and catechumens.

Testamentum Domini 2.8 [34]

This text, absent from his sources, is added by the author of the TD. *As Martimort has observed, because this text is not present in the* DA *and is inserted by the author of the* TD, *it may reflect actual practice in his community.*[35]

> Let the women [to be baptized] be anointed (*ungantur*) by the widows who sit in front, while the presbyter recites over them the formula. And also at the baptism let those widows receive the women wrapped in a veil while the bishop offers the formulas of profession; and again while he offers the formulas of renunciation.

Here the presence of the female ministers—in this case, widows, not deaconesses—is compulsory, and the concern for propriety and decency is especially pronounced. Martimort correctly observes that this is one of the texts in which the *TD* reveals its special preoccupation "with the problems of decency and modesty that arose in connection with the baptism of women." Here, the provisions are "much more strict" than in, for example, the *DA*, as the involvement of the widows is compulsory, as is the wrapping in the veil.[36] Notice that the ministry is entrusted here, not to the deaconess, as in the *DA*, but to the widow.

Testamentum Domini 2.19 (Order of Dismissal during the Paschal Feast)[37]

Let the faithful, having been dismissed, go according to their orders.
Let the women go with their husbands . . .
Let the widows[38] remain until the dawn (tempus matutinum) in the temple, having food there.
Let the female presbyters (*presbyterae*)[39] remain with the bishop until the dawn, praying and resting.

Notable here is that everything about the paschal liturgy is carefully orchestrated and organized, even the dismissal, which proceeds in orderly and regular fashion. The widows (clearly distinguished from the women in the populace), pre-supplied with food, do not leave the service but remain in the church in prayer. As in *TD* 1.35, the widows are distinguished from the female presbyters. The latter have a higher place in the congregational hierarchy and are seated in a place of prominence during the liturgy. In a context such as this, *presbyterae* could simply be translated "elderly women," but their special role alongside the bishop suggests a special status and role. As everywhere in the *TD*, they are found in prayer, their primary responsibility as female presbyters in the congregation.

Canon of Clement

This very mysterious text was translated by J. A. Assemani into Latin from a Syriac text of unknown date—probably composed sometime between the late third and early fifth century—called the Nomokanon *of Bar Hebraeus.[40] It is thus clear on linguistic grounds alone that it was not written by the first-century Roman presbyter Clement, who wrote, if at all, in Greek.[41] In a chapter section devoted to the constitution of deaconesses, the Syriac author attributed the canons of his work to the apostles Peter and Andrew and, here, to Clement. This is just one of the many texts in the ancient church attributed to Clement of Rome in order to enhance its authority.*

Let that widow be chosen who has remained for a long time without a husband, even though she has been coerced (*compressa*). If she has not consented but persevered in prayer and chastity, let her be ordained (*ordinetur*), constituted on the steps of the altar; and let the bishop pray upon her head in silence the appropriate prayer. When she has been instituted, let her pray without ceasing. And if she is menstruating, let her remain in the nave (*in templo*) and not approach the altar, not because she is unclean (*immunda*) but for the honor of the altar.[42] Afterward when she has fasted and has been taken away, let her be assiduous in the paschal feast, let her wash and thus pray. In the days of Pentecost, let her not fast.

It is clear on nonlinguistic grounds as well that the document does not go back to the first century. As Mayer points out, it bears some resemblance to a fifth-century Monophysite document entitled "Constitutions of the Egyptian Church."[43] But it also bears an even more striking resemblance to, perhaps even dependence on, *TD* 1.40 and 1.42. Thus, there is some complex literary relationship and dependence, unlikely direct, between these texts. It is possible that this text, too, depends on some form of the *AT*. What makes that hypothesis complicated (among other things) is that in *AT* 11 it is quite explicitly stated that when a widow is appointed, "she is not ordained" but chosen. Here she is most definitely ordained, as she is in the *TD*, with the imposition of hands that is reserved for the three major male orders in the *TD*. The anxiety about the menstruating widow's proximity to the altar, seen also in the *TD*, suggests that the canonical age of sixty was not being observed and that younger widows were being ordained.

Constitutions of the Egyptian Church 37.1–6[44]

The provenance, authorship, literary genealogy and other aspects of this Egyptian Church Order are all in doubt. It seems to have originated in Monophysite communities sometime in the fifth century. That it depended on earlier church orders is also not in doubt. It seems to bear some literary relationship to some form of Hippolytus' AT, perhaps the Coptic "Canons of Hippolytus," as well as to the TD and Book 8 of the AC. Though it was probably written originally in Greek, an ancient Latin translation of the document was discovered in 1900. The following canons include instruction on the appointment, character, and function of appointed widows.

1. If a widow is appointed (*constituitur*), let her not be ordained (*ordinetur*), but chosen (*eligatur*) by name.
2. If her husband died a long time previously, let her be appointed.
3. If, however, not much time has passed since her husband died, do not place trust in her.
4. Even if she is advanced in age (*aetate provecta*), let her be proved for a time; often those passions grow old with him who gives a place in himself for them.

    5. Let a widow be appointed by word only (*verbo tantum*) and with the other [widows then] be united, nor let her be blessed by imposition of hands (*nec vero manus ei imponatur*) because she does not offer the sacrifice, nor does she perform the liturgy (*quia non oblationem offert neque liturgiam facit*).

    6. The clergy are ordained (*Ordinatio fit in clero*). However, let the widow be appointed (*constituatur*) for prayer, which is common to all.

One of the major differences between these *Constitutions* and the *AT* is grammatical mood. What was indicative in Hippolytus becomes subjunctive jussive here. In other words, what is described in the *AT* is commanded here. "Let her not be ordained" (*AT:* "she is not ordained"); "let the widow be appointed" (*AT:* "the widow is appointed"). It is difficult what to make of this grammatical change, if anything. Perhaps the author simply wanted to underline more emphatically than Hippolytus that widows were not to be ordained. Perhaps, alternatively, widows were being ordained in his community, and he wanted to stop the practice. These *Constitutions* also differ from the *AT* in explicitly indicating, in Canon 6, the rationale for ordaining clergy and not widows. (In the *AT*, Hippolytus makes the rationale implicit.) The widow is simply named and appointed—not ordained—and she is not ordained because she does not offer the eucharistic sacrifice or have any liturgical function. Throughout, there is a marked distinction between *ordinatio* and *constitutio*—that is, between ordination and appointment—and the distinction has to do with involvement in liturgical sacrifice and service. Thus, whatever rite marks her induction onto the roll of widows, it is not the imposition of hands. For the author of these *Constitutions*, the widow's sole function is prayer, and, as he observes in the sixth canon, this is a function she shares with all Christians. She differs from them only in the intensity of her dedication to it.

CONCLUSION

To find discussion of ordained widows so late in the development of church office is surprising. The *Testamentum Domini* and a few related texts must stand independently of earlier, and even contemporaneous, legislation because they witness to the unusual customs of a group of Eastern churches that had several different types of office for women, including widow, presbyter, and deaconess, thus perhaps being related in some way to the Church structures revealed in the *Acts of Philip* and the *Martyrdom of Matthew* (see chapter 8). Another unusual aspect is that in these texts widows have higher status than deaconesses. As was said in chapter 1, distinctions must always be made among membership in the clergy, ordination, liturgical ministry, and sacramental ministry. It does not seem that any of these women exercised sacramental ministry, yet some of them clearly belonged among the clergy and were ordained.

Notes

1. *Testamentum Domini Nostri Jesu Christi,* ed. and trans. Ignatius Ephraem II Rahmani (Mainz: F. Kirchheim, 1899), 27. Rahmani used three Syrian texts, and the Syrian edition he produced is also included on facing pages with the Latin. When interpreting texts like the *TD* and other ancient church orders, it is well to remember Bernard Botte's warning that such documents reflect the ideals of the compiler at least as much, probably more than, contemporary ecclesiastical realities. See *L'Orient Syrien: Revue trimestrielle d'études et de recherches sur les Eglises de langue syriaque,* vol. 5 (Paris, 1960), 346.

2. "Vorläufige Bemerkungen zu dem jüngst syrisch und lateinisch publizierten 'Testamentum Domini nostri Jesu Christi,'" in *Sitzungberichte der Berliner Adademie der Wissenschaften* (1899): 878–91. Rahmani unconvincingly proposes a much earlier date (*Testamentum Domini,* xliii, xlviii).

3. *Testamentum Domini éthiopen,* ed. and trans. R. Beylot (Louvain: Peeters, 1984).

4. Rahmani's proposed date of the second century for the *TD* has nonetheless not received wide acceptance among scholars.

5. Neither this nor any other edition meets the standard of a modern critical edition. The Arabic text is not edited. See the English translation of selections from Syriac and Greek, with excellent, up-to-date introduction and notes by Grant Sperry-White, *The Testamentum Domini: A Text for Students, with Introduction, Translation, and Notes* (Bramcote: Grove, 1991). The Latin of all the translations has been checked against the Syriac with the help of J. F. Coakley of the Department of Near Eastern Languages and Civilization, Harvard University.

6. Syriac: *armlāthā.*

7. Syriac: *mshamshānyāthā.*

8. *Ministry of Women,* 66.

9. *Deaconesses,* 49.

10. Rahmani, *Testamentum Domini,* 35, 37.

11. Rahmani, *Testamentum Domini,* 47.

12. Syriac: *kāhnē.*

13. I.e., the rest of the men.

14. Rahmani, *Testamentum Domini,* 83.

15. Rahmani, *Testamentum Domini,* 85, 87.

16. Syriac: *qashishāthā.*

17. *Women Officeholders,* 125–27.

18. Rahmani, *Testamentum Domini,* 95, 97.

19. Syriac: *tettasrah.*

20. I.e., ignorant women.

21. I.e., the sick women.

22. Syriac: *madbha.*

23. Rahmani speculates that the Syriac translator confused two Greek words here—φιαλη and φυλη—and that the sentence should read, not *obviam ire phialis sanctis* but *obviam ire turmis sanctis*—"to go against the holy squadrons" (*Testamentum Domini,* 97 n. 2).

24. Ibid., 91–95. This is observed, too, by Gryson, *Ministry of Women,* 64–65.

25. *Ministry of Women,* 66.

26. Rahmani, *Testamentum Domini,* 99.

27. Syriac: *mettasrhanuta.*

28. The "infirm" and "powerful" are in the masculine plural in the Syriac.

29. The Syriac word here would be translated into English "handmaid."

30. *Deaconesses,* 51.

31. Rahmani, *Testamentum Domini,* 101.

32. Ibid., 100 n. 2.

33. Ibid., 119.

34. Ibid., 129, 131.

35. *Deaconesses,* 47.

36. Ibid., 47–49.

37. Rahmani, *Testamentum Domini,* 141.

38. Syriac: *armlāthā.*

39. Syriac: *qashishatha,* literally "female elders," not widows or presbyters.

40. The Syriac text is edited by Paul Bedjan, *Nomocanon Gregorii Barhebraei* (Paris, 1898). There is reason to believe that Assemani's translation from the Syriac is less than adequate. See *Dictionnaire de droit canonique* 2, s.v. "Bar Hebraeus," where Carlo de Clercq calls it "assez defecteuse." For this information, as well as other helpful details regarding this text, we are grateful to William Monroe of Brown University. For help in checking the Latin against the Syriac of the Bedjan edition, we are grateful to J. F. Coakley of Harvard University.

41. Though Mayer unequivocally identifies Clement both as the author and as the fourth pope of Rome, (*Monumenta,* 5 n.1).

42. See *Scriptorum veterum nova collectio e vaticanis codicibus,* ed. Angelo Mai (Rome: Typis Vaticanis, 1825–),10/2, 7.7, which contains part of the text, on the menstruating widow, that Mayer does not include in her edition.

43. Mayer, *Monumenta,* 5 n.1.

44. *Die allgemeine Kirchenordnung, fruhchristliche Liturgien und kirchliche Uberlieferung,* ed. Theodor Schermann (Paderborn: F. Schoeningh, 1914–16) 1.52–53; *DA* 2.105–6.

Chapter Eight

WOMEN PRESBYTERS

The title of presbyter is always subject to contextual interpretation. Whether of males or females, it can refer to an elderly person, as for example the *presbyteroi* and *presbyterai* in 1 Tim 5:1–2, while the *presbyteroi* of 5:17 are probably in some position of authority. Moreover, the female title *presbytera* can also sometimes mean the wife of a male presbyter. As we see below, however, sometimes neither is the case.

IN THE EAST

While synods and councils, both East and West, repeatedly condemned the practice of women presbyters, the epigraphical and literary evidence suggests their ongoing existence, even if in small numbers. Of the few references presented here, more are from the West than from the East. The lines between "orthodoxy" and "heresy" cannot be finely drawn in these examples, except where a known group is identified (e.g., the Montanists by Epiphanius and Augustine).

LITERARY TEXTS, CANONS, AND LEGENDS

The Council of Laodicea and the Church Father Epiphanius condemned the establishment of women presbyters, while the *Acts of Philip* and the *Martyrdom of Matthew* do not argue for female presbyters but rather assume their existence. Was it from communities such as these that others were taking their example?

Council of Laodicea Canon 11[1]

There are two possible councils of Laodicea in Phrygia, both of uncertain date. The first council, from which this decree comes, was probably held in the late fourth or early fifth century, though some scholars think its canons represent a collection of decrees formulated over a number of years. The second council, whose decrees have not survived, probably took place between 478 and 481. It was convened to judge the case of Stephen bishop of Antioch, who was acquitted of the charge of Nestorianism.

> Concerning those who are called presbytides or female presiders (*prokathēmenai*), it is not permitted to appoint them in the Church.

Presbytides, the first of two difficult terms used here, carries the same ambiguity as its masculine counterpart *presbyteros,* which can mean either elderly man or "elder" in office, an officer or presbyter. The context must suggest a meaning. There is little context, but what little there is suggests some kind of church function or office, thus perhaps "female elder" or presbyter. The second term, *prokathēmenai,* means females who take the front seat, or the position of leader or presider. The word carries with it connotations of honor, privilege, and status. The term used here for appointment, *kathistasthai,* differs from the usual language of ordination (*cheirotonia* or *cheirothesia*).

The result is confusion: while the terms for the women suggest church offices, the term for their appointment does not. Of course, the canon attempts to put an end to the practice—whatever it was. One possibility is that the decree speaks of head deaconesses who bear a special title and responsibility with regard to other deaconesses and women in the church generally, perhaps by presiding over groups of women and assuming some kind of quasi-presbyteral role. Another possibility is that these women did exercise some kind of genuine presbyteral role with a kind of ordination in the whole church, which the writers wanted to put a stop to. One way to do that is to demean the office by using a term that negates their ordination by reducing it simply to an "appointment." Canon 45 of the same collection seems to have a similar purpose: "Women should not approach the altar." Such legislation is only enacted to attempt to end an established practice.[2]

Epiphanius, *Medicine Box* 49.2.1–3 (Against the Quintillians . . . to whom are joined the Artotyritai)[3]

Epiphanius (c. 315–403), a native of Palestine, was bishop of Salamis in Cyprus and a tireless combatant for orthodox faith. His principal work is the Panarion *or "medicine box" containing diagnosis and treatment against all heresies; it also is called* Contra Haereses *or* Against Heresies. *A polemical and sometimes careless work, it is dependent on earlier catalogs of heresies, especially that of Hippolytus. When he refers to the Quintillians, he is actually speaking of the Montanists, a charismatic movement that arose in Phrygia in the second half of the second century and soon spread over much of the Mediterranean world.*

They use both the Old and New Testament and also speak in the same way of a resurrection of the dead. They consider Quintilla together with Priscilla as founder, the same as the Cataphrygians. They bring with them many useless testimonies, attributing a special grace to Eve because she first ate of the tree of knowledge. They acknowledge the sister of Moses as a prophetess as support for their practice of appointing women to the clergy. Also, they say, Philip had four daughters who prophesied. Often in their assembly seven virgins dressed in white enter carrying lamps, having come in to prophesy to the people. They deceive the people present by giving the appearance of ecstasy; they pretend to weep as if showing the grief of repentance by shedding tears and by their appearance lamenting human life. Women among them are bishops, presbyters, and the rest, as if there were no difference of nature. "For in Christ Jesus there is neither male nor female" [Gal 3:28]. These are the things we have learned. They are called Artotyritai because in their mysteries they use bread and cheese and in this fashion they perform their rites.

The passage provides interesting evidence of the use of biblical texts as "proof texts" by many groups who argued pro and con leadership roles for women in the early church. This is also the only description of a uniquely Montanist liturgical ritual. The use of bread and cheese as sacramentals is otherwise unknown. One always suspects that when Epiphanius is the only one to report an odd account, his imagination has gotten away with him. However, the assertion that these groups have women bishops and presbyters is well founded in what we know of their openness to the leadership of women.

Epiphanius, *Medicine Box* 78.23.2, 79.3.6–79.4.1[4]

Others hold this nonsense about the holy ever-Virgin: acting thunderstruck and crazy, they have been and still are eager to put her in the place of God. For it is related that some women in Arabia, who come from the region of Thrace, put forward this silly idea: they prepare a kind of cake in the name of the ever-Virgin, assemble together, and in the name of the holy Virgin they attempt to undertake a deed that is irreverent and blasphemous beyond measure—in her name they function as priests for women.

Of course Epiphanius totally denigrates this practice reported to him, about which we know nothing else. He then continues in defense of legitimate honor to Mary, but not taken to excess. He runs through references in the Hebrew and Christian Scriptures, arguing that no woman was appointed priest, not even the four daughters of Philip or Mary herself, who would certainly have been chosen. Christ could even have been baptized by her but chose instead to be baptized by John.

It is clear that there is an order of deaconesses in the church, but this is not for the function of priesthood (*hierateuein*) or anything such to be entrusted to them, but for the sake of female appropriateness either at baptism or for the examination of some illness or trouble and when a woman's body must be unclothed, that it not be seen by the male priest (*anēr hierargōn*) but by the female minister who is appointed by the priest on the occasion so that she can care for the needs of the woman whose body must be unclothed. Thus regularity and order are carefully provided according to custom. This is also why the word of God does not permit a woman to speak in church[5] or to rule over a man.[6] Much more could be said about this.

Certainly only the order of deaconesses was needed in the church, but widows are also named, and among them older women or "elders," but female presbyters or female priests are not mentioned anywhere. Surely not even deacons in the order of the church are entrusted with enactment of the mystery but only to minister once the mysteries have been accomplished.

This statement comes in Epiphanius' treatment of the Collyridians, a group of women in Arabia who perform a sort of feminist eucharistic liturgy in honor of Mary, a practice otherwise unknown in this time. After rehearsing the honor due to Mary and the male priesthood of the Old Testament, he gives one of the earliest witnesses to the argument that if Jesus wanted women priests he would have ordained Mary. The entire passage is condescending and insulting in tone (e.g., "The female sex is mistaken, fallible, and poor in intelligence . . . Come now, servants of God, let us put on a manly mind and disperse the mania of these women"). It reiterates the exclusion of women from altar ministry and confines their role to assistance in the baptism of women.

The word *diakonissa* is used for deaconess. Female presbyters are *presbytides* (see Canon 11 of the Council of Laodicea), and female priests are *presbyterides,* a term that more closely approximates the male word *presbyteroi.*

Acts of Philip 1.12.8–9[7]

The Acts of Philip *probably date to the late fourth or early fifth century and come from an ascetic group that felt itself under persecution from the majority church. It may have arisen among the Encratites, known to have advocated abstinence from marriage, meat, and wine as essential to the practice of Christianity by the faithful who must thus keep themselves pure. Some scholars suggest the period of the text as immediately after*

381–83 CE, when Theodosius I enacted edicts condemning ascetic dissidents, and its location in rural Phrygia, where there was a history of fertility cults led by women.

The context of the passage is that the apostle Philip has encountered on his way from Galilee a mother mourning the death of her son. Philip raises the young man from the dead, and he recites what he had experienced while dead: a visit to hell, similar in form to others of the same genre (e.g., the Apocalypse of Peter*). There he saw various people in various kinds of torments and was instructed by the angel Michael, his tour guide, or by the sufferers themselves, what evil they had done to merit such torment. The biggest sin seems to have been attempts to corrupt or even despise and hold in contempt the "pure" ones (e.g., members of this community). Those who most symbolize and embody this purity are the wide variety of officeholders in the church.*

The context of the passage is that the young man has been told by Michael that he is summoned back to the world. The presence of Cerberus is an interesting combination of Christian with classical themes.

> When I heard this, I hastened to leave, and going out, I saw at the gate a man and a woman, and the great dog called Cerberus with three mouths was tied to the gate with fiery chains. He was devouring the man and the woman and held their liver in his paws. And they, half-dead, were crying out: "Have mercy on us! Help!" But no one helped them. So I went to pull the dog away, but Michael told me: "Leave them, because they also blasphemed against the male presbyters (*presbyteroi*), female presbyters (*presbytides*), eunuchs, deacons, deaconesses (*diakonissai*), and virgins, by false accusations of impurity and adultery, and once they had done this, they encountered me, Michael, as well as Raphael and Uriel, and we gave them as feed to this dog until the great day of judgment."

Elsewhere in book 1 of the *Acts of Philip,* there are other lists of church officers: in all, *episkopoi,* presbyters, virgins, and *eunuchs* (1.6.8; 7.8–9, 17, 22–23; 8.23; 10.10–11). Only here is the list complete, adding female presbyters, deacons, and deaconesses. The term *presbytides* here cannot mean just "older women" as it sometimes does (e.g., 1 Tim 5:2; Titus 2:3), since it is embedded here in a list of other recognized church functions. It must refer to some kind of official church ministries. Because there are also deaconesses to perform diaconal functions, it is likely that the work of the *presbytides* is somehow liturgical and complementary to that of the male presbyters. The commentator on the critical edition remarks that perhaps these Encratites had preserved "the ancient Christian tradition" of the presence of women in the ministries, though the presence of female presbyters may also have been influenced by the religious climate of Asia Minor, where archaeological and literary evidence seems to indicate a greater prominence of women in religious leadership roles in Greco-Roman religions.

Martyrdom of Matthew 28 [8]

The origin of this document, and even its original form, is unknown. The manuscript history is complicated, with several early medieval Greek manuscripts surviving, as well as Latin, Old Slavonic, and Armenian translations. There are numerous possibilities of literary interpolation with other late apocryphal apostle traditions. While here it seems the evangelist Matthew is the martyr in question, there are possible relationships with another text, the Acts of Andrew and Matthias (see Acts 1:26). The names Matthew and Matthias are sometimes confused in the later traditions. Because the surviving manuscripts are so late, there is little that can be said about time or place of origin.

Matthew is accompanied by his fellow disciple, Plato. When Matthew is martyred by burning on a funerary bier, he is seen ascending to heaven. Later, he speaks to Plato giving him directions for celebration of the eucharist. Plato sees Matthew standing on the sea, accompanied by two men in bright garments and a beautiful child. The king who had ordered the execution also sees the vision and is instantly repentant and converted. Plato baptizes him, whereupon Matthew appears and gives new names to the king, his wife, his son, and daughter-in-law. Three different versions are given by Bonnet.

> 1. Greek ms. PF: And in that hour Matthew appointed (*katestēsan*) the king (*basileus*) presbyter, being thirty-seven years old, and the son of the king he appointed deacon, he being seventeen years old, and the wife of the king he appointed presbyter (*presbytida*), and the wife of his son he appointed deaconess (*diakonissa*), she being seventeen years old. There was great joy in the church, and everyone said to each other: "Amen! Praised be the priesthood (*hierosynē*) and blessing[9] in Christ. Amen."
>
> 2. Greek ms. VUE: Blessed Matthew ordained (*echeirotonēsen*) the king presbyter, his son deacon, and likewise his wife and his bride[10] deaconesses (*diakonissai*). Then they praised them saying: "The praise and grace of our Lord Jesus Christ will be with you forever."
>
> 3. Latin ms. EQ: In that same hour holy Matthew ordained (*ordinavit*) the king (*imperator*) presbyter: he was thirty-seven. And the wife of the king he ordained deaconess (*diakonissa*): she was thirty. And the son of the king he ordained deacon: he was seventeen. And his wife he ordained deaconess (*diakonissa*), who was seventeen. Then there was great joy in the church of the Lord, and all said: "Alleluia, amen. Jerusalem is glorified in the name of Christ."

The obvious clerical interest of the text takes different forms. Versions 1 and 3 are more closely related, but the wife of the king is presbyter in the Greek and deaconess in the Latin version. She is assigned an age only in the Latin. The care to specify ages is interesting, given that seventeen would have been too young in any known list of age requirements for ordination. Justinian's *Novellae* 123.13 give the age of thirty for presbyteral ordination, twenty-five for deacon, and forty for deaconess. The age for the ordination of a deaconess varied by time and place, but seventeen would have been too young anywhere. The second Greek version drops out the ages of all. The term for ordination in version 1 is less clear, while in versions 2 and 3 it is the usually accepted terminology. The title of presbyter for the king's wife in version 1 is unlikely to be simply given her as a presbyter's wife because the same language of constitution is used for all four, and the title deaconess is rarely, if ever, used for a deacon's wife. In the alterations in the text the tendency to avoid the suggestion of the presbyteral ordination of women is apparent.

INSCRIPTIONS

The first inscription, that of Ammion, has often been understood as Montanist because of its time and place, but this is not certain. The others are unlikely to be Montanist, and for the reasons given below, are unlikely to refer simply to an elderly woman.

Ammion Presbyter[11]

A funerary inscription of the first half of the third century from Uçak in Phrygia, Asia Minor. It is one of three inscriptions naming a certain bishop Diogas. In another inscription, Diogas dedicates the memorial of a bishop Artemidoros, which is paid for by church funds. The other is the memorial of Diogas himself, erected by his wife Aurelia Tatianē while she was still living and he deceased. The editors assume that all three inscriptions refer to the same person and thus come from approximately the same time. There has also been an assumption that the texts come from a Montanist community because they are found in Phrygia, the origin of Montanism, and because of Epiphanius' witness of Montanist female presbyters (Medicine Box 49.2; see above) against the presumed absence of women presbyters in the "orthodox" church. But there are no other distinguishing characteristics of Montanism in these inscriptions, and others have doubted the connection in this somewhat circular argument.[12]

Bishop Diogas to the memory of Ammion the presbyter

Ammion is a common female name in central Asia Minor, but is Ammion's title, *presbytera*, a title of office or a designation of her as an older woman? There is no comparative factor in the inscription, that is, she is not compared to anyone else who is younger. Moreover, why would the local bishop, rather than her relatives, be the one to commemorate her if the meaning of the title is simply "elderly woman"? And if Diogas were her relative, would he not have stated this in the inscription? In one of the other inscriptions, Diogas commemorates another bishop. It would seem, then, that the bishop was the appropriate commemorator of those in church office.

Artemidora, Presbyter[13]

From a mummy inscription in Egypt, second or third century.

(Mummy) of Artemidora, daughter of Mikkalos and mother Paniskiainē, presbyter, slept in the Lord

The title *pres'b'* is sometimes taken to mean "elder" in the sense of advanced age, but is more often a title of office. The order of words follows the usual form of such inscriptions: name, father, mother, age, origin, title, and date.[14] Here age, origin, and date are missing. This is the likely reading. However, all three names are in the genitive case, so another reading is possible, though less likely: that Artemidora is wife of Mikkalos and mother of Paniskiainē. In this case, it would be possible that Paniskiainē is the presbyter in the family. Her function in this capacity is not known, but such inscriptions should be understood in the context of Canon 11 of the late-fourth-century Council of Laodicea, which attempted to abolish perhaps just what was being done by this woman.

Epiktō Presbytis[15]

A brief inscription from the island of Thera, one of the Cyclades islands in the Aegean Sea.

Angel of Epiktō presbyter

There are about forty-seven inscriptions from Thera introduced by the word ange-los, most followed by a proper name in the genitive case. There is some discussion as to whether the inscriptions are pagan, Jewish, or Christian. Most accept them as Christian. The idea of a guardian angel of a tomb is found elsewhere (see Agalia-sis from the nearby island of Melos) but is most pronounced in this collection from Thera. The term for presbyter, *presbytis*, could mean simply older woman, but this is unlikely in a tomb commemoration, where functional and honorary titles are used (for background, see Canon 11 of the Council of Laodicea, above).[16]

Kalē Presbytis[17]

An inscription from Centuripae, Sicily, probably from the fourth or fifth century.

Here lies Kalē presbyter, who lived fifty years blamelessly. She died on the nineteenth kalends of October [September 14].

Kalē's title is abbreviated *preb*, an abbreviation for "presbyter" that appears elsewhere in both Greek and Latin inscriptions. The abbreviation could refer to *presbytis* or *presbytera*, two forms with more or less the same meaning. Both could mean "older woman," but Manni Piraino and Eisen point out that this designation for such a woman does not appear elsewhere in the inscriptions of Sicily. The term could also mean wife of a presbyter, but that is unlikely here since no husband is named or titled. The expression "Here lies . . ." (*enthade keitai*) is common in Italy, especially in Jewish inscriptions of Rome.

IN THE WEST

Some of the best evidence for women presbyters, both literary and epigraphical, is from the West. Much of it, by the very nature of the dynamic of suppression against it, is circumstantial and subject to multiple interpretations.

WIVES OF CLERICS

With titles such as *presbytera*, there is always the possibility that the wife of a male presbyter is meant, and indeed, this was the custom even in the West at certain periods; even the title of deaconess was used for the wife of a deacon.[18] Good examples are Canon 19 of the Second Council of Tours, the Synod of Auxerre, and the later Synod of Rome (743). They are included here to contrast with the material that follows, where it is highly unlikely that this is the case.

Second Council of Tours Canon 19[19]

This council met in November 567 in the Basilica of St. Martin. Nine bishops attended; they issued twenty-seven canons, several of which deal with relations between married male clergy, including bishops, and their wives. Canon 12 commands married bishops to live celibately, surrounded by their clergy, and separately from their wives. Canon 19 begins with a reference to misgiving that many rural archpriests, as well as deacons and subdeacons, "rest under suspicion of continuing intercourse with their wives." It goes on to declare:

> If a presbyter has been found with his presbyteress (*presbiteria*) or a deacon with his deaconess (*diaconissa*) or a subdeacon with his subdeaconess (*subdiaconissa*), let him be excommunicate (*excommunis*) for an entire year, deposed from every clerical office and put among the laity.

Both the language of this particular canon and the overall scope of the canons at the Council indicate that the presbyteresses, deaconesses, and subdeaconesses are the wives, respectively, of presbyters, deacons, and subdeacons. Thus the canon is talking about the wives of men who were married before ordination. The men were not expected to separate from their wives when ordained, but they were expected to remain celibate. That the bishops felt compelled to issue the decree, and that they begin it by announcing that the requirement of continence is being ignored, indicates that such men were not, in fact, abstaining from conjugal relations. In any case, once married, their wives were called *presbyterae* (or, as here, *presbiteriae*), *diaconissae*, or *subdiaconissae*, as the case might be. It is not enough to say, for example, that deaconesses at this point simply means, as Martimort suggests, "the wives of deacons."[20] While true, that does not go far enough. For a deaconess had also by this time surely consecrated herself to virginity. But Martimort is correct to point out that here we are really talking about a new category when we use the word "deaconess." According to this document, the deaconess and the presbyteress and the episcopess are intended to be consecrated celibates who remain in nonsexual relationship with their ordained husbands. That they have no liturgical role or clerical status is simply assumed.

Synod of Auxerre Canon 21[21]

This small diocesan Synod was presided over by the Bishop of Auxerre, Annacharius, in 578. In attendance were seven abbots, thirty-four priests, and three deacons. Though small, the Synod issued forty-five canons. One prohibited the performance of choruses or songs in church by girls. Another, Canon 22, forbade the widow of a priest, deacon, or subdeacon to marry again. Another (Canon 36) disallowed a woman from receiving the eucharist with an uncovered hand. Not surprisingly, given the number of abbots present, several of the decrees have to do with monastic discipline, including Canon 24, which forbids an abbot or monk from defecting from the cloister to marry. Canon 21 shows that sometimes the title presbytera *does not indicate church office.*

> It is not allowed to any presbyter after having accepted the blessing of ordination to sleep in the same bed with his presbytera (*presbytera*) or to unite in carnal sin (*in peccato carnali miscere*); nor may a deacon or subdeacon.

This synod took place just a decade or so after the Second Council of Tours. Both Frankish assemblies use *presbytera* in the same sense. Here, as at Tours, the term refers to the wife of a priest who has been ordained after being married. He and his wife are commanded to live in chastity, and even to sleep separately (if under the same roof) after his ordination, and this command applies to those in minor orders as well. Again, the necessity of enacting the decree probably indicates that such couples were not living chastely after priestly or diaconal ordination. What is certain is that *presbytera* here does not refer to a woman presbyter exercising sacerdotal functions.

Synod of Rome[22]

In 743, a synod was held at Rome under the presidency of Pope Zachary (741–52). Sixty bishops attended. The synod was convoked to consider a variety of matters related to church discipline. It issued fourteen canons on such matters, which included questions on fourth-degree marriages and offerings of sacrifices to pagan gods. The fifth canon is of especial interest to us.

> No one should presume to join himself physically to an abominable consort, like a presbyteress (*presbyteram*), deaconess (*diaconam*), nun (*nonnam*) or female monk (*monacham*) or a spiritual matron (*spiritualem commatrem*). Anyone who commits an act of this kind, should know he is bound by the fetters of anathema (*anathematis vinculo*) and condemned by the judgment of God and excluded from the sacred body and blood of the Lord Jesus Christ.

Ironically, the formula for excommunication was drawn up by Pope Zachary himself. He distinguished three sorts of excommunication, of which the anathema was the penalty reserved for the most serious offenses against ecclesiastical discipline. When promulgating his sentence, the pope was to be solemnly vested, sit in front of the altar, and intone the formula of anathema: "We deprive N., himself and all his accomplices and all his abettors, of the Communion of the Body and Blood of Our Lord; we separate him from the society of all Christians; we exclude him from the bosom of our Holy Mother the Church in Heaven and on earth, we declare him excommunicated and anathematized; and we judge him condemned to eternal fire with Satan and his angels and all the reprobate, so long as he will not burst the fetters of the demon, do penance, and satisfy the Church; we deliver him to Satan to mortify his body, that his soul may be saved on the day of judgment." Written notice is then sent to neighboring bishops and priests warning them to have no communion with the anathematized. This is precisely the harsh penalty envisaged here. The presbyteresses and deaconesses in question were spouses of priests and deacons who were married before they were ordained and were subsequently bound by chastity.

THREE NORTH AFRICANS AGAINST WOMEN PRESBYTERS

Tertullian had a clear understanding that women possessed the gift of prophecy but no right of access to the altar. Sometimes he identifies those he is attacking as "heretical," but in the case of the Thecla story (*On Baptism* 17.4), he does not. At the same time, it is evident in *On Modesty* 13.7 and *To His Wife* 1.7 that members of the order of widows, even if they performed no sacerdotal functions, were considered members of the clergy in his Carthaginian church. Firmilian's letter in Cyprian's collection probably indicates the presence of Montanist influence, though one would think that by the middle of the third century, there would be a clear delineation in Asia Minor between Montanists and others, and that condemning something as part of the "New Prophecy" would be sufficient. Firmilian does not make such a delineation in this text. Augustine simply repeats the stock descriptions of Montanist egalitarian practices in the selection of clergy (see Epiphanius).

Tertullian, *On the Remedy of Heretics* 41.5 [23]

Born in Carthage, North Africa, Quintus Septimius Florens Tertullianus (c. 160–225) was one of the most influential and brilliant of the Latin fathers. He could also be quite vituperative, especially on the subject of women, though most of all these abusive remarks need to be carefully contextualized and interpreted.[24] A convert from paganism, Tertullian nonetheless became a prolific and effective apologist for Christianity. In his theological works, he did much (along with the Latin Bible, probably already available at the end of the second century) to augment and develop the theological vocabulary of the church, so much, in fact, that he is often designated "the father of Latin theology." Though he was a moral rigorist, the influence on him of the New Prophecy or Montanist movement has been exaggerated. Though he was probably not, as is sometimes heard, the editor of the Passion *of Perpetua and Felicitas, he had much to say about women and their exercise of ministry (though he said nothing of deaconesses).*

In his anti-heretical work De praescriptione haereticorum, *written around 200 when the author was in what scholars once designated his "Catholic period" (that is, before his thinking manifests signs of Montanist influence), Tertullian lays out his famous argument that heretics have no right to interpret the scriptures because they do not own them. At the end of the treatise, he turns to an account of the behavior of his opponents, in the course of which he considers the ministerial activity of women in these sects.*

These heretical women: how bold (*procaces*) they are! They dare to teach (*audeant docere*), to debate, to perform exorcisms, to attempt cures—perhaps even to baptize (*fortasse an et tingere*).

Taken in isolation, this text appears as if aimed primarily at the irregularities of female ministry among the heretical sects Tertullian deplores. Read in context, however, it is clear that Tertullian's main complaint is against the indiscipline of heretical sects as such and that he has in mind primarily the deviations of heretical men. In this connection, the "bold" practices of the women serve as illustrations of the irregularity, capriciousness, and arrogance of the heretical men, whose inability to control the women in the sects is sufficient evidence of more comprehensive defects.

Even if not directed primarily against heretical women, the text is valuable for indicating unambiguously what ministerial functions women were, in Tertullian's mind, *not* permitted to assume. The proscription against teaching will reappear in Tertullian's writings (on which, see the text from *Against Marcion* 5.8.11 below), which he also bases on a Pauline text (1 Cor 11:5), and there it will apply also to women who are unimpeachably orthodox. Notable in the proscription against exorcizing and healing is that Tertullian elsewhere seems to allow orthodox lay Christian males to perform these functions. In his *Apology,* for example, he says that exorcism may be performed *a quolibet Christiano*—that is, by any Christian.[25] In other words, these activities were not, so far as Tertullian saw it, the prerogative of priests or of any other category of clergy. (Indeed, exorcists would not become members of the Christian clergy until long after Tertullian completed this work.) Thus one is forced to conclude that, at least here, it was *not* her nonordained status that barred a woman from casting out demons and curing; it was her sex.

If she was not allowed to exorcize or heal, she was not, *a fortiori,* permitted to teach. This view may rest implicitly here, as explicitly elsewhere in Tertullian, on the Pauline pronouncements to keep silent and not to teach at 1 Cor 14:34–35 and 1 Tim 2:12. Also notable in light of the prohibition on teaching is Tertullian's sympathetic view of female prophesying (on which, see the text from *Against Marcion* 5.8.11, below), which he also bases on a Pauline text (1 Cor 11:5). The language Tertullian uses to describe baptizing by women suggests not only that he regards this as the gravest of offenses he has discussed here ("*even*" to baptize) but also that he cannot be sure ("*perhaps*") that women are actually guilty of it.

Tertullian, *On the Dress of Women* 2.12.1[26]

Originally, the work we now know as De cultu feminarum *(c. 200) was composed of two distinct works written by Tertullian; they have now been united. As a result, the two books that make up* On the Dress of Women *are not coherent or continuous. Nonetheless, in both works, Tertullian pursues the same themes, focusing in some detail on the specifics of hairdressing, pigments, dyeing of hair, elaborate dressing, excess in dress, and other such matters, admonishing women to shun all of these both because they are of diabolical origin and as an outward sign of inner chastity. (He also warns men [2.8] that they are not exempt from his comments.) In the work's penultimate chapter, he uses the word "priestess" in relation to women. But it is a special kind of priesthood he has in mind for them.*

> **Let us wish only that we are not cause of just blasphemy. How great a cause of blasphemy (*blasphemabile*) is it if you, who are said to be the priestesses of chastity (*sacerdotes pudicitiae*) should turn out in public dressed and painted (*cultae et expictae*) in the style of the unchaste.**

This text indicates clearly the only priestly role Tertullian is willing to grant to women. If they may not teach or debate or baptize, or even to cure or exorcise, they may serve as "priestesses" of chastity. In using this term, Tertullian presumably did not envisage "priestess" as an actual social role or ecclesiastical category, as he would "widow," even less as an office that would be recognized in a ritual of anointing or ordination. Rather, he uses it to suggest that women, above all in their dress and public bearing, would exemplify and "mediate" the virtue of chastity. As is obvious, this is a role that is expressed implicitly and by silence rather than in the public, explicit, often verbal acts of the presbyterate. In this sense, they had an "apologetical" role to play in their priesthood insofar as they manifested to the Roman world the high moral virtue characteristic of the Christian Church. In other words, they did not have a ministry of prayer or teaching that would make them sacerdotal mediators in the strict sense of the term.

The term *sacerdotes pudicitiae* of course is redolent of the vestal virgins in ancient Roman religion, though whether Tertullian connected these Christian priestesses to those ancient Roman ones may be questioned. However, elsewhere, in his *Exhortation to Chastity* 13, he uses them as exemplars of chastity to be imitated by Christian widows.

Tertullian, *On Baptism* 17.4 [27]

Precious as a source for the history of the rite of initiation, Tertullian's On Baptism *(c. 200) was apparently occasioned by the criticisms of one Quintilla, a "viper of the Cainite heresy," (*De Bapt. 1), *a sect whose "venomous" work was to attempt to do away with baptism. In response Tertullian wrote a short tract on the sources, significance, and proper administration of the baptismal rite, near the end of which he challenged both a woman's right to instruct and, though the Cainites had rejected the sacrament, to baptize. Apparently, Tertullian was reacting to the practice of some women, relying on the example of the self-baptism of Thecla in the ditch-water of the Antiochene amphitheater (*Acts of Paul and Thecla 34), *to claim the right to baptize.*

However, the impudence of that woman (*petulantia mulieris*) who has wrong-fully seized the right to teach will not also spawn for herself the right to bap-tize (*tinguendi ius*),[28] unless some new serpent were to come forth, like the first one, so that, just as that one [i.e., Quintilla] destroyed baptism, so another should of her own authority (*per se*) confer it. But if the writings wrongfully thought to have been written by Paul [i.e., *Acts of Paul*] assert the example of Thecla for allowing women to teach and baptize, let it be known that in Asia the priest who forged that writing (as if augmenting the prestige of Paul by his own) was discovered and, though he confessed that he had done it out of love of Paul, lost his position. How credible is it that one would give a female the power to teach and baptize who has not even allowed a woman to learn by right? "Let them keep silent," he says, "and ask their husbands at home" [1 Cor 14:34–35].

Once again, Tertullian gainsays a woman's right to teach. If, according to apostolic fiat, she may not even learn, then it follows (again, *a fortiori*) that she may not lic-itly teach or baptize. (But that some *may* have been doing so nonetheless appears possible to Tertullian.) In addition, it is not simply *what* she has taught that Ter-tullian finds problematic, but *that* she has asserted her personal authority and that of a recognizably apocryphal work against explicit apostolic authority. So the issue is not primarily that a woman is teaching heretical doctrine so much as it is mag-isterial authority; Tertullian would not have her teach at all, even if hers were a strictly orthodox pedagogy of baptism.

Tertullian, *Against Marcion* 5.8.11[29]

Written around 206–12, the five books against Marcion make up the lengthiest of all of Tertullian's works. They are also among the very most important sources for the thought of Marcion. After treating Marcion's doctrine of God and his christological thought in the first three books of the treatise, Tertullian turns in his final two books to a commentary on Marcion's Antitheses *and to his interpretation of the Bible in gen-eral. The following text occurs in a discussion of gifts of the Spirit that had been fore-told in "the Law," that is, in the Pentateuch and, more generally, in other parts of the Hebrew Bible. Here, Tertullian is intent on demonstrating that "the Apostle" (i.e., Paul) is in conformity with the Hebrew prophets (one of the points Marcion was at pains to deny in the* Antitheses*) and uses them as his authority when he speaks (espe-cially in 1 Corinthians) of spiritual gifts. Part of Tertullian's intention, in addition to demonstrating the continued authority of the Hebrew scriptures, is to challenge Mar-cion to produce men and women who have prophesied, for Tertullian certain evidence of authority and authenticity.*

Similarly, when directing (*praescribens*) women to be silent in church, that
they not speak for the purpose of learning [1 Cor 14:34–35]—although he
[Paul] has already shown that even they have the right of prophesying, when
he puts a veil on the woman prophesying [1 Cor 11:5–6]—he took his
authority for setting woman in subjection (*subiciendae feminae*) from the law
(*ex lege*) . . . let him [Marcion] also show to me any from those especially holy
women in his community who has prophesied . . .

Once again, the issue of the rights and limits of female speech in church is inci-
dental to the matter centrally under discussion. In the course of a larger discussion
on the continued validity of the Law and the possession of the Spirit, Tertullian
again alludes to the apostolic proscription on female speech in church, at least
speech connected with teaching and learning. Yet, again appealing to Paul, and
perhaps reflecting the influence of his attachment to Montanism, Tertullian
explicitly allows women the right to prophesy (cf. 1 Cor 11:5: "but any woman
who prays or prophesies with her head unveiled dishonors her head"). The "law"
to which Tertullian refers is possibly Gen 3:16. Here, as elsewhere, Tertullian will
not allow women to teach or perform a sacramental act, but he does allow them
to prophesy and indeed regards it as a sign of the possession of the Spirit and thus
of authority.

Tertullian, *On the Veiling of Virgins* 9.1[30]

*Tertullian regarded the veiling of virgins as a topic significant enough to warrant
treatment not only in* De virginibus velandis *(c. 207?) but in two of his other
Latin works and one Greek one. In the course of a lengthy discussion of this topic,
Tertullian considers what rules in general govern the activity of women in the church.
In particular, he asks whether they should be allowed to teach, baptize, or to function
as priests.*

A woman is not permitted to speak in church (*Non permittitur mulieri in
ecclesia loqui*). Neither may she teach (*docere*), baptize, offer (*offere*), nor claim
for herself (*sibi uindicare*) any function proper to a man (*nec ullius uirilis
muneris*), especially the sacerdotal office (*nedum sacerdotalis officii*).

This is among the most complete catalogues in Tertullian's works of the priestly
functions women were *not* permitted to assume. Although this text was written
during the time Tertullian was under the influence of Montanism and thus sympathetic to prophesying by women, he still was unwilling to allow women to
undertake any sacerdotal duties or office. Moreover, he clearly states that women
are not to perform sacerdotal tasks because these are proper for men alone. By the
term *offere,* Tertullian means celebrating the eucharist.

Tertullian, *On the Veiling of Virgins* 9.2 [31]

In the same text, Tertullian gives his fullest description of the order of widows, which includes details regarding their physical place in the worshipping congregation, requirements for being admitted to the order, and the ministry its members exercised. They were to be at least sixty years of age, married just once, known for having educated their children well, and wise and sufficiently experienced to give good counsel. The following text refers to a bishop's incorrect decision to induct a virgin into the order of widows.

> I know for sure that in a certain place (*alicubi*) a virgin was placed in the order of widows (*in viduatu*). If the bishop had been obliged to provide her some relief, he could certainly have done so in some other way, so as to have preserved respect for discipline, lest such a miracle (I will not say a monster) as a virgin-widow (*virgo vidua*) be pointed out in the church.

This text demonstrates the existence of an order of widows in the North African church. It is clear that Tertullian's objection here is not to the bishop's desire to provide relief to a needy virgin but his decision to initiate her into an order whose criteria—here, most probably, the age criterion—for induction she had not satisfied. The result is not only embarrassing ecclesiastical indiscipline but a deficit in the respect properly owed to the order of widows. The "virgin-widow" would have been easily identifiable by her sitting in the area of prominence in the church normally reserved for widows. It is clear, then, that Tertullian was determined to preserve the distinct and special status of the order of widows in Carthage.

Tertullian, *Exhortation to Chastity* 10.5 [32]

Tertullian urges his friend not to remarry and recommends to him a life of continence. In the tenth chapter of the treatise, he dwells on the advantages of widowhood. Drawing on examples from the Hebrew scriptures and Paul on the desirability of purity, Tertullian then turns to what was revealed in an oracle of the Montantist prophet Prisca.

> Again through the holy prophetess (*prophētidem*) Prisca is the gospel preached in this way [i.e., through prophecy], that the holy minister knows to minister sanctity. "Purity," she says, "brings harmony, and they see visions and, turning their face to the ground, they also hear distinct voices, as salutary as they are mysterious."

While Tertullian generally, and often vehemently, opposes women exercising a teaching role, he does recognize here (as he does in *On the Soul* 9.4) that some women (like Prisca), under the inspiration of the Holy Spirit, do utter authoritative prophecies. Tertullian places Prisca's oracle as an authority alongside the Hebrew scriptures and the Apostle. All are effected by the action of the Holy Spirit.

Tertullian, *On Monogamy* 11.1[33]

Written around 213, this is one of the three treatises Tertullian wrote on marriage and remarriage, probably written under the influence of Montanism. Tertullian decisively repudiates second marriages. Indeed, he regards them as morally adjacent to adultery. Here, in the first chapter of the treatise, Tertullian inquires how one can ask monogamist clergy to sanctify a second marriage when they themselves are committed to a single marriage. Of course, monogamy implies the obligation to have only one marriage per lifetime (not more than one marriage simultaneously).

> **How do you ask for a blessing on a matrimony that those of whom you ask it are not themselves permitted to have—namely from the monogamist bishops, from presbyters and deacons, bound by the same promise, and from widows whose way (*sectam*) you have refused for yourself?**

This text proves by grammatical parallelism (as does Tertullian's *On Modesty* 13.7, infra, in its emphasis on the place of widows in liturgical assemblies) that Tertullian placed widows among the clergy.[34]

Tertullian, *On Modesty* 13.7[35]

> **Why do you . . . lead the penitent adulterer into the middle of the church and have him kneel, in haircloth and ashes . . . before the widows, before the presbyters (*ante uiduas, ante presbyteros*), imploring the tears of all, kissing the footprints of all, clutching the knees of all?**

This passage, composed between 217 and 222, is another that suggests that widows in Carthage sat separately from the laity and with the presbyters, an arrangement also implied in the *AC* and *TD*. Here a penitent is seeking forgiveness from all the assembled, segregated clergy—presbyters and widows. The placement of the widows in church and their grouping with the presbyters suggests that, as Daniel Hoffman has observed, "This practice recognized that these women were involved in important ministries. They were not mere charity recipients."[36]

Tertullian, *To His Wife* 1.7[37]

Of the several works on marriage and remarriage written by Tertullian, Ad Uxorem is probably the best known and certainly the most significant for our purposes. For the most part, the treatise contains counsel (or commands) Tertullian's wife is to observe after her husband's death. The following text is of interest for its reference to the Pauline injunction (1 Tim 5.9) regarding admission to widowhood and, even more, for Ter-

*tullian's explicit conviction that "widows" made up an "order" (*ordo*)—that is, a special and official class within ecclesiastical society. It is less explicit, indeed silent, about what ministry, if any, is exercised by this* ordo.

> Insofar as we can, let us love the opportunity of continence. When it first presents itself, let us resolve to accept it, so that what we could not take on in marriage, we might embrace in widowhood (*in viduitate*). The occasion must be embraced which concludes what necessity used to command. How harmful to faith, and what an impediment to sanctity, second marriages are, the discipline of the church and the restriction (*praescriptio*) of the Apostle declare, since he does not allow twice-married men to preside [I Tim 3.11], and when he would not allow a widow into the order (*in ordinem*) unless she had been married to only one man (*univiram*) . . . Indeed, it is fitting that the altar of God be presented pure (*mundam*).[38]

Tertullian used the term *ordo* to describe an officially recognized social category within the church. In applying the use of the term here to women, Tertullian implies that widows are part of the Christian clergy, even if there is no explicit profession of widowhood. At the time of Tertullian's writing, widows were in fact recognized by the entire Christian community as a special class of Christian, symbolized spatially in liturgical assembly by their occupying a place apart and by penitent sinners seeking reconciliation before them and the presbyters. Even by Tertullian's time, the conditions of admission into the category—that the woman be at least sixty years of age, have married only once and raised her children well—were well established and recognized.

Cyprian of Carthage, *Letter* 75, from Firmilian, Bishop of Caesarea in Cappadocia[39]

Born a pagan and trained in rhetoric, Cyprian converted to Christianity around 246. Within two years he was consecrated Bishop of Carthage, the most powerful ecclesiastical position in North Africa. For many years he was involved in quite a bitter dispute with Bishop Stephen of Rome (d. 257) over the possibility of reconciliation of the lapsed in the Decian persecution and then on the issue of whether heretics (in this case, Novatianist missionaries in North Africa) could licitly baptize. Cyprian's view was that such heretics had to be rebaptized. Stephen disagreed and disparaged Cyprian as a "false Christ." Correspondence between the two men became increasingly virulent, involving the rival claims of two powerful bishoprics and ancient traditions, Carthaginian and Roman, two ecclesiologies and two views on sacramental theology. Cyprian managed to secure support from the church in Cappadocia, not least of all from Bishop

Firmilian of Caesarea, who had taken a rigorous, Cyprianic view toward Montanists in Phrygia. In the course of his letter, from around 256, Firmilian writes to Cyprian and identifies heretics with false prophets. He then gives the example of a certain unnamed woman active in Cappadocia who had proclaimed herself a prophetess some two decades prior.

> There rose up suddenly then a certain woman who, in a state of ecstasy, presented herself as a prophet (*prophētēn*) and acted as if filled with the Holy Spirit . . . But that woman, who previously through the illusions and treacheries of the Demon in order to deceive the faithful . . . had also often dared this . . . to sanctify the bread and to pretend to confect the eucharist and make the sacrifice to the Lord . . . and she also baptized many, usurping the usual and legitimate mode of questioning, so that nothing might seem to deviate from ecclesiastical rule.

The prophetess Firmilian has in mind was probably Montanist, but it is interesting that he labels her not as member of a deviant group but as deviant within the church itself. The prominent role she assumes in the administration of sacraments is consistent with the exalted status and functions of women prophetesses in Montanism. This text is good evidence that before the definition and boundaries of the "Catholic" or "orthodox" church became clear, some communities allowed women a significant, in this case *presbyteral* (as well as prophetic) role.

Augustine, *On Heresies* 27[40]

In 427 or 428 Quodvultdeus, a deacon (and later bishop) of Carthage, requested of Augustine that he write a tract on heresy for the use of the clergy. Augustine proceeded to compile a handbook of heresy in 428–29, though its completion was prevented by his death in 430. The work is essentially a register and description of heresies from the time of Simon Magus to Pelagius. (Almost one-sixth of the book is given over to discussion of the Manichees.) Augustine drew heavily on a compendium of Epiphanius's Medicine Box, *as is evident in his discussion of the Pepuzians in this chapter.*

> The Pepuzians or Quintillians are named from a certain place, which Epiphanius says is a deserted city. Judging it however to be something divine (*divinum aliquid*), they call it Jerusalem. They give such positions of leadership (*tantum principatum*) that among them some are honored even with the priesthood (*sacerdotio*). They say that in the same city of Pepuza, Christ in the form of a woman (*specie feminae*) was revealed to Quintilla and Priscilla, and thus they are also called Quintillians. They also do with the blood of an infant what we have said above that the Cataphrygians do, as they are said to have arisen from them.

According to Augustine *On Heresies* 26, the Cataphrygians are "those who were begun by Montanus."[41] The ritual to which he refers here is a "gruesome sacrament" in which the Cataphyrgians are said to confect the eucharist by making tiny puncture wounds in the body of an infant, then mixing the blood they draw with wheat.[42] This odd ritual (itself imaginatively confected), which resembles the later medieval blood-libel, is attributed to the Cataphyrgians by Epiphanius, *Medicine Box* 48.14 and 15.7.[43] Actually, this whole chapter depends heavily on the epitome of Epiphanius. In *Medicine Box* 49, Epiphanius maintains that these related groups have "women bishops, women presbyters and everything else," which, he asserts, they base on the Pauline text, "In Christ there is neither male nor female" (Gal 3:28).[44] If the material on the use of the blood of infants can safely be regarded as antiheretical vilification, Augustine does preserve the genuine recognition that the Montanists held a special place for women prophets and leaders, though, unlike Epiphanius, he says nothing about women bishops.

The apparition of Christ *specie feminae* is very rare in ancient Christian literature.[45]

CANONS AND EPISCOPAL LETTERS

From the late fourth century, a movement was stirring in the West toward greater leadership roles for women, spurred on in part by the movement of Priscillian. The letter of Gelasius at the end of the fifth century requires some context. Not only Gelasius but also the three bishops of Gaul a few years later, and Fulgentius Ferrandus in Africa half a century later, suggest that the practice of women serving at the altars had happened in certain times and places in the West. Fulgentius connects the office of women presbyters with the Greek East, whose influence was strong in southern Italy, the destination of Gelasius' letter. Finally, we give a later, tenth-century opinion of Atto of Vercelli that in the early church, women were ordained presbyters.

First Synod of Saragossa[46]

According to Sulpicius Severus (363–420), a contemporary of Jerome and Augustine and hagiographer for Martin of Tours, a synod was held in 380 in Saragossa and was attended by bishops from Spain and Aquitaine (see Sacred History *3). The synod was convoked mainly to combat the errors of Priscillianism. Priscillianism was a movement that began in Spain around 370 and spread rapidly throughout the entire country and from there to southern Gaul. Among the followers it attracted were Instantius and Salvianus, two bishops. A strictly ascetical group, the Priscillianists had pronounced sim-*

ilarities to the Manichaeans, with whom they may be confused in the canons here. A chain of objections to the practices and beliefs of the sect from the Bishop of Córdoba, to his metropolitan, to Pope Damasus, back to the Synod of Saragossa (380) and finally to the Imperial Court in Trier resulted in the beheading of Priscillian. Whatever the emperor's intentions, the execution had the effect of making Priscillian a martyr and of radicalizing the movement that traced itself to his name. Indeed, it became immediately more heterodox, as the Synod of Toledo (c. 398) noted to its horror. In any case, none of the heretics, though invited, appeared at Saragossa. Nonetheless, the synod condemned them and threatened to excommunicate any who communed with them. In his Epistle *237, Augustine refers to the attendance at Priscillianist conventicles of those interested in the interpretation of both the canonical and apocryphal scriptures, to which the following canon appears to allude.*

> Let all believing women who belong to the Catholic Church absent themselves from lectures and conventicles of foreign men, and from women giving lectures, either out of zeal for teaching or learning, since this is what the Apostle commands. [1 Cor 14:34–35; and 1 Tim 2:12: "I permit no woman to teach . . ."]

Clearly, the "foreign men" to whom the canon alludes are members of the Priscillianist sect. It seems likely that Catholic women were attending Priscillianist meetings. Of perhaps greater importance is the implication that women themselves were organizing and giving lectures for the purpose of teaching and instruction. According to Sulpicius Severus, these conventicles were particularly popular with women,[47] and the emperor condemned Priscillianism in part because Priscillian and his followers were charged with organizing on a nightly basis these conventicles with "dissolute" women.

Synod of Nîmes Canon 2[48]

*A reference in the writings of Sulpicius Severus (*Dialogues *2.15) establishes that a Gallican National Synod occurred at Nîmes (apud Nemausum) in approximately 394. Despite its proximity to his episcopal see, Martin of Tours did not attend. The synod was virtually forgotten until the eighteenth century, when its acta were finally published. These reveal that, though the Bishop of Tours did not attend, at least seventeen other Gallican bishops (two of whom signed the canons for one other colleague) from seven provinces did. They produced only seven brief canons, most directed against the Manichaeans (*de ultimis Orientis partibus venientes, *as the first canon describes them) and, especially, the Priscillianists. Among the heterodox practices observed with alarm by the bishops assembled at Nîmes, just a few years after the Synod of Toledo, was the elevation of women to clerical offices reserved, in their minds, for men.*

The following was suggested by certain individuals, that contrary to apostolic teaching (*apostolicam disciplinam*), unbeknownst, women seemed to have been assumed into levitical service (*in ministerium . . . leuiticum videantur adsumptae*) in some place or another (*nescio quo loco*). Ecclesiastical discipline does not permit this because it is inappropriate (*indecens*), and such ordination should be undone (*distruatur*) when it is effected contrary to reason (*contra rationem*). It should be seen to that no one so presume in the future.[49]

This brief text is fascinating both for the details it supplies and frustratingly tantalizing for those it omits. The notion that women had been assumed into "levitical" service is of course of significant *prima facie* interest, even if in a group denounced by orthodox authorities as heretical. One would, of course, like to know more about just what this service implied. Gryson has argued that "levitical service" implied diaconal activity. But even he acknowledges that the words "deaconess" and "diaconate" are not used at all.[50] Martimort translates the key phrase *in ministerium . . . leuiticum videantur adsumptae* as "raised to the ministry of deacons."[51]

Such a translation is certainly possible, but it is not certain that "levitical ministry" should be rendered as "diaconal ministry." In the West at the end of the fourth century, "levitical" and "sacerdotal" often could be, and often were, used synonymously.[52] So there are philological grounds for believing that these Priscillianist women were functioning as presbyters.

There are strong historical grounds for believing the same. The Priscillianist attitude toward matter and the body made gender a matter of indifference in many respects. Thus, it is entirely possible that women exercised the same priestly roles and enjoyed the same sacerdotal status as the group's male priesthood. Perhaps it is, above all, this *indecens* and unreasonable conduct that better accounts for the vigor of the council's response, which Gryson has also noted. Nonetheless, we are again frustrated by the philological imprecision of a key term, and it is better not to inject more precision into the term than it can bear.

Also of interest is the geographical ambiguity *nescio quo loco,* though Priscillianism had certainly spread to southern Gaul at the time the synod was held. The synod is quite unanalytical in its rejection of female priesthood, noting only that it is not traditional, because *indecens,* and that it is unreasonable. Finally, the forceful recommendation that such ordinations be undone ties into the debate, occurring at almost the same time in North Africa, over the permanence of priestly ordination and episcopal consecration. The "orthodox" position worked out by Augustine in his conflict with the Donatists is that such ordinations could not be undone. Medieval scholastics developed this position with more philosophical texture, as those theologians insisted that ordination effects a *character* on the soul of the ordinand that can be neither reversed nor erased. The bishops assembled here assume not only that it can be reversed but that it must.

Pope Gelasius I, Letter 14, to bishops in southern Italy [53]

In his brief pontificate (492–96), Pope Gelasius had an important impact in several spheres of ecclesial life, particularly in the domains of relations between the Eastern and Western churches and between the Emperor and the church. He was an extremely prolific letter writer and a vigorous champion of what he took to be ancient and unchangeable ecclesiastical tradition. The following excerpt is taken from a very lengthy letter dated March 11, 494, and consisting of twenty-seven canons. Sent to the bishops in the provinces of Lucania and Bruttium in southern Italy and of the province of Sicily, it dealt with a variety of organizational and disciplinary issues. Four of the decrees treat virgins and widows. Canon 26 deals with the report Gelasius had received that women were serving at the altars in the south of Italy with the presumed knowledge of the bishops there.

> We have heard to our distress that contempt of divine things has reached such a state that women are encouraged (*firmentur*) to serve at the sacred altars (*ministrare sacris altaribus*) and to perform all the other tasks (*cunctaque*) that are assigned only to the service of men (*non nisi virorum famulatui sexum*), and for which they [women] are not appropriate (*cui non competunt*).

This text is crucially important for addressing the questions of if, when, where, how, and on what basis women functioned as presbyters in early Latin Christianity. However, its meaning and significance are not absolutely clear. Because of several textual ambiguities and silences, the letter is open to more than one interpretation. Not surprisingly, scholars have been polarized about its meaning. Some interpretations seem, regrettably, to be driven by agenda that are not wholly historical. Jean Daniélou, for example, has come to the conclusion that "there has never been any mention of women filling strictly sacerdotal offices. We never see a woman offering the Eucharistic Sacrifice, or ordaining, or preaching in the Church."[54] Perhaps overemphasizing the ambiguity of the text, Gryson asserts that it is "difficult to form an idea of the situation which Pope Gelasius opposed" and observes that "it is regrettable that more details" about the situation are not available. Nonetheless, like Daniélou, he is persuaded that "women bishops or women priests have never been known in the Catholic Church."[55]

On the other hand, Giorgo Otranto, much closer to the truth, reads the text as evidence for the argument that "at the end of the fifth century, some women, having been ordained by bishops, were exercising a true and proper ministerial priesthood in a vast area of southern Italy, as well as perhaps in other unnamed regions of Italy."[56]

While this conclusion is certainly sound, some of his arguments supporting it are not. For example, Otranto too confidently translates *ministrare* as "to officiate," and he asserts, without argument, that it corresponds to the Greek *leitourgein*. While one can certainly agree with Otranto that this "indicates indubitably the *involvement* of a liturgical service at the altars," the verb *ministrare* alone is not sufficient to indicate that women were officiating in a sacerdotal capacity at the altars. This is especially the case when one recalls, as Otranto does,[57] that *ministra* could be used, as it possibly was in Pliny's *Letter* to Trajan, to refer to female deacons, who would not have undertaken sacerdotal service at the altars.[58] Beyond that, a letter from Pope Zachary (741–52) to Pippin and Frankish ecclesiastical authorities written in January 747, which explicitly invokes this Gelasian letter, interprets *sacris altaribus ministrare* to mean "to serve at the divine altars." By this, they mean publicly reading the Bible during Mass, singing at Mass, or offering an Alleluia or an antiphonal song. It never occurred to Zachary to believe that *ministrare* might mean to officiate as a presbyter.[59] A later letter from Frankish bishops to emperor Louis the Pious, also invoking the decree of Gelasius, interprets "to minister" in what we might call diaconal terms: entering the sanctuary, holding the consecrated vessels, handing the sacerdotal vestments to priests, and administering the consecrated elements to the congregation.[60] So the term *ministrare* is, by itself, insufficient to suggest female presbyteral activity.

What does clinch Otranto's interpretation is the single Latin word with enclitic *cunctaque:* "and *all the other things*" (emphasis added) that male presbyters do and for which women, in Gelasius' view, are not competent. Otranto captures the significance of *cuncta* very well: this word, he correctly notes, implies "all the attributes of the male services: liturgical, juridical, and magisterial." When that piece of philological evidence is introduced, then we can agree with Otranto that: "The functions exercised by women at the altars, therefore, can refer only to the administration of the sacraments, to the liturgical service, and to the public and official announcement of the evangelical message, all of which comprise the duties of ministerial priesthood . . . Hence . . . Gelasius . . . intended to stigmatize and condemn not the exercise of a feminine liturgical service, but an abuse that appeared to him a great deal more serious: that of true and proper presbyters who were performing all the duties traditionally reserved for men alone."[61]

As we shall see, there is some inscriptional evidence from southern Italy some four decades before Gelasius was writing that fortifies Otranto's interpretation that women were functioning as presbyters, in the full sense of the term, in Bruttium at the close of the fifth century. In his letter, Gelasius goes on to censure the south Italian bishops in sharply worded and menacing tones. For this condemnation, Gelasius has recourse, characteristically, mainly to the tradition and canons of the church: the "ecclesiastical rules" and canons for which, he argues, the south Italian bishops have no respect.[62] He proceeds to warn the bishops apocalyptically that, if such a situation is not corrected, not only will their positions be jeopardized, but even the fate of the universal church could be affected.[63] The warning is a typical instance of the deep conservatism that, as several commentators have remarked, runs throughout the Gelasian correspondence.

Otranto concludes that Gelasius also intended to condemn "the conferring of the sacrament of priesthood on women," a "mandate specifically conferred by some bishops on women for the exercise of sacerdotal ministry."[64] He qualifies this as a "hypothesis" and states, somewhat weakly, "it is my conviction" that the bishops had authorized and legitimated the female presbyterate.[65] It might have strengthened his argument to observe that the letter itself states (albeit in the passive voice) that women are "encouraged" (*firmentur*) to serve at the altars. By whom? The bishops? It is certainly possible but, on the basis of this text, far from certain, especially since Gelasius implies some of the bishops simply *condoned* this behavior rather than encouraged it. Be that as it may, this text, especially when put in context of contemporary inscriptional evidence, constitutes very strong evidence that some women in the south Italian dioceses were functioning as fully fledged presbyters with the knowledge of their bishops. It is crucial to observe that these were not women in heretical sects but in churches claiming to be "Catholic" or in communion with the Church of Rome.[66]

Letter of three Gallic bishops [67]

Written in 511 by three bishops from the northern Gallic dioceses of Tours, Rennes, and Angers, this letter is addressed to two Breton priests. All five clerics are named in the first sentence of the letter, which reprehends a situation (in their eyes an abomination) very like the one described by Gelasius less than two decades before.

Bishops Licinius, Melanius, and Eustochius to priests Lovocatus and Catihernius, our most blessed lords and brothers in Christ. We have learned through a report of the priest Speratus, a venerable man, that you have not desisted from carrying certain altars (*tabulas*) through the domiciles of several citizens and presume to say masses there with women, whom you call *conhospitae,* who are employed (*adhibitis mulieribus*) in the divine sacrifice; so that, while you are distributing the eucharist, they hold the chalices and presume to administer the blood of Christ to the people of God. This novelty and unheard-of superstition saddens us not a little, as such a horrendous sect, which by no means has ever existed in Gaul, seems to be emerging in our times. This sect the Eastern fathers call the Pepodian, because Pepodius was the founder of this schismatic group. Because this sect presumed to have women associates in the divine sacrifice, the fathers ordered that anyone who wished to be involved in this error be put outside (*extraneus*) ecclesiastical communion. Accordingly, we believe Your Charity ought to be admonished, first of all, in the love of Christ for the unity of the church and of the Catholic faith. We pray you then, that, when the pages of these letters reach you, a correction of the aforesaid things follow immediately: that is, of the aforementioned altars, which . . . we do not doubt were consecrated by priests; and from those women, whom you call *conhospitae*—which term is neither said nor heard without a certain danger to the soul, as it brings infamy upon the clergy and because so detestable a name incurs shame and horror for holy religion. Therefore, following the statutes of the holy fathers, we admonish Your Charity, not only that silly little women of this sort (*huiuscemodi mulierculae*) not pollute the divine sacraments by illicit assistance, but also that anyone who should wish to have under the roof of his little cell anyone—except for mother, aunt, sister, or granddaughter—for the purposes of cohabitation should, by canonical decree [probably Canon 3 of Nicaea I] be kept from the sacrosanct boundaries (*sacrosanctis liminibus*) of the church. It seems right to us, therefore, dearest brothers, that if it is as we have heard concerning this business, that you very rapidly execute a change, because it is right, for the salvation of souls and for the edification of the people, such depraved practices be swiftly corrected, so that the pertinacity of this stubbornness not bring you to greater confusion, and so that it is not necessary for us to come to you with an apostolic scepter [1 Cor 5:5], should you decline our charity, and be given over to Satan in the destruction of the flesh, so that your spirit might be saved. To be given over Satan is this: when anyone has been separated from the ecclesiastical flock for his fault, let him not doubt that he will be devoured by demons as well as wolves.

This letter is addressed to two Breton priests who constructed portable altars in order to circulate into the countryside and to celebrate Mass in the houses of peasants. They distributed the eucharist with the help of women, here called "cohabiters" (*conhospitae*), who traveled and dwelt with them. The term *conhospita*[68] seems synonymous with the earlier term *subintroducta*, which referred to the practice in the second, third, fourth, and perhaps first centuries in which a woman would live celibately with a man, including male clerics. This practice was condemned explicitly in the third canon of the Council of Nicaea (325). It seems to be this canon the three Gallic bishops had in mind when they referred to the "statutes of the holy fathers," as they quote it almost verbatim here. Neither this canon nor the canons that reiterate the condemnation succeeded in stopping the practice entirely. Pepodian is probably a nominalization of the place-name Pepuza, a town in Phrygia near which Montanus, in the late second century, prophesied the heavenly kingdom would soon descend.[69] Montanus was accompanied by two women prophetesses, Prisca and Maximilla. Thus the bishops feared in this small group the novel emergence in Gaul of ecstatic, prophetic, apocalyptic Montanism, which had been condemned as a heresy by several Eastern synods. For that reason, and because they were angry at the pollution of sacred space by the presence of women, they reprehend their priest-brothers with considerable vigor. A sign of the depth of their outrage comes in the tone and threat with which the letter concludes.

Canon of Fulgentius Ferrandus of Carthage [70]

Fulgentius was a deacon of the Carthaginian church and a known theological and canonical authority of the time. Just at the end of his life, perhaps in the year of his death (547), he compiled a list of 232 canons, his Breviatio Canonum. *In it, he attempted to summarize the teaching of the earliest Greek and African councils. The following canon treats the issue of widows and ordination.*

> **That it is not fitting for women who among the Greeks are called presbyter-esses (*presbyterae*), and who among us are called widows, or elders (*seniores*), once-married (*uniuirae*), and the enrolled (*matriculae*), to be appointed as if ordained (*tanquam ordinatas*) in the church.**

Definitive interpretation is ruled out with this, as with any collection of canons, precisely because it is a compilation from other canonical collections assembled as much as two centuries earlier and in a very different cultural and ecclesiastical world than sixth-century North Africa. Nonetheless, Fulgentius was selective with his material, and he chose to put this canon in his collection. It may thus be an indication, which we see especially marked in the West, above all in Gaul in the same century, of increasingly vehement opposition to the ordination of widows or deaconesses.

Ancient Canons of the Church [71]

A variety of canonical collections published in the early modern period refer to a "Fourth Carthaginian Synod," supposed to have taken place, with 214 bishops in attendance, in 398 and alleged to have produced 104 canons. Throughout the nineteenth and twentieth centuries, a number of scholars have given very good reason to doubt that such a synod occurred in that year. Other collections of decrees contain the same (or nearly same) group of 104 canons but group them, with more accuracy, under the general title Statuta Ecclesiae Antiqua. *In fact, this collection of 104 canons does not originate from any single synod. Rather, it is a compilation by an obscure Gallic priest named Gennadius of Marseilles, who gathered the canons partly from African synods and partly from Oriental sources, especially the* Apostolic Constitutions. *(Thus Italian manuscripts of the collection are entitled* Statuta Orientis.*) The canons are addressed, among other things, to a variety of heresies, including the Pelagian and Monophysite.*

These references constitute the strongest possible proof that the canons had to have been produced well after the year 398, while internal evidence also suggests that the collection was completed before the end of the sixth century. They were eventually to wield considerable influence, as they were included in the False Decretals of Pseudo-Isidore and made their way, thus, into Gratian's Decretum *in the twelfth century. While the canons address the issues of heresies, they also deal with a wide variety of other matters, above all the conduct of clergymen. About a tenth of them deal with women and consecrated office. Two of these, Canons 37 and 41, treat matters of women's offices.*

> 37. A woman, though she be learned and holy (*quamuis docta et sancta*), ought not to presume to teach in a gathering of men (*viros in conuentu*) . . .
> 41. A woman ought not presume to baptize (*baptizare non praesumat*).

Unfortunately, the chronological and geographical ambiguity that surrounds this Western collection, and its heavy reliance on a fourth-century Syrian text, allows us to draw very few factual conclusions from these records, especially about Western European Christianity and women in the fifth century. Nonetheless, the canons, if not voluble, are not entirely silent. First of all, that both were produced and replicated at all strongly suggests that the prohibited behavior was actually being practiced somewhere and sometime in the south European, African, or Oriental contexts in the fourth–sixth centuries. The specificity of Canon 37, in particular the prohibition against teaching *in a gathering of men* seems to suggest that teaching by women was occurring in precisely such contexts. Otherwise, why forbid it? Similarly, that women were in fact baptizing seems suggested by the prohibition against it. It is usual in ecclesiastical history for canons to be produced reactively, not prospectively. If this principle of interpretation is applied in this case, then women do appear to have been teaching men and baptizing in some places in the Mediterranean world in the late antique period. Perhaps the fourth-century Syrian context is the likeliest, as both prohibitions are expressed in the *Apostolic Constitutions* (3.6, 3.9). Whether Gennadius reproduced them mechanically or to combat perceived irregularities in Gaul is a more difficult question to answer, thus making it impossible to say on the basis of this document alone with any certainty whether women were teaching and baptizing in Gaul in the fifth and sixth centuries.

Letter of Atto, Bishop of Vercelli, to Ambrose the Priest [72]

Atto was an accomplished canon lawyer and bishop of Vercelli, a town in the Piedmont, in the early tenth century. Among his writings are a commentary on the epistles of Paul, collections of various canons, and several letters; the following is taken from his Letter 8, to an otherwise unknown priest named Ambrose, who had apparently writ-

ten to him to inquire about the meaning of the terms presbytera *and* diacona *in the ancient canons. Atto replies that the terms could refer to women who had married priests and deacons before their ordination. But he also says:*

> Because your prudence has moved you to inquire how we should understand "female priest" (*presbyteram*) or "female deacon" (*diaconam*) in the canons: it seems to me that in the primitive church, according to the word of the Lord, "the harvest was great and laborers few";[73] religious women (*religiosae mulieres*) used also to be ordained as caretakers (*cultrices ordinabantur*) in the holy church, as Blessed Paul shows in the *Letter* to the Romans, when he says, "I commend to you my sister Phoebe, who is in the ministry of the church at Cenchrea."[74] Here it is understood that not only men but also women presided over the churches (*sed etiam feminae praeerat ecclesiis*) because of their great usefulness. For women, long accustomed to the rites of the pagans and instructed also in philosophical teachings, were, for these reasons, converted more easily and taught more liberally in the worship of religion. This the eleventh canon of the Council of Laodicea[75] prohibits when it says it is not fitting for those women who are called female presbyters (*presbyterae*) or presiders (*praesidentes*) to be ordained in the churches. We believe female deacons truly to have been ministers of such things. For we say that a minister is a deacon (*diaconum*), from which we perceive female deacon (*diaconam*) to have been derived. Finally, we read in the fifteenth canon of the Council of Chalcedon that a female deacon is not to be ordained before her fortieth year—and this was the highest gravity. We believe women were enjoined to the office of baptizing so that the bodies of other women might be handled by them without any deeply felt sense of shame . . . just as those who were called female presbyters (*presbyterae*) assumed the office of preaching, leading and teaching, so female deacons had taken up the office of ministry and of baptizing, a custom that no longer is expedient.

Atto clearly believes that before the fourth century, women had been ordained leaders of the churches, had presided over, preached in and led them. They were ordained, he thinks, because of their fitness for ministry and also because of the paucity of other male presbyters; only the Council of Laodicea in the second half of the fourth century put an end to this practice. This letter is a rare witness from the early Middle Ages to *belief* among some male clergy (including, in this case, a bishop) that women once exercised the presbyteral office in the ancient church. Partly because the document was written some six centuries after the events it purports to describe, it does not, however, constitute unambiguous witness to the *existence* of female presbyters in the early church. Yet it does certainly demolish the notion that "the tradition" is unanimous in denying the existence of female priests.

INSCRIPTIONS

Even in the inscriptions of Leta and Flavia Vitalia, it is not clear just what function these *presbyterae* had. In most cases, they may not have performed sacramental ministry but possibly served as agents for official church business. When these inscriptions are put alongside the high anxiety expressed in the contemporary documents cited above, however, we are not so sure.

Episcopa Q[76]

This versified inscription comes from a fragmented marble stone in the Basilican Cemetery of St. Paul's in Rome. The damage to the marble makes the text of the first line uncertain. The second line reads:

> Here lies the venerable woman, bishop Q (*uenerabilis fem[ina] episcopa Q*),
> Buried in peace for five [years] . . . +Olybrio.

Much about this fragmentary inscription is uncertain, beginning with its date. It is not impossible, as Muratori suggested, that the tombstone was dedicated in the late fifth or early sixth century. But that suggestion is uncertain.[77] The date could be, and perhaps more likely is, earlier. The consular date indicated in the last line may place the inscription in the late fourth century, as there was an Anicius Olybrius who served, at a very young age, as Western consul in 395; he died in 410, as the Vandals sacked the city. Jerome refers to him in *Epistle* 130.3 to Demetrias, the noble virgin and daughter of Olybrius.[78] If this is the Olybrius to whom the inscription alludes, the date of Q's death could be very precisely fixed in the year 390. (Olybrius's son would be emperor for a few months in 472.) She then could have been mother or wife of Pope Siricius (384–99). Being in such a position alone would have created numerous possibilities for ministry, perhaps above all to women. Given Siricius' fierce opposition to Priscillianism, in which women seem to have played an important pedagogical and leadership role (see canon from the First Synod of Saragossa), it is highly unlikely that Q exercised similar responsibilities in the Church of Rome. Nonetheless, such a woman would have likely been among the most prominent female ecclesiastical leaders in the community.

Leta the Presbytera[79]

> Sacred to her good memory. Leta the presbyter[ess]
> lived forty years, eight months and nine days.
> Her husband made [this tombstone].

Figure 13. Leta Presbytera (*CIL* 10.8079; *ILCV* 1.1192). Photo courtesy of Giorgio Otranto, *Italia meridionale e Puglia paleocristiane. Saggi storici* (Bari: Edipuglia, 1991), 110

She preceded him in peace on the day before the ides of May.[80]

This is a fourth- or fifth-century inscription from Tropea, Calabria. The consensus on the interpretation of this inscription, until the pathbreaking article by Otranto,[81] had been that Leta was the wife of a presbyter.[82] One commentator observes that the memory of a presbyter, Monsis, from Tropea, was recorded inscriptionally at about the same time as Leta's tombstone was made and suggests that Leta was his spouse.[83] But it would be hazardous, to say the least, to link Monsis and Leta as husband and wife. Eisen is very much on the mark when cautioning that we ought not over-hastily to conclude that "every reference to a *presbytera, diaconissa,* or *subdiacona* is to the wife of a man holding the corresponding office."[84]

More recently, scholars, led by Otranto, have argued, correctly in our view, that the inscriptional evidence here has to be interpreted in light of the Gelasian letter. Whether we will want to go all the way with Otranto and conclude Leta was "a true and proper presbyter" (*una vera e propria presbytera*)[85] is another question. But several pieces of evidence do seem to point in this direction. Both pieces of evidence are roughly coterminous. Both come from the same part of Italy. Additionally, inscriptional custom, according to Otranto, suggests "every time a presbyter prepares a tomb for his wife, he always refers to her by the term *coniux* ('wife') or *amantissima* ('most loving')."[86] Finally, Eisen correctly observes that Leta's husband is identified, but not as an officeholder.[87]

The evidence put forward by Otranto and Eisen is, to say the least, intriguing. The coincidence of time and place of literary and inscriptional evidence is particularly suggestive. Still, the data are scanty, too meager on which to rest such large and sweeping conclusions as those made by Otranto. In the end, we are talking about two pieces of evidence for the south of Italy, and the inscriptional one is, unfortunately, especially ambiguous. Beyond the tiny quantum of evidence, there is the uncomfortable fact that *presbytera* can, as Eisen concedes, refer in certain Latin ecclesiastical documents from late antiquity to the wife of a priest.

In the end, we can conclude that it is definitely possible but not certain that Leta was "a true and proper presbyter." More archaeological work could conceivably strengthen the case made by Otranto and Eisen. The inscription of a "sacerdota" from Salona in Dalmatia comes, so to speak, from the same cultural and ecclesiastical orbit as that from Tropea, not to mention from roughly the same time period. It may shed some additional light on the question.

Martia Presbyteress [?][88]

This is a graffito found near Poitiers in Gaul. The date is unknown. It may be from the late fourth or early fifth century. Other evidence, including conciliar and epistolary writings considered in this volume, may place it in the sixth century.

Martia the presbyteress (*presbyteria*) made (*ferit*)[89] the offering (*obblata*) together with Olybrius and Nepos.

The interpretation of this graffito has to begin with dating and with a philological analysis of *presbyteria*. Unfortunately, on both questions, particularly the former, there is considerable ambiguity. Some scholars have dated it to the fifth century; others have placed it later. Then there is the question of the meaning of *presbyteria*. Some scholars regard it as an adjective modifying *obblata* ("priestly offerings," i.e., the unconsecrated eucharistic elements). Others, including Otranto, see it as a noun and as a title.[90] We agree with Otranto.

First of all, the Council of Tours (567) would use *presbyteria* as a title at roughly the same time this graffito was made; the slightly later Council of Auxerre (578) would use *presbytera* as a title as well.[91] All three pieces of evidence come from Gaul. We also agree with Otranto that "Olybrius and Nepos are almost certainly two presbyters who were officiating in the community to which Martia also belonged; and it is probable that this woman collaborated with them during the eucharistic celebration."[92] However, we disagree partially with Otranto's reasoning. Otranto wants to interpret this graffito in light of the two Gallish councils just mentioned. All three texts refer to "presbyteresses," but it is quite clear, as Otranto seems not to realize, that the presbyteresses mentioned in the Gallish councils refer to the wives of priests who have no particular liturgical or diaconal role. Otranto is on much stronger ground when discussing the motives of the author of the graffito: "The fact that there had been a desire to record an action performed by Martia during a liturgical celebration would seem to signify not the usual service of the faithful at the moment of the offertory, but rather an act habitually performed by a deacon or another member of the clergy." Otranto is right to interpret this letter in light of the letter of three Gallic bishops (see text above).[93] Both texts are found in roughly the same period; both refer to activities in Gaul; both refer to the participation by women in the eucharistic celebration. In light of this roughly contemporary literary evidence, and of the existence of the graffito, it seems likely that Martia had an important role as a minister in the celebration of the eucharistic service in Poitiers.

Flavia Vitalia, Presbytera[94]

This inscription, dated 425, was found in Solin, in modern-day Croatia, then Salona in the Roman colonial province of Dalmatia on the Adriatic. Ironically, Salona, an important early Christian center, may well have been the birthplace of one of its severest persecutors, the Emperor Diocletian (284–303). In fact, it became so important that the bishop of Salona became metropolitan bishop for the province. In the fifth and sixth centuries, the town was destroyed by barbarian invaders; it remains ruined still. In the decades before it was reduced to ruins, Flavia Vitalia, a leader in the Christian community, lived and died there. A tombstone bought by a man named Theodosius tells us some interesting things about her.

> **Under our Lord Theodosius, consul for the eleventh time, and Valentinian, most noble man of Caesar, I, Theodosius, bought [a burial tomb] from the matron (*matrona*) Flavia Vitalia, the holy presbyter[a] (*presbytera sancta*) for three golden solids.**

What can we say with certainty about Flavia Vitalia? First of all, the description of her as *matrona* tells us she was free-born and married. Second, the title *presbytera* tells us, in all likelihood, that she occupied an official and recognized place as a leader in the ecclesiastical community of Salona. Unfortunately, we cannot know all we would like about exactly what this implied. By the fourth and fifth century, sales and administration of burial plots in Rome had passed to ecclesiastical officials, including presbyters,[95] a practice that seems to be reflected here in the sale for three solids of gold of a plot in Salona to Theodosius. We cannot, in particular, say with any certainty what that title *presbytera* implied, particularly whether it encompassed the full spectrum of sacerdotal activities, including leadership in liturgy and ritual.

Still, this piece of evidence emerges from a similar ecclesiastical-cultural milieu as the one reprehended by Pope Gelasius, and Flavia was functioning as *presbytera* at about the same time as those whose activities so infuriated the pope. In this light, it is equally impossible to conclude that Flavia Vitalia was not a presbyter in the full and proper sense of the term, invested with the status and all the functions of the sacerdotal office.

A Sacerdota from Solin[96]

Another important piece of epigraphical evidence also suggests, perhaps even more strongly, that women were functioning as priestesses in Salona in the fifth century.

> . . . of/to [?] a priestess[97] . . .

The epigraph on this tombstone is fragmentary. It is the genitive or dative form of *sacerdota*, "priestess." The only other bit of the epigraph remaining is a cross. This indicates the entombed was a Christian, not a pagan priestess. Obviously, as this tombstone comes from Solin, it has to be interpreted in light of the Flavia Vitalia inscription and vice versa. Taken together, they suggest a strong possibility, minimally, that women were functioning as presbyters in the community. Eisen even suggests that "it is possible that the epigraphically attested *sacerdota* was the bishop" of the community.[98]

Eisen is correct. It *is* possible. Such a possibility is strengthened, philologically, by the use of *sacerdota* rather than *presbytera*. This is clearly not the wife of a priest, nor is it merely a respected elderly woman in the community. She is a "priestess" or "sacerdotess," a woman with high official status and some sort of important official function in the community of Solin. Here the fragment of a single word, when interpreted in conjunction with contemporaneous inscriptional evidence, *can* bear at least that much historical weight.

Guilia Runa, Presbyteress of Hippo[99]

This inscription comes from a medallion mosaic in the church of St. Augustine in Hippo, North Africa, from the period of Vandal occupation, after 431.

> Guilia Runa the presbyteress (*presbiterissa*), rest in peace, lived for fifty years.

Figure 14. Guilia Runa Presbiterissa, Basilica of St. Augustine, Hippo (*AE* 1953, no. 107). Photo by David Brecht

Guilia seems to be a Vandal by name. This is important, as she would have been baptized an Arian Christian. Justinian (527–65) reconquered all North Africa by 534. Arian Christianity virtually disappeared with the Vandal kingdom that supported it. Many clerics fled, and many of the surviving Vandals were captured and transported East to serve as slaves. Justinian, who was not at all tolerant of heresy, restored to the now reestablished Catholic Church all rights and privileges it had held before the Vandal occupation, and he spent great sums renovating old churches and building new ones. It is impossible to know whether Guilia died an Arian or "converted," with the small remnant of Vandal Christians, to Catholic Christianity after Justinian's reconquest.

The title *presbiterissa* suggests she had some recognized role as a leader in the community. Minimally, she seems to have held status and role as something like a widow or deacon. While it is unlikely that she exercised routine "presybteral" functions, she was probably among the leading female ministers of the community.

CONCLUSION

As is so often the case in Church history, the sources do not tell us what we would most like to know. Conciliar or episcopal prohibitions exist alongside evidence of exactly the practice they are prohibiting, and often the evidence for the continuing existence of practices postdates the prohibitions. It does seem that in some times and places, there were women presbyters in the Church, even in "orthodox" circles, in both East and West, but most clearly in the West. Exactly what they did remains unclear, with the exception of Flavia Vitalia, who was an agent in her own right for the sale of church property. Celibacy was not always a requirement, for Leta predeceased her husband. Guilia Runa is a precious piece of evidence of church office in Arian churches, of which we know very little.

The Letter of Gelasius and that of the three bishops of Gaul suggest knowledge of women serving at the altar, at least in a quasi-diaconal service of chalice administration. That women were standing at the altar at all by that time constituted an affront to purity- and status-conscious male prelates. Quite to the contrary, the tenth-century writer Atto of Vercelli was warmest in his estimations of church office in the early apostolic and post-apostolic years, and he had no problem recognizing full presbyteral leadership of women then, though he knew that the same no longer existed in his own church. Perhaps he was engaging in a bit of nostalgia for imagined "good old days."

Beyond these rather unsatisfying and disparate assertions, the evidence does not allow us to go.

Notes

1. Text: Mansi, *Sacrorum Conciliorum,* 2.565–66; Mayer, *Monumenta,* 11; full English text with comment, NPNF n.s. 14.130–31.

2. See further discussion in Eisen, *Women Officeholders,* 116–23.

3. Text: *PG* 41.879–82. Translation of the whole available in Frank Williams, ed., *The Panarion of Epiphanius of Salamis,* vol. 2 (Leiden: Brill, 1994).

4. Text: *PG* 42.735–46.

5. 1 Cor 14:34.

6. 1 Tim 2:12.

7. Text: *Acta Philippi,* ed. François Bovon, Bertand Bouvier, and Frédéric Amsler (Turnhout: Brepols, 1999), 385 (commentary in French by F. Amsler, 515–16).

8. Greek and Latin texts in Maximilian Bonnet, ed., *Acta Apostolorum Apocrypha* (Darmstadt: Wissenschaftliche Buchgesellschaft, 1959), 2.259; discussion of ms. traditions, ibid., xxxiii–xxxv; discussion of the document by Arelio de Santos Otero in *New Testament Apocrypha,* ed. Wilhelm Schneemelcher (Louisville, KY: Westminster/John Knox, 1992), 2.458–60.

9. Text: *enlogismos,* error for *eulogismos* (Lampe, *Lexicon,* s.v.) with reference to this passage.

10. The text does not specify which woman is which.

11. Text: Elsa Gibson, "Montanist Epitaphs at Uçak," *GRBS* 16 (1975): 433–42, at 437–38, and *The "Christians for Christians" Inscriptions of Phrygia. Greek Texts, Translation and Commentary,* Harvard Theological Studies 32 (Missoula: Scholars, 1978), 136; *NewDocs* 4.122.7, p. 240; Eisen, *Women Officeholders,* 116–17; translation in Kraemer, *Women's Religions,* 256–57.

12. Detailed discussion in Eisen, *Women Officeholders,* 116–23.

13. Text: François Baratte and Bernard Boyaval, "Catalogue des étiquettes de momies du Musée du Louvre (C.E.M.L.)—texts grecs," *Cahiers de Recherches de l'Institut de Papyrologie et d'Egyptologie de Lille* 5 (1979): 237–339, at 264 no. 1115; *NewDocs* 4.240, no. 122.6; Eisen, *Women Officeholders,* 125–26.

14. Eisen, *Women Officeholders,* 126.

15. Text: Grégoire, *Recueil* 167, p. 58; Eisen, *Women Officeholders,* 123–25; discussion, Eisen and Denis Feissel, *BCH* 101 (1977): 209–28, at 210, 212 (fig. 2, p. 211).

16. Further discussion in Eisen, *Women Officeholders,* 123–25.

17. Text: *AE* 1975.454, p. 114; Eisen, *Women Officeholders,* 128–29, with discussion; Maria Teresa and Manni Piraino, *Iscrizioni greche lipidarie del Museo di Palermo* (Palermo: S. F. Flaccovio, 1972), 36–37, no. 13 (plate 7); translation in Kraemer, *Women's Religions,* 256; mentioned in *NewDocs* 1.79, p. 121.

18. For more discussion, see Brian Brennan, "'Episcopae': Bishops' Wives Viewed in Sixth-Century Gaul," *Church History* 54.3 (1985): 311–23. The article deals with wives of bishops and shows how they too exercised important leadership roles.

19. *Concilia Galliae,* ed. C. de Clercq, *CCL* 148A (1963): 184.

20. *Deaconesses,* 201.

21. In *Concilia Gallia,* ed. C. de Clercq, *CCL* 148A (1963): 268.

22. Mansi, *Sacrorum Conciliorum,*12.383; Mayer, *Monumenta,* 50.

23. *De praescriptione haereticorum,* ed. R. F. Refoulé, *CCL* 1 (1954): 221.

24. A recent study has argued that "Tertullian's views toward women, when considered within his own cultural and theological context, were not unusually negative, but were relatively positive"; and that "there are several statements [in his writings] that support the idea that he

considered women ontologically equal with men." See Daniel Hoffmann, *The Status of Women and Gnosticism in Irenaeus and Tertullian* (Lewiston, NY: Mellen, 1995), 148, 152.

25. *Apologeticum* 23.4, *CCL* 1 (1954): 131.

26. *De cultu feminarum* 2.12.1, ed. E. Kroymann, *CCL* 1 (1954): 367.

27. *De Baptismo*, ed. J. Borleffs, *CCL* 1 (1954): 291–92.

28. In his writings, Tertullian often used the legal term *ius,* which signifies a right to exercise some privilege.

29. *Aduersus Marcionem,* ed. E. Kroymann, *CCL* 1 (1954): 688.

30. *De virginibus velandis,* ed. E. Dekkers, *CCL* 2 (1954): 1218–19.

31. *CCL* 2 (1954): 1219.

32. *De exhortatione castitatis,* ed. J.-C Fredouille, in *SC* 319 (1985): 106.

33. *De Monogamia,* in *SC* 343 (1988): 178, and ed. E. Dekkers, *CCL* 2 (1954): 1–5.

34. Modern scholars agree. See Daniélou, *Ministry of Women in the Early Church,* trans. G. Simon (London: The Faith Press, 1961), 17, and Gryson, *Ministry of Women,* 20.

35. *De Pudicitia,* ed. C. Munier, *SC* 394 (1993): 2.208.

36. *The Status of Women and Gnosticism in Irenaeus and Tertullian* (Lewston, NY: Mellen, 1995), 164.

37. *Ad Uxorem,* ed E. Kroymann, *CCL* 1 (1954): 381.

38. On the widow as altar, see C. Osiek, "The Widow as Altar: The Rise and Fall of a Symbol," *Second Century* 3 (1983): 159–69.

39. *CCL* 3C (1996): 590–92.

40. Ed. R. Vander Plaetse and C. Beukers, *CCL* 46 (1969): 302–3.

41. The adherents of the movement we call Montanism called themselves "The New Prophecy." The term "Cataphyrgians" was applied to them abusively by their enemies. See D. Powell, "Tertullianists and Cataphrygians," *Vigiliae Christianae* 29 (1975): 33–54.

42. *Sacramenta perhibentur habere funesta: nam de infantis anniculi sanguine, quem de toto ejus corpore minutis punctionum vulneribus extorquent, quasi eucharistiam suam conficere perhibentur, miscentes eum farinae, panemque inde facientes: qui puer si mortuus fuerit, habetur apud eos pro martyre; si autem vixerit, pro magno sacerdote (CCL* 46 [1969]: 302).

43. As it is also by Pseudo-Jerome, *Indiculus* 32.20 (*PL* 81.641).

44. Jürgen Dummer, *Epiphanius, II. Panarion Haer. 34–64,* GCS 31 (Berlin: Akademie-Verlag, 1980), 49.2.2–5, 49.3.2, pp. 244 ff.

45. See Carolyn Osiek, "The Social Function of Female Imagery in Second-Century Prophecy," *Vetus Christianorum* 29.1 (1992): 54–074. Augustine's description of the Cataphyrgians and Pepuzians and Quintillians likely influenced another handbook of heresies written not long after his death, the *Praedestinatus* of Arnobius the Younger (*CCL* 25B [2001]), chaps. 26–27.

46. Mansi, *Sacrorum conciliorum,* 3.633–34.

47. See *Chronicle* 2.46.6 (*CSEL* 1.99, 31–100, 2).

48. *Concilia Galliae, CCL* 148A (1964): 50.

49. We would like to thank Carol Neel of Colorado College for assistance with the translation of this text.

50. *Ministry of Women,* 101.

51. *Deaconesses,* 193.

52. See, e.g., Jerome's *Commentarii in Ezechielem* 14: *qui videntur laici nec pervenire ad sacerdotalem et leuiticum gradum,* ed. F. Glorie, *CCL* 75 (1964): 737. See also Jerome's translation in the Vulgate of 2 Esdras 13.29: *qui pollunt sacerdotium ius que sacerdotale et leviticum.*

53. A. Thiel, *Epistulae Romanorum Pontificum Genuinae* (Braunsberg: E. Peter, 1874), 360–79.

54. *Ministry of Women in the Early Church,* 7.

55. Gryson, *Ministry of Women,* 105, 112.

56. Otranto/Rossi, "Priesthood," 84.

57. Ibid., 81.

58. Note, however, that Otranto/Rossi argue that Julian Pomerius, a fifth century North African writer who had migrated to Gaul, had used *ministrare* to mean "officiate at altars" (ibid., 81). See *De Vita Contemplativa* 2.7.3: *qui aut propriis illud confessionibus produnt, aut nescientibus aliis quales occulti sunt, ipsi in se voluntariae excommunicationis sententiam ferunt, et ab altari cui ministrabant, non animo, sed officio separati, vitam suam tanquam mortuam plangent . . .* (*PL* 59.452B). An English translation has simply rendered the critical phrase thus: "who either reveal it in their own confession or who, if others do not know what they are in secret, bring sentence of voluntary excommunication against themselves; and separating themselves not in heart but in duties from the altar from which they *ministered . . .*" Julianus Pomerius, *The Contemplative Life,* trans. Sr. M. J. Suelzer (Westminster, MD: Newman, 1947), 70 (emphasis added).

59. Pope Zachary, *Letter 8, PL* 89.933.

60. Letter taken from H. van der Meer, *Priestertum der Frau? Eine theologiegeschichtliche Untersuchung, Quaestiones Disputatae* 42 (Freiburg: Herder, 1969), 118.

61. Otranto/Rossi, "Priesthood," 82.

62. ". . . *sine ullo respectu regulae Christianae praecipitia funesta sectentur*" (Thiel, *Epistulae Romanorum Pontificum Genuinae,* 377).

63. ". . . *quae non solum ipsos videatur obruere, sed et ecclesiis universis mortiferam, si non sanentur, inferre perniciem*" (ibid.).

64. Otranto/Rossi, "Priesthood," 83.

65. Ibid.

66. Otranto unfortunately goes on to suggest that "Gelasius probably intended to address problems that were not exclusive to the regions mentioned" (ibid.). But if that were the case, why address a papal letter only to three Italian provinces?

67. Mayer, *Monumenta,* 46–47. Text and French translation in P. de Labriolle, *Les sources de l'histoire du montanisme* (Paris: Leroux, 1913), 226–30.

68. The title *hospita* appears in one Christian inscription from Trier (*ILCV* 2.3082B; *CIL* 13.3795) and two from Rome: *Inscriptiones Christianae Urbis Romae,* n.s., ed. P. Silvagni (Rome: Pontifical Institute of Christian Archaeology, 1922), 6.1595 and 9.24780. The meaning of this term is unknown, but it may be related. Thanks to Janet Tulloch for this reference.

69. As suggested by Gryson, *Ministry of Women,* 106. Note that John of Damascus (*De haeresibus,* 49) does refer to the "Pepuzians," whom he also calls "Quintillians." See brief discussion in Martimort, *Deaconesses,* 195–96.

70. *Breviatio Canonum,* ed. C. Munier, *CCL* 148 (1974): 305.

71. *Statuta Ecclesiae Antiqua,* in *Concilia Galliae, CCL* 148 (1963): 172–73. These prohibitions were repeated in almost identical form by later canonical collections. See, e.g., *Concilia Africa sec. trad. Coll. Hispanae,* ed. C. Munier, *CCL* 149 (1974): 352.

72. *PL* 134.114–15. For comment, see Martimort, *Deaconesses,* 209–10, and Otranto/Rossi, "Priesthood," 90–92.

73. Luke 10:2.

74. Rom 16:1.

75. Fourth century.

76. *CIL* 11.4339, *ILCV* 85; *Anthologia Latina, sive Poesis Latinae supplementum,* ed. F. Buecheler and A. Riese (Amsterdam: Hakkert, 1964), 2.3, no. 2026, p. 64.

77. See brief analysis in *CIL* 11.4339, where it is noted that other scholars have simply left the date of the inscription *in ambiguo.*

78. *PL* 22.1108.

79. *CIL* 10.8079; *ILCV* 1.1192:

BMS LETA PRESBITERA

VIXIT ANN. XL MVIII DVIIII

QVEI BENE FECIT MARITUS

PRECESSIT IN PACE PRIDIE

IDUS MAIAS

80. That is, on May 14.

81. See comment on Pope Gelasius' *Letter* 14, above.

82. See, e.g., Carl Kaufmann, *Handbuch der altchristlichen Epigraphik* (Freiburg: Herder, 1917), 256; Anna Crispo, "Antichità cristiane della Calabria prebyzantina," in *Archivo Storico per La Calabria e La Lucania* 14 (1945): 127–41, 209–10; and Antonio Ferrua, "Note su Tropea Paleocristiana," in *Archivo Storico per La Calabria e La Lucania* 23 (1954): 9–29.

83. Ferrua, "Note su Tropea Paleocristiana," 11. The inscription may be found at *ILCV* 1150.

84. Eisen, *Women Officeholders,* 131. Eisen here is commenting on Canon 19 of the Council of Tours (567), where, as she implicitly concedes, the canon *is* referring to the wives of male clergy.

85. Otranto, "Sacerdozio femminile," 352; Otranto/Rossi, "Priesthood," 86.

86. Otranto/Rossi, "Priesthood," 87.

87. *Women Officeholders,* 131.

88. *Martia presbyteria/ferit obblata Olebri/o par[iter] et Nepote* (*CIL* 13.1183; *ILCV* 1191). On the issue of dating, see brief discussion in note, *CIL* 13.1183.

89. =*tulit.*

90. Otranto/Rossi, "Priesthood," 89.

91. Otranto incorrectly implies that the same term is used in the graffito and the two councils (ibid.).

92. Ibid.

93. Ibid.

94. *Dominis nostris Thaeodosio consule XI et Valentiniano viro nobelissimo Caesare. Ego Thaedosius emi a Flavia Vitalia presbytera sancta matrona auri solidis III. Sub die, CIL* 3.14900; F. Bulic, "Iscrizioni Inediti. Salona (Solin)," *Bollettino di Archaeologia e Storia Dalmata* 21 (1989): 141–48, at 147, n. 2428. See also discussion by Otranto/Rossi, "Priesthood," 87–88, and Eisen, *Women Officeholders,* 131–32.

95. See P. Testini, *Le catacombe e gli antichi cimiteri cristiani in Roma* (Bologna, 1966), 221–26.

96. *CIL* 3.14900; see also Bulic, "Iscrizioni Inediti. Salona (Solin)," 141–48; discussion in Otranto/Rossi, "Priesthood," 88, and Eisen, *Women Officeholders,* 132–33.

97. ([SAC]ERDOTAE+).

98. Eisen, *Women Officeholders,* 133.

99. "*Guilia Runa presbiterissa quiebit* [sic] *in pace, vixi[t] an[nos]L*" (*AE* 1953.107, p. 36; 1958.290, p. 72; 1962, p. 81).

Chapter Nine

CONCLUSION

In the preceding pages, we have presented what we believe to be all the extant evidence in Latin and Greek for women holding the offices of deacon and presbyter in both the Eastern and Western Church. Also included are a few references from the Syriac-speaking churches of the East of which we are aware, though we make no claim to completeness there.

The earliest reference to a female deacon occurs in the Pauline letters, Phoebe in Rom 16:1. At this point, there is no distinction by sex. The few other first- and second-century references are ambiguous for various reasons. By the third century, the special office of female deacon or deaconess had developed in the East, intended especially for ministry to women. It is clear that in most churches that reflected this custom in the fourth, fifth, and sixth centuries, the deaconess was considered an ordained member of the clergy with special tasks. Some of the literary texts referring to female deacons or presbyters indicate that for some tasks (e.g., representation of the church in business or political contexts), their roles overlapped with the male deacons.'

The title *diakonos* did not give way to the newer *diakonissa;* rather, the original term *diakonos* continued to exist side by side with the later term *diakonissa* after the fourth century, often in contexts that seem to suggest the complete interchangeability of the two titles. For the sake of accuracy, we have maintained the distinctiveness of each title in translation.

The overwhelming preponderance of evidence for female deacons comes from the Greek East. Presented here are approximately sixty-one Eastern and four Western inscriptions of known women deacons, along with forty Eastern and two Western literary references to real women who held the office.[1] In the East, after a hiatus between the New Testament and Pliny the Younger on one hand and the *Didascalia* in the third century on the other, female deacons began to appear in good numbers and continued through the period of our study and further. Comments from a few later writers show that they fully accepted the existence of ordained female deacons at an earlier period, even if they did not recognize the continuance of the office in their own day.

Here is a rich source of information about female deacons as they exercised liturgical roles, supervised the life of women faithful, provided ongoing care for women baptizands, and were seen going on pilgrimage and interacting with their own families and the general population in a variety of ways. The number of widows commemorating husbands casts doubt on the assumption that everywhere and at all times female deacons had to have been celibate, though the majority witness is that either virginity or widowhood was requisite. The largest number of deacon inscriptions and other references comes from central Asia Minor, where there is also the best evidence for interaction with the deacons' own families. Perhaps in this geographical region that had been influenced substantially by Montanism, variant qualifications and practices were tried that were seldom implemented elsewhere.

In the West, the institution of female deacons did not even seem to arise until the fifth century, long after they were active and well known in the East. Perhaps it was only then that the Eastern custom began to influence certain ecclesiastical circles in the West, perhaps because of the issue of female presbyters, which seems to have arisen earlier. Yet the definite impression left on the reader is that most Western episcopal councils did not accept either practice. This did not deter certain respected groups from ordaining women as deacons, however, as is shown by the four Western inscriptions and two literary references, all from the sixth century. The two literary references to female deacons, both from monastic contexts, suggest a close relationship between monastic profession and diaconal ordination. In the case of Respecta, Pope Gregory the Great used the language of ordination for the abbess of a monastery. However, in the case of the other Western reference, St. Radegunda, the legendary character of the story does not hide the fact that it is her monastic profession, not leadership office, that occasions the diaconal ordination.

The full story of female deacons remains unknown. Unfortunately, the wide geographical distribution of evidence and small number in any given area does not permit clear conclusions about the emergence of any kind of regional patterns. There are more family contexts given for deacons in central Asia Minor than anywhere else. There are no family references for deacons in Palestine. Does that mean the female deacons of Palestine never lived or had any significant contact with their families, but those of Asia Minor did? Given what we know about the popularity of monasticism in Palestine by the late fourth century, it is possible that none of the female deacons of Palestine whose testimony is preserved originated there, but rather came from elsewhere to enter monastic life. This would explain the absence of family contexts. The numbers are just too small to arrive at firm conclusions, however.

The story of female presbyters is even more elusive. Surprisingly, there is stronger testimony for them in the West than in the East, yet the numbers are still so small that there is no way of knowing if they are representative. Those in the

East may have been under the influence of Montanism. In the West, the issue of female presbyters first arose in the late fourth century, probably due to the influence of Priscillian, whose Spanish-based movement favored women in ministry. The inscriptions of Episcopa Q and Martia may possibly derive from that movement. Guilia Runa, of course, is probably a Vandal Arian in Hippo sometime after the Vandal invasion. The same cannot be said of Leta or Flavia Vitalia in late fifth-century Bruttium and Gaul. The witness of their lives, along with the letter of Pope Gelasius to his own churches of south Italy, indicates a movement more central to "orthodox" circles.

Echoes of women in clerical office continued into the medieval period in both East and West, as witnessed by the sacramental symbols and powers of early medieval abbesses, who wore elements of priestly vesture in procession, gave blessings, and received the confessions of their nuns. Yet for the most part, the highest level of church office for women was on the decline already by the end of the sixth century. Various reasons are suggested by historians. Certainly the rise of cultic sacramentalism that highlighted cultic purity as requisite for approaching the increasingly sacred sacramental celebration was a key factor. Anthropological research rather consistently shows that in a variety of cultures, norms of cultic purity have been controlled by males, who exclude females from the sacred because of the awesome fear of contamination associated with the blood of menstruation and childbirth and project their fear of impurity onto women themselves. Cultic purity becomes associated with males, impurity with females. This was the biggest argument against women presbyters. Already by the fourth-century Council of Elvira in Spain, the normal marital sexual activity of male presbyters and bishops was questioned from this perspective. For this reason, the virginity or celibacy of women clergy was requisite in most times and places, even as it was either ignored or only counseled for male clergy.

Another reason often advanced for the decline of women's offices in the church is that the female diaconate was instituted primarily because of the custom of baptizing adults by immersion, which required total nudity and the anointing of the entire body by the baptizing clergy. Thus women clergy were required to continue the rite for newly baptized women after the bishop or presbyter had discretely anointed the women's head. When infant baptism became more the norm and when adult baptism by immersion ceased, there was no further need for deaconesses. In the legislation of the *Didascalia* and *Apostolic Constitutions* this part of the deaconess' role is indeed emphasized. There was more to their role than that, however: the deaconess was also to be liaison of bishop and deacons with believing women, providing some of the baptismal and post-baptismal instruction, doing pastoral visits of sick women, and accompanying women in their dealings with deacons and bishop. All of this is to be seen in the context of traditional cultures, more typical of East than West, in which the stricter separation of the sexes and the seclusion of women in their homes made it distinctly improper for male deacons to do the instruction or make such visitations. The problem with this argument is that this pattern of cultural seclusion and separation did not cease as the centuries went on. It does, however, perhaps explain the absence of women deacons in the West at the time they were thriving in the East, as Western customs were never quite as strict about seclusion and separation.

As we ponder the evidence that we have, and as we wait for more to emerge from the dust of the centuries in order better to fill in the picture, we are grateful for the material remains in manuscript and stone that have allowed us to catch some glimpses of the lives of these Christian women of long ago.

Note

1. Exact numbering is problematic and open to interpretation. It is unclear whether the Syriac deaconess Zaōrtha and the reference in the Canon of Rabbula (preserved in Latin) should be included in the Greek East or whether uncertain inscriptions should be counted or not. Furthermore, three of the most charming stories about female deacons, those of Eusebia Xenē, Justina and Theodula, are probably completely legendary. Approximate numbers are therefore more significant than exact ones.

Appendixes

A. Locations of Deacon Inscriptions

EAST

Total number: 61. Two inscriptions (Alexandra of Elis, Eneon)
are uncertain, having been read differently by different editors.

Asia Minor
  Cappadocia
    Maria of Archelais

  Caria
    Aretē, from Aphrodisias

  Cilicia, Korykos
    Athanasia
    Charitina
    Theodora
    Theophila
    Timothea

  Galatia
    Domna
    Nonna
    Philogonis

  Lycaonia
    Basilissa, from Iconium
    Goulasis
    Kyria
    Unnamed

  Lydia
    Epiphaneia
    Epiphania
    Lampadia, from Smyrna

  Phrygia
    Laodicea Combusta
      Aurelia Faustina
      Celsa
      Elaphia
      Magna
      Masa
      Mesalina
      Paula
      Unnamed

  Elsewhere in Phrygia
    Dipha
    Eistrategis
    Matrona of Axylos
    Nunē
    Pribis
    Severa

  Pontus-Bithynia
    Aeria
    Alexandra
    Basilikē
    Eugenia

Greece
  Aegean
    Agaliasis
    Unnamed, from Thasos

  Mainland
    Agrippianē, from Patras
    Athanasia, from Delphi
    Eirēnē, from Thessaly
    Nikagora, from Athens
    Tetradia, from Thessaly

  Pelopponesus
    Alexandria, from Elis
    Andromacha, from Achaia

  Macedonia
    Agathē, from Philippi
    Agathokleia
    Matrona of Stobi
    Posidonia, from Philippi
    Theodosia
    Theoprepeia

Thrace
  Eugenia, from Nicopolis

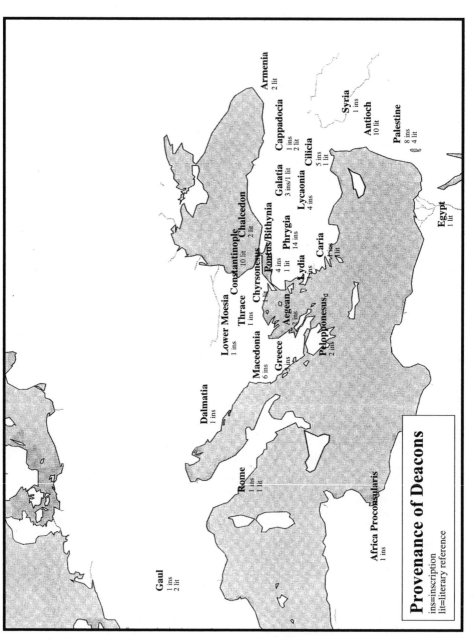

Figure 15. Provenance of Deacons

Lower Moesia
  Celerina

Palestine
  Anastasia
  Basilis
  Elladis
  Eneon?

Maria of Moab
Nonna
Sophia
Zoe

Syria
  Zaortha

WEST
Total number: 4

Africa Proconsularis
  Accepta

Dalmatia
  Ausonia

Rome
  Anna

Gaul
  Theodora of Ticini

B. Locations of Deacons in Literary Sources

EAST
Total number, including Phoebe (Rom 16:1–2) and Graptē (Hermas Vis. 2.4.3), and assuming two daughters of Count Terentius (actual number unknown): 40.

Armenia
  Dionysia
  Nektaria?

Asia Minor
  Constantinople
    Amproukla (Procla?)
    Basilina
    Celerina
    Elisanthia, Martyria, Palladia
    Eusebia
    Nicarete
    Olympias
    Pentadia
    Sabiniana

  Cappadocia
    Daughters of Count Terentius (at
      least two; number unknown)

  Caria
    Eusebia Xenē (legendary)

  Cilicia
    Marthana

Chalcedon area
  Matrona of Cosila
  Unnamed, by Callinicos

Chersonesus
  Theophila

Galatia
  Magna of Ancyra

Pontus
  Lampadion

Egypt
  Theodula (legendary?)

Palestine
  Manaris of Gaza
  Severa of Jerusalem
  Susanna
  Unnamed of Caesarea, by Palladius

Syria, mostly Antioch
  Anastasia
  Axia
  Casiana
  Eugenia

Jannia
Justina (legendary)
Publia

Romana
Valeriana
Unnamed, by Theodoret

WEST
Total number: 2

Gaul
Radegunda
Respecta

C. Locations of Presbyters

EAST AND WEST
Total number, including Episcopa Q: 11

Egypt
Artemidora, mummy

Phrygia
Ammion, inscription

Cappadocia
Firmilian's prophet (description in letter
to Cyprian)

Aegean
Epiktō, inscription

Dalmatia
Flavia Vitalia, inscription
Unnamed Sacerdota, inscription

Bruttium
Leta, inscription

Rome
Episcopa Q, inscription

Sicily
Kalē, inscription

Africa (Hippo)
Guilia Runa, mosaic inscription

Gaul
Martia, inscription

D. Family Relationships Identified for Commemorated Women in Inscriptions

EASTERN DEACONS
Agaliasis, sister and daughter, from the Cyclades
Agathē, wife (?), from Philippi
Alexandra, mother (?), from Achaia
Aretē, daughter, from Aphrodisias
Athanasia, foster mother, from Korykos
Aurelia Faustina, mother, from Phrygia
Basilissa, wife and mother, from Lycaonia

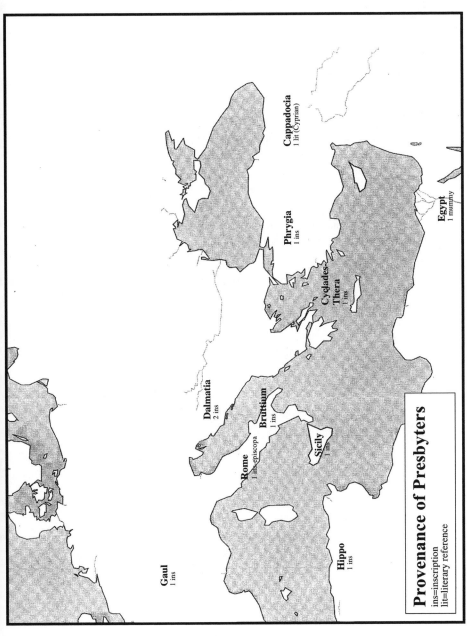

Gaul
1 ins

Dalmatia
2 ins

Rome
1 ins-episcopa

Bruttium
1 ins

Sicily
1 ins

Hippo
1 ins

Cyclades-
Thera
1 ins

Phrygia
1 ins

Cappadocia
1 lit (Cyprian)

Egypt
1 mummy

Provenance of Presbyters

ins=inscription
lit=literary reference

Figure 16. Provenance of Presbyters

Celsa, wife and daughter, from Phrygia
Charitina, daughter, from Korykos
Domna, wife and daughter-in-law, from Galatia
Eistrategis, wife, mother, and sister-in-law, from Phrygia
Elaphia, aunt, from Phrygia
Eneon (?), daughter (?), Jerusalem
Epiphaneia, mother and grandmother, from Lydia
Goulasis, sister, from Lycaonia
Lampadia, daughter, from Smyrna
Maria of Archelais, mother, from Cappadocia
Maria, daughter, from Moab
Masa, daughter and sister, from Phrygia
Matrona of Axylos, mother and grandmother, from Phrygia
Mesalina, sister and aunt, from Phrygia
Nonna, mother, from Galatia
Nunē, daughter, from Phrygia
Paula, sister, from Phrygia
Philogonis, daughter, from Galatia
Pribis, mother and grandmother, from Phrygia
Unnamed, mother(?) sister(?), from Iconium

WESTERN DEACONS

Anna, sister, from Rome
Ausonia, mother, from Dalmatia

EASTERN PRESBYTERS

Artemidora, daughter, from Egypt

WESTERN PRESBYTERS

Leta, wife, from Bruttium

Index of Ancient Names

Index of Deaconesses, Presbyters, and Episcopa

Pentadia, 15, 28, 44–45, 47–48, 209
Philogonis, 88, 207, 212
Phoebe, 4, 8, 12–18, 25, 203, 209
Posidonia, 3, 88–89, 207
Pribis, 89, 207, 212
Procla, 44–45, 48, 209. *See also* Amproukla
Publia, 48–50, 99n50, 210

Radegunda, 142–43, 210
Respecta, 141–42, 204, 210
Romana, 6, 50–51, 204, 210

Sabiniana, 8, 52, 209
Severa, 90, 207
Severa of Jerusalem, 6, 52–54, 209
Sophia, 90–91, 93, 209
Susanna, 6, 55–56, 209
Syntyche, 11

Tetradia of Volos, 3, 91–92, 207
Theodora of Korykos, 92, 207
Theodora of Ticini, 8, 144–45, 209
Theodosia, 3, 92–93, 207
Theodula, 6, 55–61, 206n1, 209
Theophila, 93, 207
Theophila of Chersonesus, 6, 61, 209
Theoprepeia, 93, 207
Timothea, 94, 207

Unnamed, by Callinicos, 62–63, 209
Unnamed, by Cyril, 7
Unnamed, by John Moschus, 66–67
Unnamed, by Pliny, 27
Unnamed, by Pseudo–Ignatius, 65–66
Unnamed, by Theodoret, 63–64, 210
Unnamed, *Life of Hypatius,* 62–63

Unnamed Daughters of Count Terentius, 62, 209
Unnamed of Caesarea, 6, 64–65, 209
Unnamed of Eleutheropolis, 55–56
Unnamed of Iconium, 95–96, 207, 212
Unnamed of Phrygia (near Iconium), 95, 207
Unnamed of Thasos, 95, 207

Valeriana, 6, 61, 210

Xenē. *See* Eusebia (also called Xenē)

Zaōrtha, 7, 94, 206n1, 209
Zoe, 94–95, 209

Presbyters
Ammion, 169–70, 210
Artemidora, 170, 210, 212

Epiktō, 170, 210

Firmilian's prophet, 181–82, 210
Flavia Vitalia, 196, 198, 205, 210

Guilia Runa, 197–98, 205, 210

Kalē, 171, 210

Leta, 3, 193–95, 198, 205, 210, 212

Martia, 195–96, 205, 210

Unnamed Sacerdota, 197, 210

Episcopa
Episcopa Q, 193, 205, 210

Index of Modern Authors

ERRATUM

page 81

Kyria of Lycaonia [1]

This fragment of a funerary monument on blue stone was found in 1885 as a support for the door jamb of a mosque in the village of Armutlu near Konya (Iconium), in the ancient region of Lycaonia. Thus nothing is known of its original location or context.

... of his parents, Conon presbyter and Kyria deaconess and of his wife Markas (?) Matrona

The inscription is broken at the beginning and the surviving fragment takes up in the middle of the dedication to or from an unnamed and unknown man. The persons whose names are mentioned may be the dedicators, but those names are usually in the nominative case, while these are in the genitive case. Alternatively, it may be this unnamed man who has survived his parents and wife and dedicated the memorial to them, but then the surviving names should be in the dative case. What is most interesting for our purposes is that both of the man's parents hold church office, and both may still be alive. The woman's title is diakonissa. In most cases of a deaconess who has children, it is not clear whether she is married or widowed, and it is often thought that still-married women could not be deacons. This does not seem to be so in the case of Kyria. If the first alternative is correct, that the parents are dedicating the monument to their son, they are married and both are holders of church office simultaneously. Here, clearly, Kyria does not carry her title as wife of someone else, which would be a possible interpretation if her husband were a deacon. Rather, since she is a presbyter, she holds her title in her own right.

Note

1. ... ΓΟΝΕΩΝ ΑΥΤΟΥ ΚΟΝΩΝΟΣ ΠΡΕΣΒΥΤΕ[ΡΟΥ] Κ(ΑΙ) ΚΥΡΙΗΣ ΔΙΑΚΟΝΙΟΥΣΗΣ Κ(ΑΙ) ΤΗ(Σ) ΣΥ[Ν]ΒΙ(ΟΥ) ΑΥΤΟΥ ΜΑΡΚΑΣ (?) ΜΑΤΡΩΝΗΣ, as rendered by J. R. Sitlington Sterrett, "The Wolfe Expedition to Asia Minor," *Papers of the American School of Classical Studies at Athens* 3 (1884/1885) (Boston: Damrell and Upham, 1888): 198 no. 326; line breaks are not given. Ref., Elm, Virgins of God, 176 n. 116.